Workbook for Social Action for Counselors, Psychologists, and Helping Professionals

Workbook for Social Action for Counselors, Psychologists, and Helping Professionals

Strength, Solidarity, Strategy, and Sustainability

Rebecca L. Toporek, Muninder Kaur Ahluwalia,
Derrick Bines, and Bryan Ovidio Rojas-Araúz

cognella®
SAN DIEGO

Bassim Hamadeh, CEO and Publisher
Amy Smith, Associate Editorial Manager
Rachel Kahn, Production Editor
Juniper Perkins, Editorial Associate
Emely Villavicencio, Senior Graphic Designer
Kylie Bartolome, Licensing Specialist
Natalie Piccotti, Director of Marketing
Kassie Graves, Senior Vice President, Editorial
Alia Bales, Director, Project Editorial and Production

Printed in the United States of America.

cognella® | ACADEMIC PUBLISHING
320 South Cedros Ave., Ste. 400, Solana Beach, CA 92075

I dedicate this book to the elders and ancestors who pursued justice, peace, and love in the face of oppression. To all who fight to survive and dismantle injustice—including new voices who strengthen the movements for justice. To the youngest generation, powerful in resistance and radical hope—finding their place in collective action, inspiring and energizing us. With deep love and gratitude, I honor my children, partner, parents, mentors, colleagues, and students who continue to teach me, show patience and love, and keep me accountable.

Rebecca

I dedicate this book to my parents who taught me about how to love and how to live the values of social justice, seva, and chardi kala. Ma and dad, you taught me that we have to fight on behalf of others because our fate is intertwined with theirs and because it was the right thing to do. Thank you to my family, community, and my beloved Henry for all the love and support. And thank you to my mentors, colleagues, and students for the solidarity in fighting the good fight.

Muninder

To the ancestors and elders whose efforts and lessons teach us that the work may be long, but it is worth it. To those with long histories of working toward justice, those just beginning, and those somewhere in between. May we all continue to find our people. To my people, thank you!

Derrick

This book is a hope for a better tomorrow for future generations, including mi pequeña Eloa X. It is written on the shoulders of giants, a promise to pay forward what we could never pay back. It is a commitment to our families, ancestors, mentors, friends, and humanity as a whole. It is a work of love and rage alongside colleagues, scholar-activists, and healers. I dedicate the words within to freedom fighters worldwide who make their communities better every day, who change the world, and who dare to DREAM of a better world in one that tried to keep us DREAMless.

Bryan

Brief Contents

Detailed Contents

Prologue

As this book goes to print, we are witnessing a critical moment in history—one in which civil rights, democratic institutions, and social protections are being rapidly dismantled at both federal and state levels. While these shifts may feel unprecedented to some, the reality is that oppression, marginalization, and systemic violence are not new. These patterns of injustice—rooted in colonialism, white supremacy, and patriarchy—have long existed in the United States and globally.

In this context, the S-Quad model and the work of this book feel more urgent than ever. From civil rights violations, the suppression of the free press, and the silencing of judges, law firms, scientists, and scholars—to illegal deportations, targeted violence against both immigrants and citizens, and escalating threats of war—these realities demand responsiveness and presence in the face of injustice.

We are also witnessing powerful resistance, solidarity, and the emergence of radical hope through collective action. We believe this book offers an important foundation for navigating and challenging systems of oppression.

We must remain informed, yet mindful of the toxicity of the current political and social climate. Now more than ever, we need one another's solidarity, thoughtful sustainability, and evolving strategies to forge the path ahead. Stay open to new tools and emerging approaches. Connect with others taking action and care for yourself, your loved ones, and (y)our communities.

Our voices and actions are essential. It is crucial that we make thoughtful decisions about where and how we engage, taking into account our positionality and vulnerability—understanding the risks and working to minimize harm.

section 1

Social Action, Social Justice, and Advocacy in the Profession: Finding Your Place

Chapter 1

Laying the Groundwork

Strength   Solidarity

Sustainability   Strategy

FIGURE 1.1 S-Quad image

"I am cognizant of the interrelatedness of all communities and states. I cannot sit idly by in Atlanta and not be concerned about what happens in Birmingham. Injustice anywhere is a threat to justice everywhere. We are caught in an inescapable network of mutuality, tied in a single garment of destiny. Whatever affects one directly affects all indirectly. Never again can we afford to live with the narrow, provincial 'outside agitator' idea. Anyone who lives inside the United States can never be considered an outsider."

—Rev. Dr. Martin Luther King Jr. *Letters from a Birmingham Jail*

The words of Dr. King Jr. continue to be as relevant today as they were in 1963, as injustices and oppression continue to be perpetuated throughout our communities, nation, and world. We are committed to joining with those who are oppressed, resisting oppression, and working toward a free and just world. We believe, as Rev. Dr. King Jr. wrote, that our fates and our abilities to seek justice for any one group is inextricably linked to justice for others. In this book, we use the S-Quad (S⁴) model as a guide to engage in social action. Taking action is purposeful and driven by passion, persistence, and lived experience. It can, however, be complex, and the magnitude of the issues we try to confront can be daunting. In fact, this complexity can stop us from engaging in *any* action. Considering this, we think that four areas of reflection, each represented by one of the S's in the model, can help us bring together tools and energy for our efforts. These areas of reflection include strength, solidarity, strategy, and sustainability. In a sense, they can act as a guide to engaging in social action.

We need to expand our work as helping professionals to more intentionally and systematically include justice, and recognize that we need to work on ourselves first. The journey to engage in social action won't always be comfortable or easy, but there will be change—openness in ourselves and growth in our work. In writing this book, we assume that you, as the reader, are willing to invest the effort to engage in social action. You can think of this first chapter, and our overview of the book, as a way to gain "informed consent" from you the reader.

We have organized this workbook into three sections. In this first section, we lay the groundwork with an introduction to context, concepts, and activities that ask you to start thinking about how to take social action in the helping professions. The second section dives deep into the four areas of reflection detailing the S-Quad framework and includes examples and activities for self-assessment. In section three, you will bring all your work together to create your personal and professional social action plan.

Before we move into the content of the book, we want to introduce ourselves, as we believe that who we are is as important as what we know. In addition, we believe that the process of working toward social change requires each of us to engage in self-reflection on our motivations, influences, positionality, and voice. After you get to know a little about us, we will introduce you to the book, including assumptions, definitions, and conceptual frameworks we use throughout the text. We also introduce the S-Quad model that shapes our discussion about social change and provides the structure for the work you will do throughout the book. Finally, we wrap up this chapter by talking about our use of the umbrella term "helping professionals" and explore how your profession is related to social change.

Our Voices

Even with our shared goals of justice, we are different individuals, with specific histories, and our respective voices are uniquely our own. We would each like to share the influence of our elders and ancestors who came before us, our salient identities and contexts, our journey to social action, and our plans for the future.

Derrick

I, Derrick, am in large part the product of people believing in me and providing me with opportunities for personal and professional development. I once had an incredibly supportive boss say to me, "You must have a lot of people pulling for you." She was right. I am from a community of people who love and challenge me, and have instilled in me the values of support, intention, and commitment. I bring each of them and their lessons (spoken and unspoken) with me as I navigate this life journey.

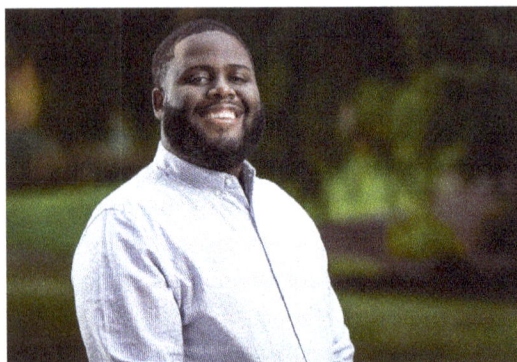

I identify as a cisgender, able-bodied, heterosexual, Black man. These identities are generally most salient for me and inform the way I navigate most places in society, and how society interacts with me. The longer I am in higher education, the more I realize how being the first in my immediate family to graduate from college

FIGURE 1.2 Photo of Derrick Bines

impacts my professional experiences. I reflect a lot on the varying levels of cultural, social, educational, and other privileges that I experience and have experienced throughout my life. I work at a university that is built on the ancestral territory of the Ramaytush Ohlone people, and I reflect daily on the privilege I have as a non-Indigenous person.

I entered the fields of counseling and psychology because, like many of us, I had a desire to help people, specifically Black people. I was aware of the history (and current experiences) of discrimination and injustice Black people faced navigating the health professions, which contributed to a mistrust within the community. I also recognized the stigma related to talking about mental health. In college, I noticed while working with other Black students to support each other navigate school, that we often discussed racism, stress, and other challenges, but never explicitly connected those to our mental health. When I met two Black psychologists, I began to make the connection. I wanted to help others make this connection—that what we feel is related to what we experience. I wanted to affirm these experiences and create systems that care for people and empower them to care for themselves and their communities. This is also part of my connection to social justice—a drive to foster supportive environments where people's needs are met. I'll share more about this in Chapter 2.

Finally, my approach to writing is influenced by the people I am in community with, the people that I hope to reach, hip-hop music, and my love for storytelling. I use quotes, stories, and analogies to communicate in ways that I hope are clear. You may notice this throughout this book. I continue to be influenced by the world around me, and as such, my writing style is constantly developing.

Bryan

Identities are dynamic, fluid, and complex. Today, I, Bryan, am a highly educated, Afroindigenous healer, an ADHDer, creative soul, and Immigrant American. I am also a brother, son, husband, Eloa's father, tío, scholar-activist, DREAMer, poet, hip-hop educator, licensed psychologist, author, speaker, and entrepreneur. My upbringing has profoundly shaped who I am and how I see the world. I was born in San José, Costa Rica, to a Costa Rican father and Panamanian mother, *el hijo de la panameña*. I have always lived in the space between. As Anzaldúa (1987) might say, I am a "Neplantero" *ni de aquí o ni de allá*. I have been called "too dark, too loud, too Panamanian" to be Costa Rican, yet I am also my Panamanian family's "Tico."

FIGURE 1.3 Photo of Bryan Rojas Araúz

For a long time, I struggled to find my place and often felt defined by what I was not. Growing up in a bicultural family taught me to appreciate both the similarities and differences between two neighboring countries and within one family. These experiences made me more tolerant, curious, and open to embracing cultural and individual differences. All of this happened before I ever set foot in the United States—a place that would challenge my identity and expand my sense of possibility.

As a previously undocumented immigrant, I learned to value the sense of opportunities that were not always present. I arrived in the United States at 13 years old to learn English, intending to return and help my family make ends meet. What was meant to be a 6-month trip became a permanent move. I did not have the privilege of growing up in a neighborhood that fostered academic progress. Instead, I faced an environment marked by violence, poverty, and misguided lessons. Thanks to the guidance of elders and mentors, I now have a place at this table. I remember my abuelo Ovidio Araúz—a successful businessman with only an elementary school education—and mentors like Dr. White, Drs. McWhirter, Dr. Toporek, Dr. Ahluwalia, and Dr. Alvarez, among many others. Their guidance and essence remind me of who I aspire to be.

In academic, clinical, and social spaces, my work is fueled by activism and a deep commitment to social justice. I live and run my private practice in Denver, Colorado, on land once belonging to the Ute, Cheyenne, and Arapaho peoples. In my path to liberation, I recognize that the echoes of colonialism and the pulse of survival coexist as integral parts of my being. With ongoing self-decolonization of mind, body, and spirit and abundant love, I have come to realize that I was whole all along—"de aquí y de allá."

Colectiva

My voice is shaped by the hope of migration
and the hard knocks lessons of the inner city
My voice is the product of learning to be unapologetically me
no longer fractions of self, no longer unshapen, broken pieces
My voice is unashamed of how it shows up when spoken or written
My voice is ESL classes growing up, *y sobrevivir a la fuerza*
My voice is an accent that gives me away if the color of my skin didn't
My voice is a stanza of resistance
to the snap of finger tips of those who came before me
My voice challenges tradition, questions what is, and pushes towards liberation
My voice is activist, slam poet, megaphone
persistence, existence, contradiction, and the places in between
My voice resounds the existence of many,
My voice is colectiva

Rebecca

I, Rebecca, am a White person committed to a constant process of working to recognize and dismantle racism and identity-based violence within myself and in my communities. I believe my purpose is to use whatever power, access, and social and economic capital I have to work toward changing oppressive systems and support powerful and insightful changemakers who are often silenced. I am, as Dr. King Jr. said, "caught in an inescapable network of mutuality, tied in a single garment of destiny" and I understand that the liberation of others is necessary for my survival. Elders who fought for racial justice have shaped who I am, lifting me and holding me accountable—Drs. Janet Helms, Derald Wing Sue, Patricia Arredondo, Don Pope-Davis, Thomas Parham, Joseph White, Judy Lewis, Tod Sloan, Shirley Kawazoe, and Jacqueline Reza, among many others. I work alongside and learn from my colleagues and friends who are fierce change agents.

FIGURE 1.4 Photo of Rebecca Toporek

I am a child of pacifist artists who were adamant about justice and fairness, and who also struggled with mental health, trauma histories, gender oppression, social class, and other challenges. I am constantly shaped by my two children in the vibrance of their early 20s, who face their own experiences of oppression and individual challenges. They have a wealth of knowledge and because they sometimes see things differently than me, they push me to learn more and be more. I am a settler in what is commonly referred to as the San Francisco Bay area, but is more accurately acknowledged as land that is the ancestral territory of the Chochenyo Ohlone people. My university is built on the occupied ancestral territory of the Ramaytush Ohlone and Coastal Miwok people. I give thanks to Sogorea Te' Land Trust and other collectives working toward rematriation and I commit to continuing to contribute in the ways they deem worthwhile.

As a professor, counselor educator, and psychologist focused on advocacy, anti-racism, and economic justice, I am grateful for the support and challenge of my students and colleagues who share experiences of oppression as well as privilege. As a White, early 60s, female-presenting person with intermittent disabilities and evolving gender and sexual identity, my focus for the past 40+ years has been on learning how to be a racially aware White person in racially oppressive systems. I am also deepening my compassion for myself and others who are trying to find their way as well as people whose perspectives differ from mine. I believe this is shaping the way I approach teaching and writing for anti-oppression and counseling more generally. At the same time, I am alarmed, dismayed and activated about what is happening in the US and around the world with greater divides between wealthy power holders and people who are marginalized and vilified in so many ways. I am increasingly understanding and integrating the importance of the relationship of our somatic and physical experience with our individual and collective well-being.

My voice and writing are a tapestry of my ancestors and elders, my learning and unlearning, my formal training, and the systems I have navigated and benefitted from. Through higher education, I adopted language shaped by White supremacy in the academy so that my own struggles could be seen as credible. I have also found academic language to be useful in advocacy for racial and economic justice. As a professor and academic writer, my writing style tends to be lengthy, often providing more context than necessary. I am working to reconnect to my authentic voice, which is closer to imagery and metaphors. In this vein, this onion skin "poppy" emerged one night while I was making dinner. For me, it is a reminder of how powerful, painful, and beautiful it can be to peel back layers of self-knowledge.

Hopefully you will see some of my authentic voice in this book in addition to the formal language I have been trained to use.

FIGURE 1.5 Onion skin "poppy"

Muninder

I, Muninder, try to live my life with intentionality and humility, and yet, sometimes fall short. I am a daughter of courageous Sikh Indian immigrant parents, a sister to overachieving brothers and sisters-in-law, and an aunt to nieces and nephews whose trajectories are more open than we could ever dream ours to be. Because of them, I remain a daughter of Guru Gobind Singh Ji in that I try to have a spiritual compass, but I am also a fierce fighter when I witness

FIGURE 1.6 Photo of Muninder K. Ahluwalia

oppression. These are the seeds of my journey to be a social justice warrior, planted and nurtured by my parents. I identify as an Indian American, Sikh cisgender, heterosexual woman who is bilingual (English/Punjabi), and wishfully almost trilingual (Spanish). I grew up in a predominantly White town in New York and moved to my beloved New York City at the age of 18 to be around people who looked and lived like me.

Aside from my parents, my mentors and close friends, Dr. Lisa Suzuki and Dr. Rebecca Toporek, are influential in my growth. They taught me how to be a better counseling psychologist and a better human being (or at least they try!). Mi prometido, Mr. Henry Tavarez, has taught me the value of patience and how even when deemed an "expert," I knew very little about the lived realities of those who come from different social locations than my own. For the past 23 years, I have worked at a public university in New Jersey that occupies land in Lenapehoking, the traditional and expropriated territory of the Lenape. I commit to dismantling practices of erasure and oppression of all people.

I am nourished by working with first-generation college students, students of color, and students who embrace the value of diversity. I also enjoy working with students who don't yet see that equity, inclusion, and justice are foundational to wellness and helping to facilitate their shift in perspective. I try to introduce and sustain anti-racist practices in my program, in the university, and in my professional organizations. In my small way, I am helping to prepare clinicians, researchers, advocates, and educators to work with vulnerable members of marginalized communities, including my own.

Lastly, I love to talk, listen, write, teach, and learn. In my personal and professional life, my spoken and written words are loud, direct, passionate, and pretty easy to understand. In graduate school and in my early career, I often felt like an outsider in academic discussions. So, as a scholar, I try to write so anyone can understand or relate to what I am saying, especially the communities I am trying to serve.

The Intertwining Paths of Our Identities and Histories

We each have different voices, shaped by our ancestors, our experiences, and by each other. To set the stage for the readers of this book, we want to share how our individual paths came together, weaving our individual voices into a collective one. For some of us, Rebecca was the *vichola*, or matchmaker. In 2000, Muninder and Rebecca met during their doctoral internship at University of California, Berkeley. They became instant allies and close friends and wrote their dissertations over scones at a local record shop. Rebecca and Bryan met in 2012 while waiting in line for the public transportation shuttle during Bryan's first couple of weeks in the master's program at San Francisco State University, where Rebecca is a professor. A discussion of shortcomings in the program and ways to improve the experiences of students of color was followed by an invitation to collaborate on social justice projects. Since then, Rebecca and Bryan have never stopped collaborating with one another. Muninder met Bryan in 2013 at the Teachers College Winter Roundtable. Soon after, the three became mentors and collaborators to each other. Bryan and Derrick met in

2015 during the interview weekend for University of Oregon's counseling psychology doctoral program. The connection was instant, and other students believed that they had known each other for years. Rebecca and Derrick met through Bryan at the Oregon Country Fair in 2016, and Derrick and Muninder met in 2017 at the Teachers College Winter Roundtable. Despite having met in 2016, it wasn't until 2020 that Rebecca and Derrick began working together when they became colleagues in the same department at San Francisco State University.

Now that you know us, you also know that our voices and what we present in this book are shaped by our demographic, sociopolitical, historical, and geographical context, among other experiences. Thus, while we believe the S-Quad framework can be adapted effectively in many countries, we also acknowledge that we situate our book for people living in the United States, with a US-based perspective. We are, however, undeniably linked to other nations and immigration stories and, where it is central to our personal or professional lives, we will speak to that.

You will notice that while we four wrote collaboratively, we each bring differences to our presentation style and our understanding. As you read the book, you will notice our different voices, lenses, and different styles. We think of our work as a jazz quartet of sorts, each contributing sound emanating from ourselves as an instrument. There is harmony, but there are also moments that seem discordant. Our work is in solidarity with each other, even when we engage differently. Throughout the book, we have also shared voices of other colleagues, elders, and mentors, some from a video interview project Muninder and Rebecca did a few years ago, *Helping Counselors and Psychologists as Advocates and Activists* (Toporek & Ahluwalia, 2019).

Acknowledging, honoring, and raising voices is the heart of social action. We encourage you to consider what your authentic voice is and how you use it. And a note about voice—using one's voice doesn't always mean speaking, but rather we mean how we present ourselves and our ideas. Also, our authentic voice may shift over space and time; how we present in one arena might be very different from how we present in another.

ACTIVITY 1.1

Questions for Reflection

We are all influenced by our identities, experiences, communities, contexts, and systems in the development of our authentic selves and expression.

1. What factors, people, and experiences have influenced you?

2. How do you—or could you—use these influences as it relates to social action?

3. Are there times that you consciously use a different voice? What prompts you to use this different voice (e.g., context, power differences)

Our Assumptions, Conceptual Frameworks, and Organization of the Book

We recognize that we come to this book with assumptions and commitments that are informed by our teaching, research, and practice; our ethics codes; multicultural competencies of our profession; and our lived experiences. In the spirit of reflexivity and transparency, we feel that it's important to share these assumptions and commitments with you.

Assumption 1: As helping professionals, engagement with social action is an ethical imperative that is intertwined with mental health and growth of individuals, families, and communities. As helping professionals, we have made a commitment to a set of ethical principles. At a minimum, we have made a promise to use our position, knowledge, and efforts to support others and society. Regardless of the professional field that we call home, we are guided by similar ethical principles. For example, the ethical principles for psychologists include: (a) beneficence and doing no harm, (b) responsibility, (c) integrity, (d) justice, and (e) respect for people's rights and dignity. Similarly for social workers it includes (a) service, (b) social justice, (c) dignity and worth of the individual, (d) importance of human relationship, (e) integrity, and (f) competence. We (Bryan, Derrick, Muninder, and Rebecca) believe professional ethics include a commitment to improving human existence at an individual, familial, and societal level. For healing and growth to occur, social action is required; we are called to take a stand in the face of oppression.

Assumption 2: You, the reader, bring expertise to this project. All of us bring expertise from our lived experiences, strengths, and resources. You may have been engaged in social action for a long time, or you may be early in that process. You may have a clear path and know where your efforts are best used. Or you may be wanting to respond but not sure how to do that, especially given your professional role. Some of us have a close understanding of privilege, oppression, power, and action. Others may be newer to understanding this and given our social reality, may have been shielded from many experiences of oppression and even functioned as a tool of oppression. Social change needs investment from everyone, and an awareness of our positionality ensures that the investment is sound.

Assumption 3: Many ancestors and elders in the helping professions provide a foundation and allow us to ground our work firmly in theory and generational knowledge. We are building upon their work. Our perspective is particularly influenced by Freire's (1970) concepts of praxis and conscientization. Action and reflection are necessary to social change and liberation, as well as moving us to greater understanding of our own social reality. Additionally, Bronfenbrenner's (1979) ecological model provides a framework for us to understand where and how we are anchored within systems and how our social reality is shaped by our environment. This helps us reflect on how we are connected to others and how social action may need to be directed in multiple arenas. Finally, the psychology of liberation (Martín-Baró, 1996) provides important grounding for this workbook. The work and wisdom of our elders, as well as advocacy by helping professionals past and present, provide powerful examples of taking action (we will talk more about this in the next chapter). If you are unfamiliar or only marginally familiar with concepts and frameworks mentioned, we strongly encourage you to do a bit of reading on these and consider how they may (or could) influence your work as a helping professional.

Assumption 4: There is a relationship and distinction between a diversity or multicultural orientation and a social justice orientation. We believe that cultural humility, multicultural responsiveness, and a pluralistic lens are necessary, but not sufficient, for social action. For our purposes, having a cultural understanding of self and others is only the beginning. That understanding must also include examining the systems within which social change must happen and the complexities of oppression and intersectionality. In a sense, the journey to multicultural competency is a precursor to social action in the best interest of our clients and their communities. Aligned with this, you may notice that we attempt to use language throughout the book that acknowledges power and systemic influence. For example, we have been intentional in using the terms "marginalized" and "minoritized" rather than "underrepresented" or "minority" when talking about groups, individuals or identities that are subject to historical and systemic oppression. Although "underrepresented" has been generally accepted in writing and may allude to representational imbalance, some have argued that it can turn the locus of responsibility to the individual or group rather than the system (e.g., Nwangwu, 2023). Critical race theory (CRT; see Crenshaw, 2011) is a helpful foundational concept to articulate the relationship between multiculturalism and social justice. Very simply put, critical race theory is rooted in a legal context examining how racism is embedded in legal decisions and policies. Further, policies, laws, and systems codify differential treatment based not only on identity but intersections of identities one holds. To move toward strategy for social action, we must understand the structural ways this oppression is embedded in policies and practices. Consider how we, as helping professionals, function within systems that oppress and can also facilitate liberation. How do we, as helping professionals, examine our systems and then move to challenge and transform? We will do a deeper dive on all of these concepts in Chapter 3.

Assumption 5: We are influenced, as authors, by our physical and societal location in the United States, and we recognize that oppression and social change is both local and global. We have to recognize that our awareness of marginalization and oppression is influenced by our experiences as people who have been raised, trained, and educated mostly in the United States of America. We know that experiences of power and privilege are not exclusive to the United States as there are global representations of social injustices. We have to consider the global representations of peoples' histories and lived experience here and abroad. It is important for us to take a world citizen perspective in which we can identify injustices and act in solidarity with those who are taking action across the world, always centering those who are most affected by current conditions. As we shared in our opening quote, Dr. Martin Luther King Jr. clearly said, "Injustice anywhere is a threat to justice everywhere." If we understand this to be true, then we are also invested in fighting for social justice as global citizens. We cannot only center the identities we carry and our geographies, but instead we must challenge ourselves to commit to social action beyond what affects us.

At the same time, there is a tendency by those in the US to focus on oppression that occurs in other parts of the world and to deny what is occurring here. While we understand there is oppression globally and the US is a part of perpetuating that oppression, there are so many examples of oppression within the United States that we cannot ignore.

Assumption 6: Strength, solidarity, strategy and sustainability (S-Quad) are useful as an effective framework for social action. In this book, we use four areas to facilitate social action: (a) strength, (b) solidarity, (c) strategy, and (d) sustainability. *Strength* refers to the skills, knowledge, and resources that we possess. These are the assets and tools we can bring to the work of social change, how we can contribute to existing action, and where we may want or need to develop ourselves further. *Solidarity* encompasses our relationships and collective power. Solidarity is both necessary for the cultural appropriateness of the action we take and to sustain the heart of who we are. We are framing *strategy* as specific approaches and avenues for social change. These strategies include a range of individual and collective actions aimed at addressing specific goals, such as unjust policies and practices and systemic oppression. Lastly, we believe that continued engagement with *sustainability*—mind, body, relational, spiritual, and collective wellness—is essential. These areas of reflection and action provide the structure and shape the journey you will take in the next 12 chapters.

The Work of "Helping Professionals"

We believe that the S-Quad framework and the activities in this workbook are relevant across professions and even to readers in the public at large. We have intentionally shaped this version of the book for readers in the "helping professions" and focused on issues relevant to those professions. We expect that readers who focus on mental health, relational wellness, and/or realization of academic or life goals for students, clients, and communities may relate more readily to some of the content than those not affiliated with this work.

Although the term is very broad, we use the term "helping professionals" in this book to refer to counseling, psychology, human services, social work, and related fields. Other professionals such as those in education, nursing, and medicine may find resonance with this book, although the examples and much of the discipline-specific information we present come from counseling and psychology. As helping professionals, we have significant overlap in the work we do, but each profession has their own perspective on that work and the language they use to describe that work, as well as specific areas of difference. Below, we share what counseling, counseling psychology, and social work organizations say about their work.

American Counseling Association:

Professional counselors help people gain personal insights, develop strategies and come up with real-life solutions to the problems and challenges they face in every area of life. As trained and credentialed professionals, they accomplish this by getting to know clients, by building safe, positive relationships and suggesting tools and techniques they believe will benefit clients ... Counseling is a professional relationship that empowers diverse individuals, families, and groups to accomplish mental health, wellness, education, and career goals. (American Counseling Association, n.d.)

American Psychological Association:

The practice of counseling psychology encompasses a broad range of culturally sensitive practices that help people improve their well-being, alleviate distress and maladjustment, resolve crises and increase their ability to function better in their lives. With its attention both to normal developmental issues and problems associated with physical, emotional and mental disorders, the specialization holds a unique perspective in the broader practice-based areas of psychology. While both counseling and clinical psychologists practice psychotherapy, counseling psychology differs from clinical in that its practitioners tend to focus on overall well-being across the lifespan, compared to clinical clients who often are experiencing more severe symptoms of mental illness. (APA, 2014)

National Association of Social Workers:

The primary mission of the social work profession is to enhance human well-being and help meet basic and complex needs of all people, with a particular focus on those who are vulnerable, oppressed, and living in poverty ... The most well-known aspect of the social work profession is providing direct services or therapy directly to clients. We help guide people to critical resources and counsel them on life-changing decisions. We also advocate for change to improve social conditions and strengthen the social net ... Social workers help relieve people's suffering, fight for social justice, and improve lives and communities. (National Association of Social Workers, n.d.)

You can see in the above three profession descriptions what each considers important. The language used and attention given to the individual, groups, communities, and systems differ, although individuals who work in all three professions would probably agree that we need to look at each level. Additionally, each profession has slightly different histories in relation to social action. There are many more fields (e.g., human services, clinical psychology, marriage and family therapy, nursing, psychiatry, traditional healers), each bringing their own set of skills and perspectives to social action.

Status Quo and Our Work

When Muninder described her work as a counseling psychologist who works as a professor in counseling programs, she mentioned work with supervision of trainees, teaching of classes, and research that she is engaged in. What she doesn't often talk about is that the bulk of her time is spent maintaining the status quo, which is really antithetical to the well-being and educational equity she hopes to promote. In fact, most of our work tasks as practitioners are about maintaining the status quo (Kivel, 2017). For example, we teach the same theories using the same texts written by individuals mostly from dominant groups, and when we talk about serving individuals from non-dominant groups, we discuss adaptation of theories and techniques.

As helping professionals, we must understand that the status quo is contrary to wellness and definitely in opposition to social action. It is doing the same thing we have always done for the same problem that continues to exist. Maintaining the status quo is like having our car in park (and sometimes in reverse), while social action is like putting it in drive and accelerating. So, as brown (2017) suggests, we must let go of the status quo, become social change agents, and engage in social action. "Social change is the process of shifting attitudes, values, and actions to address social problems in a positive way. Anyone at any age can be an agent of social change. Being an agent of social change is an active way to create a safer, healthier future for you, your relationships, your community, and your world" (National Sexual Violence Resource Center, 2014).

The term "social change agent" makes Muninder think of clandestine operations like those of James Bond (or maybe it is just the word agent), but in actuality, the activities can be quite tangible and transparent in a professional context. As social change agents working to promote well-being, we may, for example, help to change policies at our workplace that heavily penalize individuals from underserved communities for being late to appointments, while simultaneously advocating for better public transportation in those neighboring towns. Let's stop for a moment and begin to think about our professional work and its relationship to social action.

ACTIVITY 1.2

Work Tasks, Your Professional Context, and Social Action

1. List work tasks associated with your current profession as a health provider, helping professional, or educator (if not yet employed, then consider your fieldwork experience or the job you hope to hold in the future).

2. In what ways do your work tasks give attention to individuals, groups, communities, and systems?

3. What does your profession say about social action? How does it promote the status quo?

Reflection and Reflexivity in Action

Counseling and other mental health professions are rooted in the understanding of the human experience, including aspects of diversity. Dr. Patricia Arredondo argues that all forms of counseling are political in nature (also see Katz, 1985). We believe all of our actions are political as well. Whatever we choose to address or ignore is a stance. We know it would be impossible to address all issues all the time; however, through a better understanding of ourselves and our context, we can become aware of the reason we do or do not take action on certain issues. This examination also allows us to be social change agents with intentionality so we can more effectively be a catalyst for change and social justice. As you work through this book, we ask you to use both reflection and reflexivity. Tom Barrett's (2021) discussion of the distinction between these two in reference to teaching helps convey our meaning.

> **Reflection** focuses on your thoughts, feelings, and actions. It involves looking back on your teaching practice and examining what you did well, where you might improve. It's an introspective process, too, in which you look inward—it's about thinking "on" yourself. On the other hand, **reflexive thinking** is a way of being in the world that involves noticing patterns in your experience. You look at patterns and influences that affect your actions as a whole—it's about noticing how you change and grow. (Barrett, 2021, bold in original)

In Activity 1.2 you explored your professional work and its relation to social action. Now we ask you to reflect on where *you* stand in relation to social action.

ACTIVITY 1.3

Actions

Take a couple minutes to reflect on the following questions:

1. What actions are you currently taking toward social justice? Or if you are not currently taking action, what are some ideas you have about actions you could take?

2. What social movements are you committed to? Or if you are not currently committed to any movements, what movements would you like to learn more about and support?

3. What struggles are you less aware or unaware of and why?

4. What one thing can you commit to that would help you move toward intentional action?

While you were answering these questions, what emotions, and thoughts came up for you? Why do you think they came up for you? Did you feel you needed to do more? Did you feel resentment toward others for not doing enough? Whatever emotions come up, sit with them, and let go of judgment.

Where Are We Going Next? Overview of Section I

Now that you know us a little better and the ground we are standing on, we would like to give you a preview of what's coming next.

- Chapter 2 lays the foundation of the historical and professional context of social action, social justice, and advocacy. We look at ways in which our professions are working to end oppression, and we also assess the ways in which they historically (and currently) have promoted oppression, stood silently in the face of oppression, and sometimes were (are) the perpetrators.

- In Chapter 3, we ask you to assess yourself, with the goal of working more authentically and more humbly with others. We discuss foundational ideas such as privilege, power, intersectionality, and multicultural competence.

- In Chapter 4, we discuss personal, community, and professional values and ethics and how they shape our work as helping professionals. We also unpack the ways in which our ethics promote justice, the ways they inhibit it, and what we can do differently.

- Finally, in Chapter 5, we guide you toward finding your focus and articulating the need for social action in your work. We will work with you to find a vision that acts as a beacon as you move toward action that you will use in Section 2 of the book, applying the four areas of reflection in the S-Quad model: strength, solidarity, strategy, and sustainability.

History and Context for Social Action, Social Justice, and Advocacy in Mental Health Professions

"History is not the past; it's the present. We carry our history with us. We are our history."

—James Baldwin

Before you begin to read this chapter, we want you to reflect on your depth of foundational knowledge of history and context in social justice and advocacy.

ACTIVITY 2.1

Importance of History

Reflect on the following questions and record your thoughts in a place you can return to later.

1. Why is it important to know the history of your field before engaging in social action?

2. What do you know about the history of your field—in general and/or in terms of advocacy and social action?

The first time Derrick attended a professor's office hours as an undergraduate, the professor asked whether Derrick could name the first Historically Black College and University (Cheyney University of Pennsylvania). He could not. Derrick thought the question was a bit random because the professor had asked him to attend his office hours due to his performance on an exam. At the time, Derrick did not understand that the professor, an older Black man who had spent much of his life on college campuses as a student and professor, was trying to teach Derrick, a young Black man in his first year of college, the importance of understanding history and context. More accurately, the professor wanted Derrick to understand history and context as it related to him and his academic life. While Derrick didn't understand it then, over time, it became abundantly clear why understanding our pasts can help shape our future.

Similarly, Muninder recalls that when her classmates stopped listening, her high school social studies teacher yelled, "history repeats itself if left unknown or unacknowledged." He warned students of holocausts, genocides, enslavement, and other forms of oppression never ending. A select group of students always laughed when the teacher said this, but to some, including Muninder, it rang true. Muninder noticed that in the US, where we don't really learn of how enslavement *is* our history, racism may have shape-shifted over the years, but never gone away. As we write this book, history and communities are continuously under attack. For example, the teaching of Black history, critical race theory, ethnic studies, and books related to historical oppression in the US are banned in many states and there are efforts at the federal level to make teaching these subject a federal offense resulting in defunding of schools as well as prosecution. Policies that have attempted to correct historical injustice are being overturned and eliminated, including those related to diversity, equity, and inclusion, women's reproductive rights, and the rights of trans individuals.

Sankofa, a word derived from the Akan people of Ghana, represents the importance of understanding your past to inform your future. It is important that we become knowledgeable about the history of our professions. We need to know the change makers who have deeply impacted the professions through advocacy and social action—and continue to. And we have to take responsibility for the ways in which we maintain the status quo at the cost of the well-being of those who are most marginalized. We have organized this chapter aligned with an ecological framework, beginning with the broadest macro level, moving to community and organizational level, and ending with the individual level. We describe some of the sociopolitical context, as well as the history of counseling and psychology and integrate some examples from social work. We then share a bit of our own histories as they relate to advocacy, counseling, and psychology.

Prior to delving into history, we want to introduce ecological systems theory (Bronfenbrenner, 1979). Ecological systems theory considers that an individual exists within a larger context and that this context impacts development (Bronfenbrenner, 1979). We use this theory as a framework for understanding the different levels in which advocacy and harm can exist. Within this larger context are five systems: (a) the microsystem, (b) mesosystem, (c) exosystem, (d) macrosystem, and (e) chronosystem. Consider an individual student, including their identities, on a college campus in 2021. The microsystem consists of the people and places that a person engages with directly (e.g., family, peers, faculty, and staff members), and the mesosystem includes the interactions between aspects of the microsystem (e.g., parents interacting with teachers). The exosystem contains elements that may not directly interact with an individual, but do impact the individual (e.g., faculty and staff policies). Within the macrosystem are cultural elements including beliefs, values, and policies that impact an individual and the world around them (e.g. conduct policies, competitiveness, diversity of the campus). The chronosystem represents the times in which an individual is developing, including their stage of life and events occurring during their lifetime (e.g., COVID-19, virtual classrooms, technology advancements, political climate). More recently Stern and colleagues (2021) included a racial cultural lens that considers both challenges and strengths at different levels.

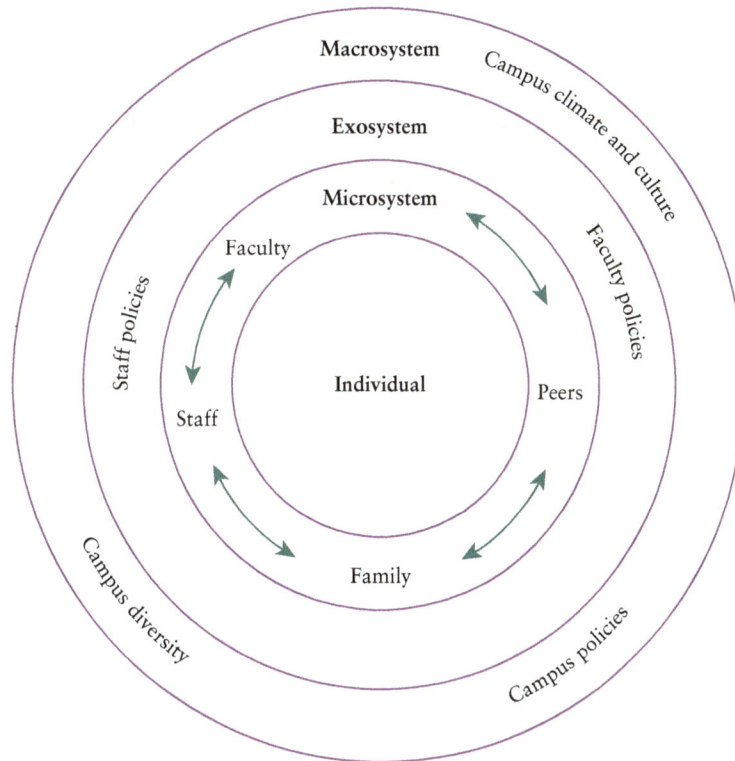

FIGURE 2.1 Ecological Model

In addition to the ecological model, consider other theories that you have encountered throughout your academic journey and how those might help address systemic oppression and liberation.

ACTIVITY 2.2

Helpful Theories

1. What theories are you familiar with that may be helpful as you develop your own approach to advocacy? See a list of helpful theories below.

2. What theories do you want to learn more about?

In addition to any theories you may identify, we (Derrick, Bryan, Muninder, and Rebecca) would like to highlight the following as important foundations for some of the work we do in this book, as well as in taking action. As you read the following list, if you are unfamiliar with a theory, please take a few moments to do a bit of research and learn more to broaden your foundation:

- Intersectionality (Crenshaw, 1989)
- Critical race theory (Delgado & Stefanic, 2001)
- LatCrit (Solórzano & Yosso, 2001)
- Disability critical race theory or DisCrit (Annamma et al., 2013)
- Community cultural wealth (Yosso, 2005)
- Liberation psychology (Martín-Baró, 1994)
- Relational cultural theory (Comstock et al., 2008)
- Empowerment theory (Rappaport, 1987)

We note that this list is not meant to be exhaustive, but rather to highlight theories across disciplines that may be useful as you develop your understanding of advocacy and social action.

Historical Context for Advocacy

The history and current state of discrimination within the United States has been and continues to be well documented. It is not within the scope of this workbook to provide a detailed history of the US or of oppression within the country. However, it is important that we acknowledge this context as it relates to psychology, counseling, social work, and other helping professions.

Helping Professions in the US: History of Oppression, Advocacy, and Attempts at Correction

A part of understanding the history of advocacy within helping professions is recognizing that much of this advocacy has come in response to (and even as the result of) exclusion, discrimination, and injustices both outside and inside of professional organizations. It is important to understand the history of mental health professions and professional organizations within the context of US history, particularly as it relates to oppression and advocacy. Though this chapter focuses on experiences within the United States, including the experiences of those who immigrate to this country, we recognize that harm and advocacy are present in the histories (and the professions' histories) of many nations globally. Below, we share just a few examples of oppressive practices by professionals and our professional associations against marginalized communities, and some attempts to repair the harm that has been caused. As we describe the history of marginalization and advocacy in the following sections, use the lens of the ecological model (Bronfenbrenner, 1979) and consider the impacts across the different ecological systems. Remember to continue breathing as you read, some of this may be hard to take in.

Scientific racism, the use of science to perpetuate the notions of superiority and inferiority, has been prevalent in many professions, including psychology. Scientific racism within psychology has supported the notion that behavior of White Americans is normative while that of minoritized groups is inferior and abnormal (Holliday 2009; Pickren, 2009). An example of scientific racism within psychology can be found in the use of intelligence testing. Intelligence testing was used to support the notion that African Americans, Mexican Americans, Indigenous Americans, and immigrants from eastern and southern Europe were inferior to individuals of Western European descent (Levine, 2015; Padilla & Olmedo, 2009; Pickren, 2009). Intelligence testing was also used in the military to show that White soldiers were more equipped than Black soldiers (Pickren, 2009). Similarly, the bell curve (Herrnstein & Murray, 1994) has been used to substantiate the idea that certain groups of people are less able, less achieving, and less cognitively capable. Norm based testing, such as intelligence testing and standardized testing, is still being used today, though many scholars continue to advocate against its use. In addition to psychology, other helping professions have a history of involvement in oppression. For example, see Wright and colleagues (2021) for a discussion of the social and political climate toward people of color during the mid-to-late 1800s, when the field of social work was established.

In addition to scientific racism, there is a history of oppression of marginalized groups by helping professions. Asian Americans have experienced a history of discrimination in the US, including immigration, citizenship, and voting discrimination dating back to the 19th century. Psychology, education, and other professions have long promoted the model minority myth (i.e., the framing of Asian Americans as a model minority in reference to educational achievement, household income, and assimilation into US society in relation to other racial and ethnic minorities [Leong & Okazaki, 2009]). Although this myth may seem positive, it leads to erasure of the challenges experienced by many Asian Americans including poverty, discrimination, and violence. Additionally, this myth has been used to criticize Black and Latinx Americans and pit these groups against each other. Discrimination against Asian and Asian Americans continues to occur, as evidenced by the rise of anti-Asian violence resulting from framing the COVID-19 pandemic as being caused by a virus from China (Grover et al., 2020).

Wright and colleagues (2021) communicate the role of colonization, legalized slavery, and other discriminatory practices in our understanding of the history of social work. For example, they highlight the bias surrounding who is credited as an important figure in social work history. They acknowledge the role of what we now refer to as White privilege in the recognition of identified founders, while other important figures of color, such as Eugene Kinckle Jones, are not mentioned as framers of the social work profession. Further, because of the treatment of Indigenous Peoples in the country, it is possible that their contributions to the field of social work or social welfare could have been omitted, ignored, or downplayed (Wright et al., 2021).

Discrimination against people who identify as LGBTQ+ has also been part of the history of psychology, counseling, medicine, and other helping professions. During the 1950s and 1960s, homosexuality was categorized as abnormal and pathological and was treated by hormones, electroconvulsive therapy, psychotherapy, and institutionalization (Kimmel & Browning, 1999). Similarly, gender nonconformity and transgender identity were pathologized, with earlier versions of the *Diagnostic and Statistical Manual of Mental Disorders* (DSM) including a diagnosis of "gender identity disorder." It was not until the 1970s that homosexuality was no longer categorized as a psychiatric disorder, and not until the most recent edition of the DSM-5 where "gender identity disorder" was replaced with "gender dysphoria" in an effort to depathologize having a gender identity that differs from sex assigned at birth and to focus more on the distress that may arise from a misalignment between gender identity and assigned sex.

However, pathologizing sexual orientation and gender expansiveness lingers in our work. Although organizations such as the National Association of Social Workers, American Counseling Association, and the American Psychological Association have explicitly banned conversion therapy, this and other forms of harm continue. Discriminatory practices are expanding through many states' legislation that support mental health providers' refusal of clients on the basis of "conscientious objection" (Cooper, 2023). Similarly, policies and legislation that discriminate against trans youth have proliferated (Novotny, 2023). As we write this book, anti-trans and anti-LGBTQIA legislation and executive orders have barraged the public, in many cases contrary to well established science and best practices. The major professional associations have spoken firmly against this discrimination but there are some individual practitioners and researchers who are supporting the oppressive measures, or at the least, staying silent or complicit.

Another example of harm within the context of the US is explained within the 2015 Hoffman Report. Independent reviewers found that the American Psychological Association colluded with the Department of Defense after the attacks on September 11, 2001, by modifying the ethical guidelines in a way that ultimately allowed for psychologists to be involved in "enhanced interrogation techniques" to obtain information about how the attacks occurred (Hoffman et al., 2015). Years before the independent review, some members of APA vocally raised concerns about the shift in ethical guidelines (e.g., Ken Pope distributed a public resignation letter denouncing these moves within APA [Pope, 2008; Pope, 2016]).

Outrage within and outside of the APA pressed for a clearer and direct stance against psychologist's involvement in interrogation and torture. This outrage, along with the results of the Hoffman Report, led to the amendment of the APA Ethics Committee's stance against torture and interrogation. What is often left out of the discussion of the impact of the findings of the Hoffman report is its harmful impact on marginalized individuals and communities, particularly those who are Muslim, Middle Eastern, and/or Arab. Gomez et al. (2016) discuss the impact of this institutional betrayal on those within the organization, those from minoritized backgrounds, and the impact on the organization itself.

APA is still contending with the harms that it has caused and continues to cause. In October 2021, APA issued an apology to people of color for its role in "promoting, perpetuating, and failing to challenge" racism and discrimination in the United States (APA, 2021). The Association of Black Psychologists rejected this apology for several reasons, including APA not adequately addressing and atoning for this history nor consulting with psychological organizations of minoritized ethnic groups on matters that impact their respective communities (Association of Black Psychology, 2021). In 2023, the Society of Indian Psychologists accepted a public apology and statement of commitment for reconciliation from the APA (APA Indigenous Apology Work Group, 2023). The apology was a result of several years of collaborative work and consultation with Indigenous scholars and community members who provided feedback and recommendations for reconciliation and repair. Other organizations are also contending with their oppressive histories. The National Association of Social Workers issued an apology in June 2021 "for racist practices in American social work" (NASW, 2021), as they struggle with the juxtaposition of being a professional organization that champions social justice and also has a history of discriminatory practices.

The above mentioned examples are in no way an exhaustive compilation of the harm caused by mental health professions. However, the movement toward challenging the oppression perpetuated by professional organizations only came about because members were aware and willing to act. The questions in Activity 2.3 are meant to guide you in learning about the history of your respective field.

ACTIVITY 2.3

Impact on Your Community and the Communities You Care About

Consider the questions below to begin to reflect on the history of your respective field:

1. What other ways have psychology, counseling, and other helping professions contributed to the oppression of people within the United States?

2. Consider the communities that you identify with. How does the history of your community relate to the history of psychology and/or other helping professions (e.g. counseling, social work)?

Awareness alone does not make change. In the next section, we will discuss some experiences of advocacy of those within the helping professions toward changing the professions, again with a focus on counseling and psychology.

Making Space Outside and Within Professional Helping Associations

Some helping professionals have been vocal about marginalization within their professions through advocacy for inclusion of oppressed groups and communities. Their leadership and action made it possible to create spaces for these groups within mainstream organizations and create new ones that are more representative of minoritized communities. Below, we present some examples from psychology illustrating history and advocacy beyond mainstream perspectives. We hope this can serve as a starting point to further study the history of other organizations and divisions that might not be present.

Like many organizations, there were no people of color or women included in the founding of the APA in 1892 (APA, 2021). In fact, APA did not acknowledge the underrepresentation and marginalization of Black psychologists within mainstream US psychology until 1963, in response to urging by a division of APA—Society for the Psychological Study of Social Issues (SPSSI; Holliday, 2009). In 1967, SPSSI invited Rev. Dr. Martin Luther King Jr. to speak at the annual APA Convention. In his address, he spoke to the role of social scientists within the Civil Rights Movement and called for (White) social scientists to research Black leadership development within organizations, examine the effectiveness of political action as a social change mechanism, and understand the psychological and ideological changes in Black people and the implications for the relationship between Black people and society and social institutions (King, 1967).

Advocacy and organizing efforts by Black people within the fields of counseling and psychology have challenged and continue to challenge structural inequity. In addition to Rev. Dr. King's charge, the Civil Rights Movement during the 1960s played a major role in shifting psychology. As anger with existing institutions, laws, and policies increased and people felt empowered to advocate for themselves, the push for change in the field of psychology was monumental. Black psychologists believed that APA was dedicated to White middle class values and was unresponsive to the needs and interests of Black psychologists and Black communities. As a result, they formed the Association of Black Psychologists (ABPsi) in 1968 and presented concerns to APA related to the low numbers of Black psychologists and graduate students, lack of effort toward ending social problems, and the limited representation of Black psychologists within APA governance (Pickren, 2009). During the same year, Black social workers disengaged from the National Conference on Social Welfare to form the National Association of Black Social Workers (NABSW) that served as an advocacy group to address the concerns of the Black community. They released a position statement with demands to be addressed by the conference executive committee (see NABSW, 1998). See https://socialwelfare.library.vcu.edu/social-work/national-association-of-black-social-workers/ for more information about NABSW.

Inspired by ABPsi, Black graduate students in psychology disrupted the 1969 presidential address at the annual APA Convention to present demands related to greater racial equality in APA (Pickren, 2009). In another example, the Black Caucus was established within the Society for Research in Child Development in an effort to advance the careers of African Americans within the organization and to improve the lives of Black children (Holliday, 2009). The institutionalization of Black psychology served as a model for other racially and ethnically focused psychology advocacy movements and organizations.

Latinx and Asian American psychological associations, similar to that of Black Psychology, were established as a result of the systemic inequities experienced by Latinx people and Asian Americans within US society and the profession of psychology. For example, early pioneers of Latinx psychology, such as Dr. George Sanchez, published articles arguing that intelligence tests lacked the validity to assess Mexican American children given that the tests were based on White samples who had different life experiences and/or English language proficiency. These scholars also highlighted the marginalization of Latinx people in the US and critiqued traditional clinical psychology training for not accounting for the experiences of Latinx people (Padilla & Olmedo, 2009).

The Lake Arrowhead Conference (1979) was the first time a large number of Latinx-identified psychologists representing diverse backgrounds (national origin, geographic regions, and disciplinary interests) came together to form an alliance. This meeting established a foundation for the National Hispanic Psychological Association, now known as the National Latinx Psychological Association, which was founded in 2002, under the leadership of Dr. Patricia Arredondo (Chavez-Korell et al., 2012). The establishment of Asian American psychology was influenced by the activism of the Civil Rights Era and developed alongside Asian American studies. Asian American studies emerged across the US from the activism on college campuses along with the Third World student movements (Leong & Okazaki, 2009). In 1972, the Asian American Psychological Association was formed with the intention of educating and training Asian American psychologists, improving mental health services, and advocating for Asian Americans (Leong & Okazaki, 2009).

The founding of the American Indian and Alaskan Native Society of Indian Psychologists, also known as the Society of Indian Psychologists, (SIP) began in the early 1970s through the efforts of Carolyn Attneave, who launched the Network of Indian Psychologists, and Joseph E. Trimble, who created an interest group within SPSSI. When they merged their efforts, they established the beginning of SIP (Trimble & Clearing-Sky, 2009). The organization serves as a space of support for Native students, professionals, and elders working in mental health professions, as well as a respite from environments in which they may be the only or one of a few Native people. Additionally, they work to further the understanding of American Indian people through culturally appropriate research and practice. This organization and other programs have been instrumental in recruiting, mentoring, and supporting Native students interested in the field of psychology (e.g., Indians into Psychology Doctoral Education [INPSYDE], Alaska Natives into Psychology [ANPsych] at the University of Alaska, Fairbanks, and the American Indian Support Project at Utah State University).

For many years, Middle Eastern, Arab American, and North African psychologists and trainees felt that their experiences were not represented in existing psychological organizations. In 2017, a coalition of psychologists established the American Arab, Middle Eastern and North

African Psychological Association (AMENA-Psy), which is dedicated to the development of Arab/MENA psychologists and psychological research and practice in North America. AMENA-Psy (2022) strives to promote the values of "amena," which comes from the Arabic root a-ma-na, including honesty, fairness, faithfulness, safety, and peace in the organization's work.

As previously mentioned, there were no women involved in the founding of APA. As a result of sexism, women have generally been marginalized within psychology. Early attempts of women to organize within APA were met with resistance. For example, during World War II, the National Council of Women Psychologists was formed to increase opportunities for women psychologists. The organization was denied as a division of APA several times and ultimately became the International Council of Psychologists (Tiefer, 1991). As the numbers of women-identified psychologists increased alongside the Women's movement of the 1960s, organizations such as the Association for Women in Psychology (AWP) were founded, separate from APA. AWP worked to combat gender discrimination and sexual harassment within the field, address the lack of research and theory related to women, and advocate for feminist psychology (AWP, n.d.). The Society for the Psychology of Women (Division 35 of APA) was established in 1973 to advocate for women's issues within APA.

Two other examples of mental health focused divisions born from advocacy within large White-centered professional associations are the Society for the Psychological Study of Culture, Ethnicity, and Race (Division 45) of APA and the Association for Multicultural Counseling and Development of the American Counseling Association (AMCD). In 1974, APA established a Minority fellowship program, and its first director, Dr. Dalmas Taylor, proposed a conference for ethnic minority psychologists. The national conference was held in 1978—initially named Expanding the Roles of Culturally Diverse People in the Profession of Psychology, but known as the Dulles conference—and focused on methods for ethnic minority psychologists to become more meaningfully involved in APA (Comas-Díaz, 2009).

Among the recommendations from this conference was the creation of a division within APA to study ethnic minority psychology and focus on issues within APA. Division 45 of APA, founded in 1986, was the result of many years of advocacy from psychologists in minoritized ethnic populations to represent "psychologists who conduct research on ethnic minority concerns or who apply psychological knowledge and techniques to ethnic minority issues" (Society for the Psychological Study of Culture, Ethnicity, and Race, n.d.). Since its inception, Division 45 has been a welcoming space within APA where psychologists and graduate students can build community and seek mentorship, as well as engage with research through conferences and programming.

The Association of Multicultural Counseling and Development (AMCD) is a division of the American Counseling Association that seeks to support and attend to the needs of racially and ethnically diverse people within the field of counseling and enhance the development, human rights, and psychological health of all people—among other things (Holliday, 2009). AMCD, originally established as the Association of Non-White Counselors, was formally recognized in 1972 as a division of the American Personnel and Guidance Association (APGA, later becoming the American Counseling Association). This came after several years of advocacy, organizing, and being denied as a formal division of AGPA.

As referenced previously, the pathologization of those who identify as LGBTQ+ is part of the history of psychology. The gay liberation movement and emerging literature critical of existing research and practices were imperative in challenging this pathologization. The Society for Sexual, Affectional, Intersex, and Gender Expansive Identities (SAIGE, a division of ACA) began as the Caucus of Gay Counselors in 1975 (SAIGE, 2020). The division is committed to advocacy for these communities within the counseling profession and beyond. In 1984, what is now known as the Society for the Psychology of Sexual Orientation and Gender Diversity (APA Division 44) was established in APA as a result of staged political action and organizing by queer psychologists and allies who presented demands and challenged discrimination within mental health organizations (Kimmel & Browning, 1999).

The organizations discussed thus far focus on centering the voices of marginalized helping professionals from specific communities. There are also examples of groups that arose from the recognition of a need for coalitions to address marginalization and oppression. For example, Counselors for Social Justice (CSJ) evolved from informal meetings that focused on how the ACA could better commit to anti-oppression and social justice through collaborative efforts. Based on the outcomes of these informal meetings, a group was convened with representatives across ACA divisions (AMCD, SAIGE [then AGLBIC], Association for Specialists in Group Work). This formal planning meeting identified the need for social justice advocacy across divisions and within ACA (Anderson et al., 2015). After considerable advocacy, CSJ was recognized as an official division of ACA in 2000 to "promote social justice in our society through confronting oppressive systems of power and privilege that affect professional counselors and our clients and to assist in the positive change in our society through the professional development of counselors" (CSJ, 2023). Similarly, within APA, a coalition of 22 divisions are allied in what is referred to as Divisions for Social Justice (DSJ) to discuss and voice human rights issues that arise both within and outside APA.

The above section highlights the actions taken by those within psychology and counseling to move the fields closer to being socially just and inclusive. There are many such examples in social work, human services, and other helping organizations. Activity 2.4 asks you to reflect on what we have shared so far and your connection and reactions to the harm and the advocacy we described.

ACTIVITY 2.4

Reflecting on the Past

1. Reflect on the instances of harm and advocacy described above and those you may have researched within your respective professions.

2. How have these and/or other instances impacted you, your communities, and/or the communities you hope to serve.

3. What do you wish was done differently?

4. Do you notice any parallels between the past and today?

Reading and reflecting about history can bring up a lot of emotions. Before moving on to the next activities, we would like you to take a moment of pause. Take the next 10 minutes to put the book down and engage in self-care. Perhaps you take this time to grab a snack, go outside, watch a funny video, or simply sit with yourself and take deep breaths. Whatever feels comfortable for you, take these next 10 minutes for yourself.

IMG 2.1

Historical Figures and Events

Now that you have taken these last 10 minutes away from the book, we can move on to the next activity. Activity 2.5 introduces examples of significant people and events within the history of the helping professions. Use this list and the questions below to explore the foundations for advocacy within your field. This will require you to research your own people, events, and/or organizations. As you answer the questions and become more familiar with people and events, pay attention to your internal process. Learning about history, and particularly inspiring history, can help us feel more connected to our identities, to ourselves as helping professionals, and to the work we do.

ACTIVITY 2.5

Pioneers, Events, and Organizations

Below is a list of significant people, events, and organizations related to the history of counseling and psychology. We have tried to create a diverse list, but we acknowledge that it is not exhaustive. We invite you to go beyond this list and to research scholars, activists, and organizations that match your own identities and histories. As you review this list, reflect on the following questions:

1. Which people and organizations on the list below do you feel particularly drawn to? Why?

2. Consider those who you feel drawn to. What influence do the people and/or events have today?

3. What or who is missing from this list? What did they accomplish and/or how have they impacted the field?

4. What organizations have been impactful and/or supportive to you throughout your life? These can be organizations outside of the field of mental health and include community and student-based organizations. How can these outside organizations inform what we do as helping professionals?

- Dr. Joseph L. White, the "Godfather" of Black psychology, published the first article outlining a vision of Black psychology in *Ebony* in 1970.
- Dr. Jessica Henderson Daniel was the first African American woman to serve as president of the American Psychological Association. She was president-elect in 2017 and president in 2018.
- Dr. Carolyn Attneave, a Delaware and Cherokee psychologist, was the first Native American woman to receive a doctoral degree in psychology (1962). She partnered with Dr. Joseph Trimble, a Lakota psychologist, to organize an American Indian Interest group within the Society for the Psychological Study of Social Issues, later the Society of Indian Psychologists.
- Dr. Janet Helms completed work in racial identity development and assessment, which has been used across disciplines, including psychology, education, and law. Testified for Supreme Court cases regarding bias in testing and other issues.
- Dr. Logan Wright, from the Osage Nation, served as the first Native American president of the American Psychological Association from 1986–1987.
- Dr. Derald W. Sue, a pioneer of Asian American psychology, coled advocacy drawing attention to the need for multicultural competencies in counseling and psychology. Sue also revitalized and expanded Dr. Chester Pierce's work on microaggressions.
- A group of counselor educators and psychologists (Drs. Derald Wing Sue, Patricia Arredondo, Thomas Parham, Allen Ivey, Michael D'Andrea, Don C. Locke, and others) worked collaboratively and strategically for over 2 decades to advocate for formal multicultural counseling competencies. Their first publication calling for cultural competence was published in 1982, with calls following in 1992 and 1996 and final adoption by ACA in 2002. This work also paved the way for the multicultural guidelines in APA and the advocacy competencies in ACA.
- Chinatown North Beach Mental Health Services and Chinatown Child Development Center in San Francisco were the first agencies to offer culturally relevant and bilingual mental health services to Asian Americans.
- Richmond Area Multi-Services (RAMS) in San Francisco (originally named Richmond Maxi Center) was established in 1974. The National Asian American Psychology Training Center was established under RAMS in 1979.
- Dr. Marigold Linton was one of the founders of the National Indian Education Association (NIEA) and the Society for the Advancement of Chicanos and Native Americans in Sciences (SACNAS). (see www.sacnas.org)
- Dr. Evelyn Hooker (1957) conducted a groundbreaking study that found that gay and heterosexual men's projective test results could not be distinguished from the other. These findings were important because of the stigma and discrimination against those who identified as gay and lesbian at the time. These findings, along with other research and advocacy efforts, were pivotal in the advocacy for LGBTQ+ rights within psychology.
- Dr. Alfredo Castaneda was the first Latino to serve on the editorial board of *Child Development* and a well-known child experimental psychologist who studied the importance of biculturalism from a psychological perspective, among other significant concepts.
- Dr. Martha Bernal was the first Latina to receive a doctorate degree in psychology in the US in 1962.
- Dr. Patricia Arredondo is known as "La Madrina" of Latinx psychology. She was the first president and one of the founders of what is now known as the National Latinx Psychological Association.

- Dr. Daya Singh Sandhu was the first Sikh president of AMCD in 2009–2010. A well-known counselor educator, he fought racial prejudice, gender inequity, and youth violence in the US and India.
- Dr. Melba Vasquez was the first Latina and woman of color to serve as president of APA in 2011.
- Dr. Martha Banks advocated for the need for attention to the intersection of disability in feminist psychology with the inclusion of the importance of race and religion.
- The Lake Arrowhead, California, conference of Hispanic psychologists (1979) established the foundation for NLPA.
- Dr. Samuel H. Johnson founded the Association of Non-White Concerns, a division of the American Counseling Association, in 1972. This organization later evolved into what is now known as the Association for Multicultural Counseling and Development.
- National Association of Black Social Workers (NABSW) was founded in 1968 in San Francisco, California, by a group of Black social workers while at the National Conference on Social Welfare (see the history of NABSW at www.nabsw.org).
- The American Arab, Middle Eastern, and North African Psychological Association (AMENA-Psy) was founded in 2017 with Germine Awad, Mona Amer, and Nabil El-Ghoroury as founding board members.
- American Rehabilitation Counseling Association was established in 1957 and is focused on providing support and advocating for those with disabilities (for more information, see http://www.arcaweb.org/).
- The Society for the Psychological Study of Culture, Ethnicity and Race (Division 45 in APA) was founded in 1986 with rotating presidential slates beginning with Esteban Olmedo (Latino Slate, 1986), Chalso Loo and John Moritsugu (Asian American Slate, 1987), Dalmas Taylor (African American Slate, 1988), and Teresa LaFromboise (Native American Slate, 1990). Dr. LaFromboise also appointed a task force on gay, lesbian and bisexual concerns and a task force on women during her tenure as president.
- The National Multicultural Conference and Summit was founded in 1999 in Newport Beach, California, when a group of scholars from several APA divisions came together to address the growing mental health needs of historically marginalized groups and disenfranchised individuals. The conference brings individuals from psychology and other mental health disciplines together to inform and inspire multicultural theory, research, practice, and advocacy. To learn more about the conference, visit https://www.multiculturalsummit.org/
- The Teacher's College Winter Roundtable on Cross Cultural Psychology and Education, convened in 1983 as one of the first annual national conferences focused on cultural issues in counseling, psychology, and education.

Personal History and Context

As demonstrated throughout the chapter, the context for advocacy in counseling and psychology includes activism as a response to inequity, discrimination, and marginalization. We have each come to this work through our own contexts. In the following pages, we will share our influences and journeys into our engagement with social justice work, and we encourage you to reflect on your personal context and motivations. At the end of the chapter, you will be asked to reflect on the experiences that have moved you into your respective fields.

DERRICK'S JOURNEY

Social justice was important to me well before I was introduced to the term. I was raised in a community that valued "looking out" for each other. This was our way of caring for one another and making sure that folks were able to get their basic needs met. Beyond the lessons of my community, involvement in several groups was key to my development. In high school, I participated in an organization that aimed to build community among Black students. As part of this group, we provided food and gifts to families during the fall and winter holidays. We also fundraised to go on college tours—an introduction to college for many of us. Many of us went on to become first-generation college students and graduates. For all of us, this organization was a space to connect to a larger community.

In college, I continued to develop this passion for supporting Black students and creating counterspaces where we could exist in community. I became actively involved in student organizations that focused on helping Black students navigate and graduate from college. In these efforts, we partnered with a community-based organization to support elementary and high school students. It was not until I was in graduate school and became exposed to more explicit language about power, privilege, positionality, and oppression that I began attending protests and marches.

Although the involvements mentioned above have impacted my journey related to social justice, the public (recorded) deaths of Black people and the movement for Black lives have been significant in my understanding and dedication to this work. My commitments continue to strengthen and broaden. It is important to note that I am very much still developing my own understanding of what it means to take action in the spaces and roles I occupy. I come to this work (and this text) as someone who is in progress and process, learning from those in the field and beyond.

REBECCA'S ONGOING JOURNEY TO AWARENESS AND ACTION AGAINST RACISM

The foundation of my story and path up to now, in relation to social action, is clearly embedded in the values of my parents, as well as my internal challenges of trying to understand injustices I observed as a child, White female identified, Polish French Canadian, living in the US, with mental illness in the family. Although we participated in some social action as a family (e.g., grape boycotts, peace rallies), it felt as though it was something we did, rather than something we *must* do. In my early 20s, when I became a counselor, all those values came to the forefront as I saw my clients face daily challenges directly related to oppression and oppressive systems. I also saw how my role and training as a counselor was not only deficient but also invalidating if I did not acknowledge, and try to address, the injustices in systems my clients were confronting. It felt worse than fraudulent to be working with them, caring about them, but not taking responsibility to directly do something about these injustices.

I began to intensively uncover the missing pieces in my understanding and skills in multicultural counseling as a White person—learning from mentors and role models who were actively working to change the field of counseling. Many experiences and pivotal moments influenced my path in social action. One example happened more than 25 years ago when my colleagues and I chose to speak out and then faced a six-year lawsuit for speaking out. This lawsuit differentially impacted us, with the greatest impact on my colleagues of color. This solidified my commitment to social action and the importance of strategy. As I began to take on more active roles, I also became clearer about the connection of activism in the community and the activism I was doing within the field and in my institutions. Over the past ten years, I have become increasingly alarmed and activated to speak out publicly, gain training for collective action, and join with community groups who are engaged in activism focused on anti-racism, as well as the rights of immigrants, trans and LGBQA+, and Indigenous communities. I continue to learn, struggle, and hold gratitude for the many, many people I have learned from and continue to learn from.

MUNINDER'S JOURNEY TO ANTI-RACISM

My desire to engage in activism started as a young child raised by Sikh parents using Sikh teachings to inspire my life's journey. To me, the teachings were clear—one needed to be an activist to be a good person. Every aspect of my religion taught me to be more like the Gurus, whose life's work was to fight for the rights and well-being of others, particularly those who are most oppressed. In fact, many were martyrs for this cause. As a child, my parents told me stories and I read comic book versions of the heroism of the Gurus and other Sikhs, and I wanted to be brave like they were. I think this is where I learned to be interpersonally brave, but my advocacy was limited to the individual level for many years.

The systemic work came during my doctoral studies as I started to learn about the interrelatedness of oppression for all groups and that systems disruption was necessary for change to happen. I gained more skills over the years—and more professional power as well. I engage in social justice work, anti-racism work in particular, in my job as a chair and professor because the university system continues to be inequitable for underrepresented and marginalized groups. I engage in justice work outside the ivory tower because I see how racism impacts the well-being of BIPOC individuals and communities.

Specific events and specific people have been catalysts in my life. After I graduated with my master's degree in counseling, I worked in an in-patient substance abuse rehabilitation center and witnessed injustice in the way clients (mostly people of color from under-resourced communities) were treated. That job was the impetus for pursuing my doctoral studies—to gain the knowledge, skills, title, and power to help create social change in systems such as the rehabilitation center. Two other pivotal moments in my life were the backlash post-9/11 that Muslims and Sikhs experienced and the summer where Black men and boys were videotaped being shot by police, with no resulting justice. Both moments were unequivocal reminders that racism is ever present and anti-racism would need to be my life's work.

BRYAN'S JOURNEY TO SCHOLAR ACTIVISM

Caring for others was a core value my family instilled in me. We lived by the golden rule—treating others as we wished to be treated. Over time, I discovered that honoring each person's unique needs was a deeper commitment to recognizing their full humanity. Despite always valuing care for others, my activist journey began when an accident stripped me of my identity as an athlete. Prior to that I jokingly said I was in high school to play sports; however, once I got injured, I had to renegotiate who I was and what it meant to no longer be an athlete. As a response and to help me grieve the loss, I channeled the energy I had once committed to sports into activism.

I first became involved with the League of United Latin American Citizens (LULAC). At that time, I had little idea what activism or advocacy truly meant. Still, I knew I wanted to support students like myself who lacked guidance. Through the League, I received mentorship and, for the first time, seriously considered a college education.

At 18, I stepped onto a college campus for the first time when I enrolled at a local community college. There I became part of the Puente program and for the first time since I had arrived in the US, I felt connected to the Latine community. I became a community organizer and helped plan the May 1, 2006, marches in my community, known as "The Great Boycott." At the time, I reached out to multiple organizations and was denied any kind of support, including those who I believed were there to support me. I was told by a Latino organization that being Latino was a "social identity not a political one." However, I could not separate my Latino identity from my immigrant identity or what it meant to be undocumented in America. Before having the language for it I understood that the political was personal. Therefore, I founded the "DREAM club" a pro-immigration, pro-education, and pro-community advocacy group. I did so with the support of other Puentistas, allies, and professors. The organization became known on campus and actively engaged in political action and advocacy for all people. I began to see my academic success as bigger than myself, as a challenge to systemic inequities and a form of resistance.

After transferring to San Jose State University, I joined a Latino-based multicultural fraternity (Sigma Lambda Beta International Fraternity Inc.) and continued to be involved in the community while developing my identity as a DREAM activist and social change agent. A promise to continue to do all I could to support undocumented immigrants eventually translated into a dissertation (*Undocumented Healing: Strengths and Resilience from the Shadows*), a doctoral degree, private practice, and a career focused on increasing access to mental health and education for marginalized communities—all while creating narratives of strength, resilience, and success. During a time period where immigrants have become the target of xenophobic attacks and dehumanization, I find myself in the same place I was over 20 years ago. Organizing in community, centering those most affected, while recognizing that this book is also part of that promise.

We have discussed the history of helping professions in terms of advocacy and shared a bit about our personal histories that brought us to this work. Now we would like you to reflect on your own history.

ACTIVITY 2.6

Your Journey

Reflect on your own history and context. What experiences have contributed to your interest in your current field and moved you toward action? Consider the organizations and/or events that you thought of in Activity 2.5.

1. Create a timeline starting with your ancestors, key influences, and historical events that impacted your current position as a healer or healer in training.

2. Map key moments in your life (and that of your family and community), including events, historical moments, experiences, and challenges within your lifetime.

3. Envision the impact you hope your actions will have on the future.

As you continue to read, reflect, and take action with this book, keep in mind this exploration of your history and the history of your profession.

"It is important for all of us to appreciate where we come from and how that history has really shaped us in ways that we might not understand."

—Sonia Sotomayor, US Supreme Court Justice

Chapter 3

Power, Privilege, and Raising Our Consciousness

"It's easy to forget who you are."

—Kendrick Lamar

"I know that people can be better than they are. We are capable of bearing a great burden, once we discover that the burden is reality and arrive where reality is."

—James Baldwin

The year 2020 brought with it the COVID-19 pandemic. The world slowed down enough to spotlight oppression, and as a result, there were many calls to action—societally, interpersonally, and intrapersonally. Simultaneously, divisions based on race, sexuality, religion, gender, poverty, and politics were made obvious by polarization; however, for those who have lived in the margins, these experiences and conversations were not new. Even with our efforts toward justice, relatively little has changed. We are still asking for the same things that so many have fought for—Martin Luther King Jr., Malcolm X, Ed Roberts, Fred Korematsu, Grace Lee Boggs, Cesar Chavez, Delores Huerta, Audre Lorde, Bayard Rustin, Colin Kaepernick, Marsha P. Johnson, and Sylvia Rivera, and others.

Conversations and reflections on our personal and institutional relationship to power, privilege, and oppression are difficult and emotional, yet they are essential in order to work effectively toward social change and liberation. Liberation commits us to use our power and privilege to fight on behalf of all who are bound by oppression. Lilla Watson, an indigenous Australian professor, artist, and activist said, "If you have come here to help me, you are wasting your time. But if you have come because your liberation is bound up with mine, then let us work together" (Watson attributes this statement to Aboriginal activists in Queensland in the 1970s; Uniting Church in Australia, n.d.). Working for change means making a commitment to challenge oppressive systems—racism, sexism, ableism, heterosexism, transphobia, xenophobia. Understanding our positionality and how that is bound up with our liberation and that of others is essential to social change.

In Chapter 2, we presented the historical context and the impact of social change within helping professions. We also explored what it means to create spaces for diversity (e.g. identity-based organizations) and how that has shaped our work and professions. While Chapter 2 focused outward on the profession, in this chapter, we focus inward on you. We provide the opportunity to reflect on your own history, identities, and how these have shaped you and your relationship to social change. This chapter challenges all of us to be honest with ourselves in order to continue to increase our consciousness while (re)committing to taking action. We recognize that there is tremendous diversity among our readers. For some, this self-reflection may be new, while for others, it may be very familiar. If you are new to these ideas, some of this reflection may be uncomfortable, and we ask that you consider that discomfort, be patient with yourself and the process, and be willing to persist. Alternatively, if you have immersed yourself in understanding power, privilege, oppression, intersectionality, and liberation, we ask that you consider how you might challenge yourself for a deeper understanding and relationship to your positionality and social action.

The activities in this chapter are intended to provide you with opportunities to reflect and readjust. We invite a mindful awareness of yourself and others into this space. Whether you are doing this workbook alone or in a group, we ask you to take the time needed to reflect, critically think, and challenge yourselves with an open mind and heart, curiosity, and compassion for yourselves and others. In the spirit of solidarity, share your insights and lessons with others.

ACTIVITY 3.1

Mindful Awareness: A Guided Activity

Take a seat, get comfortable, and close your eyes.
  Take three deep, slow breaths, each a little deeper than the last.

- Breathe in through your nose as if you were smelling flowers.
- Breathe out through your mouth as if you were blowing candles (repeat 3x).

This is a mindful moment. We will return to mindful moments throughout the book.
Focus on the now:

- Put both of your hands above your heart.
- Pay attention to the warmth of your hands.
- Pay attention to the way your hands rise and fall on your chest as you breathe.

Take a mindful moment.
  Feel gratitude for the air that gives you life. Focus on your breath. Think about the reason you are engaging with this book and continue reading with intentionality.
  Take a couple minutes to be present in the now (2 minutes of mindful breathing).

Self-Awareness, Messiness, Mosaics, and Social Action

Audre Lorde said, "There is no such thing as a single-issue struggle because we do not live single-issue lives." (Lorde, 1984). Humans are complex by nature. It's important for us to understand that we exist in spectrums— clearly not only one thing or another but a mixture of overlapping identities. We learn to tell our stories in order to make others comfortable or to fit specific narratives, often doing so at a cost to ourselves by ignoring parts of us and not showing up as whole people. Therefore, we want to invite you to sit with the messiness of existence. Like a mosaic, we are an imperfect combination of all things: oppressed and oppressor, privileged and marginalized, and agent and subject. In order to be able to support social change, we need to take the time to reflect, increase the understanding of our experiences and the experiences of others, and then leverage our positionality in the best way possible. When we provide services, advocate, or educate, regardless of our role, there is not one right way to take action. Within this context of messiness, we will ask you to reflect on positionality, power, privilege, oppression, and your experiences with these concepts.

"Positionality" refers to where you are in relation to others, given your cultural background, experiences, and identities within the society in which you live and interact. Because society is shaped by social, historical, and political forces, who we are is influenced by the identities we hold and what they mean to us and to others. For example, positionality in relation to race in the US is shaped by the country's social, political, and economic history and contemporary context, and the influence of identities in relation to access to institutional power. Since the invasion of the American continents by White Europeans, individuals with White European heritage have held political, economic, and social power. (For complexities regarding the history of "Whiteness" in the US, read David R. Roediger's 2018 book *Working Toward Whiteness*.) The positionality of people of other ethnic and national descent has also been influenced and shaped by historical and political forces, as well as existing privilege and power structures within American society. Immigration status, skin color, economic and educational resources, and many other factors reflect one's relationship to others and the power and access we have. This positionality shapes our experiences and how systems impact us. We acknowledge that our lenses as authors are anchored in the United States, but every country has a history of inclusion, exclusion, power, privilege, and oppression. Some of what we know and write about is applicable outside the United States, and we invite you to consider examples of global oppression that you are connected to, understanding how each of your contexts informs your strengths, solidarity, strategies, and methods for sustainability for social change. No matter where we are geographically situated, we can be agents for social change and take action.

Privilege and oppression are two sides of the same coin with power determining where we land. Privilege "is a special right, advantage, or immunity granted or available only to some people or group" (Oxford English Dictionary, n.d.). Power is the "possession of control, authority, or influence over others" (Merriam-Webster, n.d.-a). Consider that oppression is the force placed by those who hold structural, societal, or individual power on those who have less power. Oppression is often enacted in controlling access to resources, determination of policies and practices that perpetuate inequities, as well as systems for maintaining wealth and societal power for those with privilege individually and/or intergenerationally. In most cases, oppression and privilege coexist given the complexity of the many identities we hold and the sociopolitical and historical context (Chan et al., 2018). When we engage in a critical analysis of this experience, we are able to work toward liberation.

Pamela Hays (2012) suggested that the following assumptions can help us engage in a critical analysis from a place of love and acceptance for ourselves and for others:

1. We are all biased.
2. We don't need to belong to dominant groups to be biased.
3. Those in power reinforce biases through social structures that create systems of privilege and oppression.
4. Nonprivileged (minoritized) members are socialized to be aware of what separates those who have privilege from those who do not.
5. Privileged members of these systems are socialized to ignore these differences.
6. Privilege separates privileged and unprivileged people from important information about one another.

(Adapted from *Connecting Across Cultures: The Helper's Toolkit*, pp. 24–33)

ADDRESSING Framework: Identity in Relation to Privilege and Oppression

Pamela Hays (1996) used the acronym ADRESSING (later referred to as ADDRESSING; Hays, 2008) to outline the various identities that make up our positionality and reflect the extent to which those identities benefit from societal privilege (receive advantages based on our membership in an identity group) or face systemic and individual oppression (receive unjust treatment or be blocked from resources due to membership in an identity group). The identities that Hays lists include our age, disability (developmental and acquired), religion, ethnicity and race, socioeconomic status, sexual orientation, indigenous heritage, national origin, and gender. Even if you may think these identities don't mean much to you, it is certain that your experience is influenced by the way other people and society (e.g., economic, social, and political systems) perceive those aspects of your identity. This affects how you are treated and the opportunities you are offered. Most of us who hold privileges are not even aware of how we benefit from them on a daily basis, and we may assume that everyone is offered the same opportunities. When a person is unaware of their privilege (or even when they are aware), they may not notice oppression when they do not experience it directly. Those who are marginalized and oppressed are often more aware of those who have privilege and how that privilege is used. For example, privilege can be seen in how our professions are defined and who has defined them, what type of knowledge is considered valuable, and who gets to create that knowledge. When we think of "professionalism," we need to ask ourselves whose stories, values, and realities are centered? Why are these accepted truths? If our stories, values, and histories are prioritized then we hold privilege. Groups and individuals who have the power to silence the story of entire groups and known history (e.g. rewriting history to minimize the Holocaust or slavery) reflect privilege and power used for strategic acts of oppression and suppression. Similarly, silencing and eliminating the existence of entire populations (e.g., trans and LGBQAI) in documents, public records, and other structures represents intentional oppression and structural violence. Although many of us do not wield power at such high levels, the privilege we hold may collude with such actions if we are not aware. Thus, critical self-reflection is necessary to address oppression. Table 3.1 (adapted from Hays [2016]) presents aspects of power and privilege.

TABLE 3.1 Examples of the ADDRESSING Identities

Identity	Dominant Group (Holds Power / Privilege)	Minoritized Group
Age	Young/middle age	Children/elders
Developmental / acquired disabilities	Non-disabled folks	Neurodivergent/disabled people (cognitive, intellectual, sensory, physical, and psychiatric disabilities)
Religion / spirituality	Christian/secular	Muslim, Buddhist, Jewish, Sikh, Hindu, Atheist, etc.
Ethnic / racial identity	White	Black, Indigenous, and People of Color, including Asian, South Asian, Latino, Pacific Islander, African, Arab, Middle Eastern, (including all of the above who are also American) and multiracial
Socioeconomic status (SES)	Upper and middle class	Lower status (occupation, education, income, area of residence)
Sexual orientation	Heterosexual	Gay, lesbian, bisexual, asexual, pansexual, queer, etc.
Indigenous heritage	European heritage	Native, American Indian, Pan Indigenous or Aboriginal, Inuit, Alaska Native, Maori
National origin	US citizens and US born Americans	Refugee, immigrant, undocumented
Gender	Male identified, cisgender men	Female identified, transgender, nonbinary, genderqueer, androgynous, two-spirit, woman
Additional identities:		

Pamela A. Hays, Adapted from "Table 1.1 ADDRESSING Cultural Influences," *Connecting Across Cultures: The Helper's Toolkit*, pp. 8. Copyright © 2013 by SAGE Publications, Ltd.

The ADDRESSING framework does not capture all aspects of power and privilege. Our education, geographic location, cultural practices, professional identity, and language abilities can be forms of privilege or oppression that are not included in this model (see Arredondo et al.'s [1996] Personal Dimension of Identity for an alternative framework that includes geography and historical context). Nonetheless, we use the ADDRESSING framework as a starting point for reflection. To fully understand how power, privilege, oppression, and marginalization have shaped and continue to shape our lives, our profession, and our clients' lives, we have to understand world history, economics, and political science. Given limitations of space and keeping our focus on action, we suggest that you consider making time to investigate some of those forces specifically as they relate to the places where you and those you serve live.

In order to deepen our understanding of our relationship to power and privilege, we can reflect on our own lives with a critical lens. The following activity will help us connect our past, present, and future with mindful self-reflection. It will also invite us to step into the heart of it and away from intellectualizing our experience.

ACTIVITY 3.2

Inviting the Past, Present, and Future

Read the following instructions through before starting the exercise. Then read each step again and actively engage in the suggestion.

1. First, take three deep breaths.
2. Now think of the identities that are important to you.
3. Think of your ancestors and what it meant for them to live with the identities you share.
4. Think of yourself and what it means to live in your identities today.
5. Take a moment to think of future generations and what it will be like for them to live in those same identities. Make a wish for the lives you hope they'll live.
6. Take 2 minutes to be aware of the thoughts, feelings, and responses you had for each time period—the past, present, and future.

PAUSE

Now that you have read the above passage, take the time to actually do the practice. No really—put the book down and take 2 to 3 minutes to breathe and set your mind in a space of mindful awareness. We promise we'll be here waiting for you the moment you are done. Now take a seat and get comfortable while you give yourself a mindful moment of reflection.

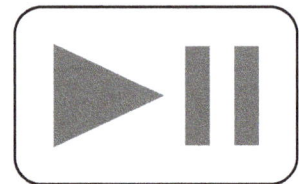

Glad to see you are back. Now that you have taken some time to reflect and breathe, hopefully you have given yourself enough time to process the activity. If you are feeling overwhelmed, tune into your needs, and check in with yourself. If you need to take some time away from this book to process, please do so. Be gentle with your steps and be gentle with your growth. Social justice work is rewarding in many ways, but it's not always easy or comfortable to reflect on our identities and how they play a role in our work.

Now we ask you to go deeper and center the aspects of identity that you identified in the previous activity. Reflect on your positionality and that of those closest to you.

ACTIVITY 3.3

Mindfully Me

Mindfully me:

- As you reflect on Activity 3.2 and the identities you chose to focus on, go back to Table 3.1 and highlight all of your identities. Map your power and privilege.
    - o Put a plus (+) sign on the identities for which you hold power / privilege.
    - o Put a minus (–) sign for the identities for which you don't.

- Go back to the ADDRESSING framework and add any identities that are important to you that are not included in the framework (e.g., psychologist, scholar, caregiver, supervisor, first-generation student, etc.). Reflect on your positionality within those identities and add plus (+) or minus (–) as see them play out in society.
- Now pay attention to the number of pluses (+) and minuses (–) that you have added.

  o What comes up for you?

  o What emotions do you feel?

  o What thoughts do you have?

Take some time to reflect on what it means to live in your identities and see your positionality (+ vs –).

- What privileges were you aware of, and how did you become aware of them?

- What privileges were you unaware of, and why do you think this is?

EXAMPLE

Derrick's Reflection on Identity and Privilege

As I reflect on the activity above, I notice the range of privilege associated with my different identities. For example, I put a (+) next to SES, given my current job and education background, and gender, given my identity as a man. I placed a (–) next to race/ethnicity because of the oppression that Black people have experienced and continue to experience. Another identity that I hold is that of a professor, which is connected to my SES and thus would also have a (+) to represent the privilege associated with this role.

As I reflect on this activity, what comes up for me are the ways that my responses in this activity have changed over time. Having done this exercise previously, I recognize the changes in privilege associated with certain identities over time (i.e., my educational background and current job). Other experiences have been constant throughout my life. The thoughts that arise for me are related to the intersectional experiences of my identities. The history and contemporary experiences of Black people in this country are well documented, and my experiences as a Black person cannot be separated from the experience of my other identities (see intersectionality below). However, it is important that I do recognize the privileges that I experience as a generally abled-bodied (glasses or contact lenses allow me to see without much challenge), cisgender man born in the US (+). Being perceived as a gender that is congruent with how I identify means that I have never been misgendered or had to worry if gendered spaces are inclusive of my gender identity (e.g., most public bathrooms, men's therapy groups, etc.). When I first did this activity, I remember feeling surprised at how easy it had been for me to overlook certain privileges. For example, I am physically able to open heavy doors and walk upstairs while not needing to use an entrance ramp or elevator that might not be easily accessible. Although being Black complicates each of these privileges, I have to understand that those who identify as Black without the privileges I described may have an even more difficult time navigating the same situations, and that it is important for me to continue to push for equity and accessible environments.

Your positionality directly influences your relationships with others, where you get support, and who influences your growth, knowledge, power and access to resources. In the next activity, we ask you to reflect on your relationships and how they shape your experience related to power and privilege (inspired by Hays, 2016).

ACTIVITY 3.4

Vicarious Oppression and Privilege

Think of three people who are close to you and map the ADDRESSING framework for their identities including plus (+) and minus (–) signs as you did for your own.

- What are the similarities?

- What are the differences?

- How do your similarities and differences in identities impact their and your experiences of the world?

- How have these three people changed, challenged, or expanded your worldview?

- Has (previously unseen) oppression become visible to you through your association with them?

- What privileges have you acquired through your association with them?

- In what ways has your life and understanding been enriched through your association with them?

We hope you've had the opportunity to reflect on the lessons these people have provided and the ways your worldview has been transformed through these relationships. Maybe send them a gratitude text later today without much need to explain. Bryan will be sending his little brother a *"Gracias por existir"* text in a bit.

The activities you've done so far in this chapter have been about exploring your identities and relationships and how those shape your experiences. There are areas of your life in which you hold power as well as areas in which you might be marginalized. We have seen in Derrick's example—and you have probably seen in your own reflections—that our relative power and how systems of power engage with us is influenced by our multiple identities. This is intersectionality.

Intersectionality

Kimberlé Crenshaw introduced intersectionality in the context of legal studies to conceptualize the experience of Black women (Crenshaw, 1989) and the gap in discrimination law to address this intersection. Laws meant to address discrimination on the basis of gender and laws meant to address discrimination on the basis of race were inadequate to address discrimination of Black women. Further, it was a call to recognize the ways feminist and anti-racist movements each failed to address these experiences.

"Intersectionality" refers to the nuanced complexity of lived experience and how power and oppression within a sociopolitical context play out in the intersections of identity (for a great overview, see Kimberlé Crenshaw's 2016 Ted Talk, The Urgency of Intersectionality). Intersectionality frameworks (Crenshaw, 1989, 1991) have been used in different areas of study, however, the concept is often watered down in that some aspects of power and privilege have been ignored or minimized (Duran & Jones, 2021). The heart of intersectionality lies in the inspections of power and privilege; therefore it is not additive, but instead, exponential in the impact it has on those who hold particular multiple marginalized identities. Adames and Chavez-Dueñas (2017) explained that the experiences of Afro Latinx women were not marked by the summation of marginalized identities, but instead the exponential effect that each distinct identity had on one another. Similarly, Misawa (2010) and colleagues described how the bullied experience of gay men of color is marked by experiences of homophobic racism and being excluded or alienated from their racial group because of their sexual orientation. In turn, they are often marginalized by LGBTQ+ communities because of their race, ultimately creating an oppressive double bind. If we were to add any other identity to this profile (e.g., disability or undocumented status) their experience of the world would be further affected by the combination of these identities exponentially.

Reflecting on the various aspects of our own identity and experiences with power, privilege, and oppression allows us to have more complex insights and opportunities for understanding the world. It is important to consider that, given these identities (especially the visible ones), we represent something to the people we encounter. As we engage in social action, it is important to have an awareness of how we use our identities, what our identities mean to us, what they mean to others, and how our identities influence our interactions with the world. In Activity 3.5, we ask you to think about the different aspects of your identity and what they may mean when you engage with others. We use Bryan's identities as examples throughout so that you can see how this activity can unfold.

ACTIVITY 3.5

How Others Perceive Us Makes a Difference

For this activity, you will create a mask to represent the aspects of your identity that are often noticed and unnoticed by others. To create this mask of identity, you can use paper or a blank mask. You can respond to the prompts by writing, drawing, collaging, or any other creative way to represent who you are.

1. Imagine that you are meeting a person for the first time. What aspects of your identity are they most likely to recognize? If it is helpful, refer to the ADDRESSING framework and Activity 3.3. On the outside of the mask (the front of the face), write or illustrate the aspects of your identity dimensions that are easily seen or recognized by others. Although this may change somewhat depending on whom you are interacting with, for now, think about the aspects of your identity that are most obvious to others.

2. What aspects of your identity may go unnoticed/unseen by this new person? Write or draw these aspects of your identity on the other side of the mask (the inside of the face).

3. Now that you have created a mask of identities (easily known or unknown to others), think about how the ways you are treated might change based on who you engage with.

CREATING MY MASK (BRYAN)

1. My skin is Brown and tatted. As an Afro Latino man, I am racially ambiguous and do not fit neatly into a lot of spaces. I wear my hair long and curly. I move freely through the world as a large able body (I do not have visible physical disabilities). Therefore, I believe the identities most obvious to people I encounter are as a large physically able-bodied, cisgender male of color (I look the way US society expects men to look). What those identities mean to others depends on what meaning they attach to what they perceive. It's also important to recognize that they do not perceive my identities as silos but instead view some combination of them.

2. I am Costa Rican and Panamanian but grew up in the United States. I'm *neplantero, ni de aquí ni de allá* (*not from here or there*), but from both cultures. I am a spiritual person. I am a husband and a father. I'm an older brother. I grew up in low SES. I am of Spanish, Indigenous, and Afro Caribbean descent. I'm bilingual. I have ADHD. These are all examples of identities others are unable to know simply by looking at me or initially engaging with me. What those identities mean to others depends on what meaning they attach to them if I choose to disclose them. These identities are also experienced in combination with my visible identities.

3. As a person of color and an immigrant, I interact with other people of color and immigrants as an insider–outsider who is given the trust of the community in a different way. In contexts where most people are White and the purpose of gathering is not related to race, they might treat me as a threat or express discomfort. For example, when walking down the street in a majority White city, people often move away from me or change the side of the street they walk on. In other spaces, like conferences or the classroom, I might stand out as one of a few people of color in the space and thus experience being tokenized or tribalized by my appearance. If I am in a group of people of color or work within communities of color, I'm able to code switch to connect with the community. I'm trusted by some communities of color, and I'm given access to knowledge and perspectives that White researchers might not have access to. In other words, the identities and experiences of the people I interact with will influence the way they interpret my identities. For some, the color of my skin and tattoos may feel safe, while others may be mistrustful of me because of their (conscious or unconscious) bias or socialization.

The way we see ourselves and the ways others perceive us shape our interactions, our opportunities, and our relationships. These identities can present strengths and challenges and are also somewhat limited in that they do not fully represent who we are. They do not reflect all of the ways that we have learned and engaged in our world or what we bring to our work. It's also important to recognize that some of our identities and what they mean to us can be fluid and change through lived experience. Our experience of the world would change if we were to change any one of our identities. One single identity shift can drastically change the way we experience the world and the way in which the world experiences us. The following activity is intended to help us imagine exactly that.

ACTIVITY 3.6

Shifting Power and Privilege

1. Reflect on all of your different identities from the earlier activity.

2. Now, imagine that one of your oppressed identities changes so that it holds more privilege in your life. For example, if you experience oppression because of ableism [disability identity], imagine what might be different without your disability. How might people treat you differently? How might your life change? What emotions come up for you when thinking about this?

3. Now think of one of your identities that holds more power and privilege and imagine losing that power and privilege. For example, if you are middle class, imagine what might be different if you lost that privilege (e.g., became unhoused). How might people treat you differently? How might your life change? What emotions come up for you when thinking about this?

Bryan has done this activity with many of his students, and it has often generated an emotional response to imagining a life drastically changed by switching a single identity. Students with many privileged identities have sometimes had difficulty identifying ways they would gain more privilege. Even in terms of economic privilege, our understanding of wealth is different if we know what it is like to grow up not having enough to eat at home versus having a home where all needs were met. At other times, students have had difficulty identifying any areas of privilege but then were able to acknowledge that others face oppression they do not. The activity is about self-reflection and the power of having one identity shift. This served as an opportunity to tune in and reflect what it meant to live with this level of privilege in their lives and learn how to leverage that privilege toward equity.

The personal dimensions of identity framework (Arredondo, 1996) discusses the differences in identity in terms of dimensions of identity that are changeable and visible, as well as those that are a result of outside forces or historical contexts. As Arredondo described, identity shifts can happen at various times of life, which can change our access to privilege. Education, social status, or the development of other identities (e.g., such as a professional identity within a specific group or field) can change our positionality toward increased privilege. Sometimes privilege is unearned, such as resources or affordances we receive because of the color of our skin, place of birth, or gender. A shift in privilege may occur when someone completes higher education or earns more money. Even in those cases, the foundation we may have due to unearned generational privilege (political and economic power due to privileged identities) influences our ability to acquire privilege. Similarly, loss of privilege due to a change in identity status (e.g., acquiring a disability) is mitigated by privilege we may have due to other identities. Activity 3.7 is intended to help you reflect on the ways in which privilege may have changed throughout your life thus far.

ACTIVITY 3.7

Transitions of Power and Privilege: How Have Your Identities Changed from Birth Until Now?

1. Think about your life, from the moment you were born to the present, and where you think you will be in the future.

2. Draw a timeline with all of your life's major events. Think about your journey, challenges, and victories. Make sure to highlight shifts in identity or privilege that may have taken place along the way (e.g., graduating college, acquiring a disability).

3. Now write up/reflect on the following:
   o How have you acquired or lost power and privilege in your life?

  ○ What has that experience been like?

  ○ How might the gain or loss of privilege and/or oppression shift the way you approach social action?

Being able to reflect on our experiences of oppression and privilege, as well as changes throughout our life, can help us understand our own movement from center to margin or vice versa. This can help us center the margins we may or may not be a part of. We do not need to be part of an oppressed community to be involved in taking action alongside them. With the changes that take place during our lifetime, we may be able to leverage our positionality for social change.

Taking Action: A Liberatory Stance

As we consider our own positionality, power, privilege, and oppression in relation to taking action to dismantle oppression and engage in social action, we challenge you to take a liberatory stance (Burton, 2012). Liberation psychology was born from a place of resistance and liberatory theology. It is described as a reconstruction of psychology in relation to the lived experiences of marginalized people, social issues, action, and movements (Burton, 2012). Through a Liberation psychology lens, psychologists are no longer objective observers, but instead are called to become active participants in transforming systems of oppression (Martín-Baró, 1994). As discussed in Chapter 2, traditional views of counseling and mental health maintain the status quo and are rooted in White supremacy and oppressive practices. Liberation psychology is one way to think about our positionality, social action, and a liberatory stance.

 In the context of rampant abuse of poor and marginalized communities by those in power in Latin America, Martín-Baró (1996) called on Latin American psychology to move away from preoccupations of scientific validity and status and instead set itself at the service of the marginalized majorities. Furthermore, he asserted that liberation can only take place if we are willing and able to seek new forms of knowledge that center the experience of those most affected by inequality and oppression. To take a liberatory stance, we must be driven by intentionality and hold ourselves and our fields accountable through critical self-reflection and committed action.

 We recognize that we have introduced some major theories, concepts, and ideas in this chapter. We invite you to further explore the expansive body of knowledge that exists for each of them. We hope you were able to reflect on your experience, the experiences of others, and the ways in which we influence and affect each other as we engage in social action.

Chapter 4

Professional Ethics and Social Action

"Justice is what love looks like in public."

—Dr. Cornel West quoting Dr. Martin Luther King, Jr.

(https://www.uua.org/ga/past/2015/ware-west)

Introduction

Ethics can embody what we believe, who we are, and what guides our passion and action—not simply the professional guidelines we are expected to follow. The personal ethics we gain through our families, communities, and lived experience are often what drive and guide us in social action. How can we translate and honor that in relation to our professional ethics? Each professional practice field (e.g., counseling, psychology, social work) has a set of ethical guidelines that practitioners are expected to use in guiding their behavior and making ethical decisions.

For us, social action is an actualization of our values, our love, and our commitment to justice. In this chapter, we want to broaden how we think about ethics beyond what our professions tell us. We invite you to explore ethics as a part of who you are and what you believe. Once we have grounded ourselves in community and our personal ethics, then we will dive into our professional ethical guidelines and how that may be connected, or disconnected, from our personal and community ethics.

In this workbook, our journey so far sets the stage for this important conversation of ethics and social action. Using the ecological framework in Chapter 2, we encouraged you to consider systemic oppression in the history of your profession and also shared examples of advocacy and justice. In Chapter 3, we asked you to explore your identities and positionality and consider how your personal context is connected to who you are as a professional as well as how those influence your roles and activism. We encourage you to become familiar with, and use, existing guidelines for multicultural and social justice practice for your profession as one piece of the foundation for social action. In this chapter, we invite you to engage in a process of reflecting and discovering the principles and lessons that have guided you thus far and then consider them in relation to professional ethics.

Before we go any further, we'd like to share a story to illustrate one example of the ways that ethics, morals, and social action may interact.

Rebecca and the Cabal of Nine

In the 1990s, I was working as a college counselor when the student government president, a young Black man, was arrested on campus due to a conflict with a fellow student leader, a White woman. A group of about 15 faculty and staff came together out of frustration and outrage, sharing examples of other previous "minor" incidents experienced by students of color and students with disabilities in student government. In the past, we had tried to provide the students with resources and information about self-advocacy, due process, and filing complaints. For those of us who were counselors, this supported the principle of autonomy (from our professional code of ethics and aligned with our training). But the complaints kept coming and the arrest of the student government president was the last straw. Morally, it felt like we were complicit in this continuing pattern of violence because we had not directly taken action in the system to prevent it.

After an 8-hour meeting, nine of us wrote a confidential memo to our academic senate expressing 12 points of concern about student government, including the role and function of the student government advisor position. Almost immediately, the administrator in that role launched a $10 million lawsuit against us as individuals, calling us a "cabal." He also sued the college. The college refused to provide legal counsel for us arguing that we had acted outside our role. In response, we asserted that our action was within the scope of our duty and cited a standard from the 1995 American Counseling Association (ACA) Code of Ethics & Standards of Practice (that was the version in place at the time). The code stated that if a counselor was aware of discrimination taking place within their organization, they were ethically bound to bring that to the attention of the organization. The college ended up paying for our legal counsel and the lawsuit settled after 6 years. But that is a story for another time.

As you can see from that story, ethics, morals, and the law are not always clear or aligned. We'd like to share a few definitions to distinguish between these concepts and how they might relate to our actions personally and professionally. *Ethics* guide behavior based on a set of values, beliefs, principles and moral thinking; what is "right," "good," and "appropriate" may vary given a particular context or community. *Professional ethics and standards* outline guiding principles and expectations for behavior and decision-making for individuals within that profession. Alternatively, *morals* reflect a system of beliefs about how we should live (The Ethics Centre, 2016) and are shaped by community, family, and culture. Ethics, morals, and laws often overlap and sometimes conflict. In Rebecca's example, the organization had specific expectations of how college personnel were expected to act. In addition, the professional ethical principle of autonomy shaped how Rebecca and her counseling colleagues initially intervened. As things devolved, the conflict between their moral sense of justice, the expectations of their organization, their professional ethical guidelines, and the perpetuation and tolerance of oppression all conflicted and compelled Rebecca and her colleagues to act differently.

Reflecting on our historical discussion in Chapter 2, let's dig a little deeper into the journey to our current professional ethics. Professional ethical standards and laws are created, shaped, and revised by a process usually involving members who hold power within an organization or discipline. The history of most professions, especially in the global north, reflects the perspectives of White men. The voices of many of our communities were excluded and marginalized in this process, but over time, more voices and communities are redefining what our professions are, or could be. This is essential to move toward more socially just and culturally relevant ethics.

As you work through this chapter, reflect on your personal sense of ethics, your communities' ethics, and what your communities expect of you and how you behave. Also, reflect on standards set by your professional associations and how these guidelines influence, hinder, and/or support social action.

An Ecological Framework: Community, Personal, and Professional Ethics

The ecological systems that influence the way we live and work (personal, community, and professional) give us a great perspective for exploring ethics. The values and principles of our communities (past and present, including our professional community) shape the way we interpret the world, our place in it, and how we engage with it. Our personal sense of ethics is shaped by our choices about what beliefs we internalize and which ones we discard. The next example illustrates these different spheres, how they guide behavior, and how they might align or conflict with one another.

EXAMPLE

Muninder and the Granola Bar

I keep granola bars and other snacks in my desk drawer in my office. Now, imagine I am meeting with a student for advising and I learn that they have not had anything to eat today, and in fact, may have challenges ensuring they have food on a regular basis. The decision about how to act in light of this information will be guided by beliefs and teachings from different sources. My profession may suggest that the scope of my role is to provide academic guidance or education and that people in other professions are better positioned to address food insecurity. My university understandably expects that I will refer the student to the food pantry, and I do share this information with all students. My religious community might expect me to give the students something to eat *and* go out into the community and remedy the fact that some people don't have access to food. My personal ethics, and the pragmatic need for immediate action, might lead me to regularly have snacks in my office and offer students a granola bar because it is the fastest way to address the issue—and then address the reason they came to me in the first place (advising).

For each of us, these arenas overlap depending on the alignment of the culture of our personal selves, our communities, and our profession. We will begin by exploring our communities, past and present, and their influence in setting the ethical stage.

Community Ethics

Consider "community" as a group of people who are connected in some way, such as with shared interests, experiences, responsibilities, attributes, beliefs, needs, goals, and sometimes geography. The influence of these communities is actually more far-reaching and specific than we might think.

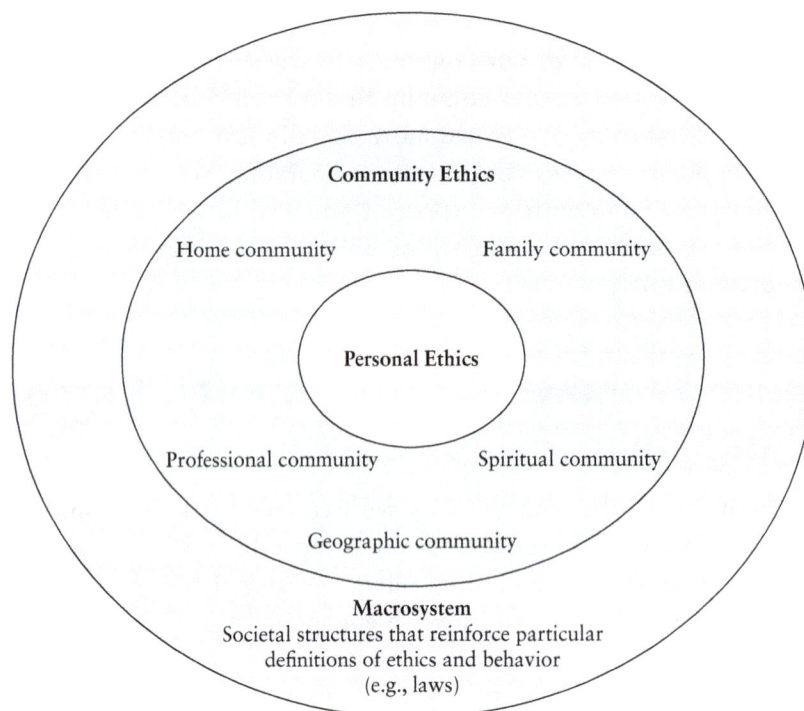

FIGURE 4.1 Ecological framework for ethics

ACTIVITY 4.1

Questions for Reflection

1. What communities shape your views and beliefs directly or indirectly?

2. How do these communities influence your behavior and expectations of others?

3. How can our communities' beliefs and perspectives guide and fuel us in social change?

We think about community ethics as the shared values, beliefs, lessons, guidance, and/ or expectations for behavior that a community shares among its members. Dr. Wade Nobles (1991) described culture as "the vast structure of behaviors, ideas, attitudes, values, habits, beliefs, customs, language, rituals, ceremonies, and practices peculiar to a particular group of people which provides them with a general design for living and patterns for interpreting reality" (p. 1). We can think about community ethics as reflections of the community's beliefs and expectations for the ways we relate to the community and to the outside world.

In reality, we belong to, and are influenced by, many communities: family communities (chosen or default), cultural communities, religious communities, communities based on interests and affiliation, neighborhood or proximity communities, workplace communities, professional communities, and more. We will start by exploring communities closer to our personal lives and then separately address professional and workplace communities (e.g., counseling, psychology, social work).

Our First Communities: Starting from the Beginning

From the time we are little, we watch others and learn from those we admire (or fear) as well as from stories that provide lessons about how the world works and how we should exist in the world. Wisdom from parents, elders, community members, religious leaders, educators, and others are often passed down through stories, parables, *dichos* (sayings), metaphors, and other ways. For example, "do unto others as you would have them do unto you," "*dime con quién andas y te diré quien eres*" (tell me who your friends are and I will tell you who you are), and "walk your talk." In Sikhism, there is the aspiration to "live in Chardi Kala," or live in a state of eternal optimism and positivity, even in the face of hardship or oppression. For Muninder, it is a central message that her family has passed down to younger generations and it is the primary principle for how she approaches life—to be positive as we fight for justice.

EXAMPLE

Bryan and *Personalismo*

I grew up between Costa Rica and Panama. My Latino upbringing shaped many of my values, including the importance of community, family, respect, and *personalismo.* I learned from a very early age that if anyone came to our home we would give them at the very least a piece of bread or a cup of coffee, *un cafecito.* Breaking bread and being willing to take care of others was the minimum we could do to show kindness and *respeto.* Acts of kindness became a representation of love and appreciation. I remember my grandmother often saying "*Donde comen dos, comen tres*" (Wherever there's enough for two to eat, there's enough for three). I learned that no matter how little we had, we always had enough to give, and no matter how hard things got, there were others going through much more difficult things.

In the next activity, recall stories or lessons you were told as a child. Write what you remember and what these stories mean to you now.

ACTIVITY 4.2

Stories and Lessons Passed Down

1. In the left column in the table below, write at least three stories, *dichos,* or lessons you remember being taught.
2. In the right column, describe how this lesson may have shaped how you aspire to live your life, how you engage with others, and/or the kind of person you hope to be.
3. As you reflect on these stories, think about how they guide your behavior, your expectations, and the decisions you make when confronted by uncertainty.

Story	What Does this Mean to You Now?
1.	
2.	
3.	
Other?	

For some of us, elders and lessons inspire us. For others of us, we may spend our lives trying to undo lessons that we find harmful or toxic; for example, we try to unlearn lessons that divide people, make us fear difference or feel superior, or develop loathing for ourselves or others. In this way, the lessons still influence us, but now as motivators to live a different way.

As we grow, more communities provide us with lessons for success, survival, and resilience. In some communities, shared expectations help the community and its members stay strong and safe. For example, in his book, *We Keep Us Safe*, Zach Norris (2020) talks about the ways communities keep themselves safe without involving police, given the history of police violence in many communities of color. Similarly, in the Sikh community, individuals often will turn to an elder or community member who is in a particular profession for advice prior to seeking assistance from a professional (e.g., asking Muninder Auntie for help working with their child before going to see a professional therapist). Or when facing religious or racial discrimination, Sikhs may contact a community based organization (e.g., Sikh Coalition) rather than contacting law enforcement as a first line. A sense of trust exists with the belief that a fellow community member will have their best interest at heart.

The examples below illustrate how lessons from our communities and loved ones have shaped our lives and provided guidance for how we move in the world.

EXAMPLE

Derrick and Keeping Safe

At an early age, I was aware of how people in positions of authority could make judgments of me based on my race or the way I dressed. This became increasingly noticeable as I began to drive. Messages from my community about driver's safety included not riding with a car full of my friends or taking off my hat (or driving without one) if I saw a police car. As you may notice, these extended beyond wearing my seat belt and using my blinker when changing lanes. While these messages were not always effective for me and historically have not been effective to keep Black folks from harm, they were passed on to me from my community and were intended to keep me safe. As I move about the world today, I consider my safety and that of those around me, though I know my actions will not always be enough to protect them or me.

Now think about your own communities—the most central ones that shape your behavior—how you view the world, and your expectations of others.

Personal Ethics

Because we have evolved from, and belong to, so many different communities, we integrate and internalize these lessons consciously or unconsciously. This shapes our "personal ethics"—the beliefs and expectations we have for our own behavior and the behavior of others. Throughout our life we learn, weigh options, try out new ways of being and behaving. We hopefully see the impact of our behavior, which then further shapes us. In the next activity, we ask you to explore the rules you live by and reflect on your application of these in your interactions with others.

ACTIVITY 4.3

My Rules for Living—AKA Personal Ethics

Consider how you might complete these statements:

- In my life, I am led by a cluster of rules for living influenced by culture, religion, and relationships. I am guided by:

- In my relationships with others, I strive to:

- I would like to be known as a person who:

- When faced with a difficult choice about how to behave, or an ethical challenge, the guiding rules I think about are:

- When I have hurt someone, I believe it is important to:

- When I see that another person has been hurt or bullied, I strive to:

- When I recognize that I have power because of my identity or access to resources, I use that power:

Now look back at how you responded to each of the questions above. How does your positionality, personal beliefs and cultural community expectations shape your sense of ethics and social action?

Below Muninder has shared her responses to Activity 4.3 to illustrate how her personal values and ethics influence her behavior and the ways she moves in the world.

Muninder and Sikhism

My personal ethics are strongly guided by Sikhism and the important people in my life, including my partner, closest friends, and family. In my relationships with others, I strive to be respectful, kind, and generous. I would like to be known as a person who will stand up against oppression, regardless of cost to self. When faced with a difficult choice about how to engage, the guiding rules I think about are being honest and transparent and recognizing that the right choice is often the hard choice. When I have hurt someone, I believe it is important to take accountability and accept that I have caused harm, apologize, acknowledge the impact, and when possible, try to ease the hurt and remedy the situation. When I see that another person has been hurt or bullied, I strive to protect them in the moment and then try to help make change so that it doesn't happen again—to them or anyone else. When I recognize that I have power, I try to share that power and use that power for good.

Our personal ethics continue to evolve over time. When we become a member of a new community, for example a profession, we are introduced to the ethics of that community. We evaluate those and consider how to integrate those ethics into the way we live and work. Like when we travel somewhere for the first time, we pay attention and try to learn how to respectfully navigate that new environment. We may not always take on values and expectations of the new environment as our own, but we must know them in order to function well. In the case of professional ethics, we have agreed to uphold those by making the choice to join the profession. How we uphold those may be influenced by our personal and community ethics.

PAUSE

Moving from personal to professional can sometimes feel abrupt, so before moving on to our discussion and examination of professional ethics, we would like you to pause for a moment. Take the next 5 minutes to put the book down and engage in self-care. Perhaps you take this time to grab a snack, go outside, stretch, and simply sit with yourself and take deep breaths. Whatever feels comfortable for you, take these next 5 minutes to take some time for yourself.

IMG 4.1

Professional Ethics

In some ways, professional ethical codes and guidelines can support us in social justice work and help us to respectfully serve the communities we want and need to serve. In other ways, professional ethical codes may not give helpful guidance, or may feel irrelevant, incongruent or even harmful and create barriers toward justice. We can think about professional disciplines and industries as communities with defined values, expectations, and standards for behavior and ethics. In the case of counseling, psychology, social work, and other helping professions, these codes of ethics or standards are established at a national level and then trickle down to influence state licensing boards as well as training programs and workplaces. These standards influence, and are influenced by, state and federal laws in place to regulate professions, protect their members, protect the public, and maintain the dominant social structure and the place of the profession in that structure (see Kivel [2017] for a deconstruction of this last point). For example, licensure laws and legal proceedings may use ethical codes to assert what is "reasonable behavior" for a person in that profession. What is defined as "reasonable behavior" reflects the perspectives of the dominant cultural group. Alternatively, professional ethics can also help support our work toward advocacy, systemic change, and human rights.

The process of establishing and revising professional standards is determined by the culture of the profession at the time, the perspectives of the people who were at the table, their definition of ethically complex situations, and what role professional helpers had in relation to clients and communities. For example, the first American Psychological Association (APA) Ethical Principles of Psychologists and Code of Conduct was created in 1953 (https://www.apa.org/ethics/code/) by an eight-member committee. It integrated ethical dilemmas contributed by 2,000 members (Smith, 2003). We know that this data came from exclusively White male psychologists, working mostly with White clients or in positions of authority and control with communities of color. Even revision processes are still dominated by the ways things have been done in the past. However, revision is one place where some of our social justice role models have intentionally advocated to change these codes to be more culturally responsive to the communities we serve and to our own lived experience. We will talk more about examples of this later.

In Activity 4.4, we invite you to begin deconstructing how your profession's code of ethics may help, limit, or discourage you from taking social action.

ACTIVITY 4.4

Your Profession's Code of Ethics or the "Industry Standard": Bridge or Barrier to Advocacy, Activism, and Social Action?

For this activity, you will need a copy of your profession's written code of ethics (or similar document). We also recommend using two different colored highlighters (or two different symbols) as you follow the steps below.

1. Review the code and highlight (or place a symbol) next to each standard that might **support or affirm social action** or social justice. If it helps you to be more concrete, think of a couple of specific social justice issues that you might find in your professional life. Create a scenario in your head about each of these issues or incidents.
2. Using a different color highlighter (or symbol), scan the code again and highlight standards that you think might be **contrary or a barrier to social action** as a helping professional.
3. Summarize your observations in the table below.

Title of Document:			
Supporting Social Action		**Limiting or Inhibiting Social Action**	
Standard (Title and Number)	**Notes (How Might this Standard Support?)**	**Standard (Title and Number)**	**Notes (How Might this Standard Inhibit?)**

- What do you notice?

- How was the code or standards taught to you?

- How culturally inclusive or responsive is this code to communities that are targets of oppression?

- How might the code be revised or modified to better support you in ethical and effective social action?

- Are there examples where your professional code of ethics has directly supported social action, or the ethics committee associated with your organization has taken stands on ethical issues? (you may need to do a little research to be able to answer this one)

In the table below, we have taken an excerpt from the ACA Code of Ethics and noted just a few examples of standards that we think might support social action and a few that might not.

EXAMPLE FOR ACTIVITY 4.4

ACA Code of Ethics

Title of Document: ACA Code of Ethics (2014)			
Supporting Social Action		Limiting or Inhibiting Social Action	
Standard (Title and Number)	Notes (How Might this Standard Support?)	Standard (Title and Number)	Notes (How Might this Standard Inhibit?)
A.7.a. Advocacy	This standard says that "when appropriate, counselors advocate at individual, group, institutional, and societal levels."	A.4. Avoiding harm	On the surface, this seems like a good thing, but it doesn't help identify harm, provide guidance, or address systems level harm that may come up due to overall systems of oppression (e.g. insurance requirements, carceral programs).
D.1.h. Negative Conditions	This standard encourages counselors to "alert their employers" and attempt to make changes in their organization if they see inappropriate policies and practices.	A.6.b. Extending counseling boundaries	Limited, doesn't provide any guidance for social action, collective action.

- **What do you notice?** *I noticed that the code is really focused on individual clinical practice and teaching, but doesn't provide much guidance about systems level change.*

When we did this exercise, we found that there were a lot of nuances as we read the standards. On the surface, the code addressed a lot of important issues regarding client's rights in relation to the counselor. However, as we think about the ecological framework, the code is very individually focused and doesn't provide as much guidance for systems-level work or being proactive. Further, it felt very limited in terms of space for cultural context, social action, and the role of the counselor outside the clinical or educator role. For a great analysis and discussion about the APA code of ethics and civil disobedience, see how Flynn and colleagues outlined the ways the ethics code "succeeds and fails to speak to the needs of psychologists who are considering civil disobedience." (Flynn et al., 2021, p. 1217). We highly recommend reading their discussion as they explicitly challenge psychologists and psychological associations to extend their practice and policies to support the ethical imperative for social action.

In a 2013 article, "Does the American Psychological Association's Code of Ethics Work for Us?" Gayle Morse and Arthur Blume described the collaborative effort of four Ethnic Minority Psychological Associations (EMPAs) to bring forward central ethical principles that shape their work. They noted a shared sense that "psychological societies worldwide would benefit from revised guidelines that more closely reflect their beliefs and values about community, spiritualism, and relationships, as well as consider the effects of historical trauma or colonialism, than the beliefs and values incorporated into the current APA code" (Morse & Blume, 2013, p. 2). Each of the four EMPAs (Association of Black Psychologists [ABPsi], National Latinx Psychological Association [NLPA], Asian American Psychological Association [AAPA], and Society of Indian Psychologists [SIP]) have a code of ethics or similar document that highlights expectations for professional behavior within the context of cultural values and perspectives.

Counselors for Social Justice (CSJ), a division of ACA, developed a code of ethics that outlined ethical principles to support and guide counselors working from a social justice perspective (CSJ, 2011). There are other examples of professionals working at organizational levels to revise codes and bring a more culturally responsive and liberatory perspective to that process or challenging the political nature of codes of ethics. For instance, in the mid 2000s, a coalition of psychologists challenged APA, charging that its members, and the organization itself, were complicit and sometimes directly involved in interrogation and torture (see APA, 2015). Alternatively, there are ways that our professional organizations have advocated for human rights at a national and international level invoking ethics as a force. Although these examples may be few, they are helpful models and can inspire us to look at ways to work with and encourage our organizations around social action "(e.g., ACA, 2025; CEO Alliance for Mental Health, 2025)". One example comes from the APA Ethics Committee's 2022 document *Frequently asked questions regarding the ethical issues related to the recent Supreme Court decision overturning Roe v. Wade (1973)* (Brabeck & Hunter, 2022). This document outlines the conflict between the APA code of ethics and that recent decision. Other examples can be seen in the work of a range of professional organizations that have addressed neglect and discrimination against clients from marginalized communities by creating practice guidelines for working with those communities. We also suggest that you recall some of the examples provided in Chapter 2.

In the following activity, we ask you to reflect on your profession's code of ethics in relation to one additional document that describes ethical behavior from a nondominant cultural perspective, for example from the EMPAs or similar groups within your profession.

A More Diverse Perspective

Locate at least one document from within your profession that describes ethics and guides professional behavior from a perspective that is culturally specific or focused specifically on social justice (for example, within psychology, the EMPAs have more culturally situated ethics; within ACA, the division of Counselors for Social Justice has created a code of ethics). Write the name of the document in one oval below and your profession's primary or official code of ethics in the other oval (e.g., for counselors it would be the ACA Code of Ethics).

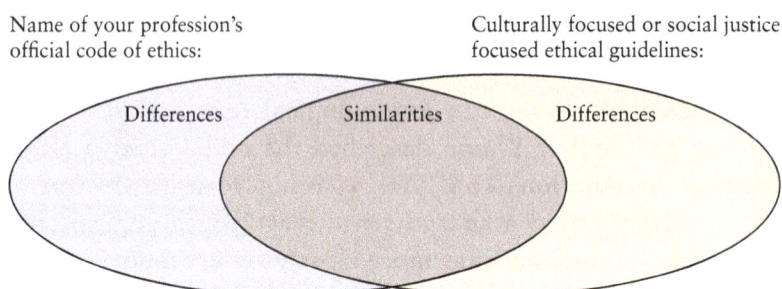

Name of your profession's official code of ethics:

Culturally focused or social justice focused ethical guidelines:

Differences   Similarities   Differences

FIGURE 4.2 Differences and similarities in ethics

1. Compare and contrast the documents and note the assumptions that are implied or stated related to social justice or social action.

2. Use the Venn diagram to write similarities and differences in the assumptions, values, standards, etc. described in the documents.

3. How do the standards and/or language leave out or negate pieces of who you are, what you value, and/or the communities that you belong to or serve?

4. How do the documents affirm pieces of who you are, what you value, and/or the communities that you belong to or serve?

5. Other observations and reflections?

Critically examining your profession's code of ethics and considering that critique in the context of alternative perspectives of professional ethics and social action can help in several ways. First, you will identify ways that the existing code of ethics can support advocacy and activism as a professional. Second, this exercise can clarify resources that already exist ("official" resources) to guide, support or defend action you might take. Third, the process can help you identify areas that may need to be changed within your profession's code. Perhaps working toward this change would be a good social action goal for you and your collaborators/accomplices, whether on committees or simply responding when calls for feedback come out.

When we bring our lived experience as people from marginalized populations, we see easily the gaps in professional ethical codes. Other times, we may not know what would be helpful until we are in situations where we need guidance or support. In Rebecca's example at the beginning of this chapter (the lawsuit) the ACA Code of Ethics both de-emphasized the role of counselors intervening in systems change (focus on autonomy) and supported the individual actions that she and her colleagues took to address injustice in their college. Since that time, the ACA Code of Ethics has been revised multiple times, and each iteration has given a little more attention to cultural responsiveness and advocacy. Still, more work is needed.

The Intersection (or Conflict) of Your Communities' Ethics, Personal Ethics, and Professional Ethics

In Activity 4.6, we invite you to reflect on the intersection of the ethics and guides for living from your communities' perspectives, your own personal sense of ethics, and your profession's ethics.

ACTIVITY 4.6

Your Intersection of Personal, Community, and Professional Ethics

For this activity, explore the intersection of your community ethics, personal ethics, and professional ethics. It may be helpful to refer back to previous activities in this chapter.
Consider the expectations for behavior and resolving complicated situations.

1. Where do your profession's ethics, your personal ethics, and your communities' ethics overlap or agree?

2. Where do they conflict?

3. What actions can you take to help move your field closer to a place of social justice and cultural relevance? How could you and your social action colleagues help move these goals to be more integrated and established in a Code of Ethics?

4. Who might join you in these actions or is already taking action to make this a reality?

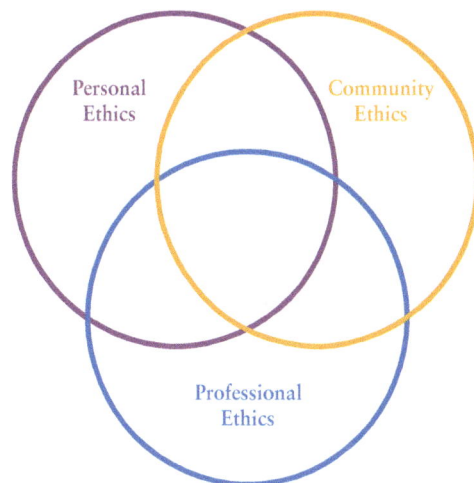

FIGURE 4.3 Intersection of personal, community, and professional ethics

Conclusion

Throughout the remainder of this workbook, we would like you to keep this perspective of ethics in mind and consider the ways in which these tools (codes and guidelines) serve as strengths or resources, help or interference with your work to build solidarity. As professionals, we have agreed to abide by the standards and ethics in place and we have a role in their evolution. How are these helpful and supportive for our clients, communities, and us? Do they guide or inhibit developing effective strategies, sustain your well-being or create conflict? This perspective can be the foundation for the work you will do throughout this book and out in the world. We would like to emphasize that the heart of ethics is not just about protecting the public and the profession but is essentially about our values and our dignity. This is also what social action is about.

Chapter 5

Articulating the Need for Social Action in Your Work

Finding Focus

"When an individual is protesting society's refusal to acknowledge his dignity as a human being, his very act of protest confers dignity on him."

—Bayard Rustin

In previous chapters, we explored more deeply the context of our work and our professions, considerations of the role of power, privilege, oppression and intersectionality, and the role of ethics in pursuing and executing social action. For some of us, we are very clear about our focus and purpose in engaging in social justice, even if we haven't articulated it. For others of us, there is so much injustice in the world that sometimes we feel like we aren't sure where or how to begin to act. This feeling of overwhelm can make it difficult to contribute to effective, meaningful change. Our task in this chapter is to help you articulate the work you do, your vision for what you want your work to be, the barriers you face in taking social action, and how to work through these barriers. Throughout this chapter, and this workbook, we use the term "vision" to represent the culmination of our hopes, intents, and dreams that focus our social actions and passions. We acknowledge that "vision" and other sight-related words (e.g., image, lens, view) have the potential to feel exclusionary for those with vision related disabilities. Our intent is a metaphorical use of these terms, and we hope that we have shared them in ways that are accessible to all readers.

What Is Our Work as Helping Professionals?

When someone asks Muninder, "What do you do?" She usually answers that she is a psychologist and a professor of counseling. Then they follow up with, "Cool. So ... what do you DO?" She describes what counselors, psychologists, and other mental health practitioners, supervisors, and educators do and why we need them for the promotion of mental health and well-being. She talks about work with clients, supervision of trainees, teaching students, and research that she is engaged in. Specifically, she emphasizes how multiculturalism and social justice are foundational to mental health. Without justice, she says, there is no wellness. She usually shares this quickly, like an elevator pitch of sorts, and then if they have follow-up questions, they can ask about anything she described. If they were just being polite, they can move on to someone more interesting.

An elevator pitch is a short (1 minute or less) script that answers the question, "What do you do and why should I care?" It is like a sales pitch about you or what matters to you, and it invites the listener to ask for more information. It allows something meaningful to be communicated in the time of an elevator ride. There are a number of models for this type of pitch (check out these examples: https://www.businessnewsdaily.com/4034-elevator-pitch-tips.html, https://icc.ucdavis.edu/sites/g/files/dgvnsk2236/files/find/resources/networking/Networking-Pitch-Handout.pdf, and https://zety.com/blog/elevator-pitch). Common threads include introducing yourself and where you come from, stating the issue and why it is important, sharing what you are doing about the issue, and making a request of the listener. Though this tool is used particularly well in the business and political arenas, we think social change-oriented mental health professionals can also use it effectively in their work. Throughout this workbook, we will guide you in developing your elevator pitch. In this chapter, you will begin creating your pitch and continue to develop it as you work through the following chapters. By the end of this process, you will have a succinct, clear, and actionable message. This message can help you stay focused on your intent, communicate the importance of your issue, engage others, and even overcome barriers you might encounter.

In the following activity, you will develop a simple elevator pitch about the job-related work you currently do. Consider this activity one that lays the groundwork for the actual elevator pitch you will begin later in this chapter.

ACTIVITY 5.1

Beginning Your "Elevator Pitch"

If you had to give an elevator pitch (two to three sentences) about your work in your job or field of study, what would you say?

- Introduce yourself.

- State what you do and why it matters.

Once you have crafted this, try it out on family and friends who are not in the helping professions. What do they think? Do they understand what you are trying to convey about your work and why you believe it is important?

As you reflect on the work you do and why it matters, reflect on the foundation—what underlies your decision to engage in this work. In this next section, we will have you begin to consider *why* you do the work that you do and how it connects to social justice.

Finding Focus

As social change agents, there has to be something that drives you to do the work you do and the way that you want to do it. In Activity 5.2, you will identify values and beliefs that you hold dear: the spark, kindling, and fuel that guide you to engage in social action. In Activity 5.2, you distill your values into words that capture what you hold dear because understanding the "why" can guide "how" we engage more effectively in social action.

ACTIVITY 5.2

Your Spark, Kindling, and Fuel

What lights your fire? Consider the values that underpin your work.

1. Circle all the words below that represent the values and beliefs that guide you or that you hold dear. The more honest you are with yourself, the more helpful this activity will be.
2. Add any values and beliefs that are important for you, but are not listed here.
3. Place an asterisk (*) by the top eight words.

Harmony with people	Communities	Peace	Passion	Fame
Justice	Relationships with animals	Happiness	Romance	Human rights
Education	Relationships with people	Freedom	Integrity	Participation in decision-making
Aesthetics	Wisdom	Religion/God	Humility	Patriotism
Economic success	Safety	Spirituality	Achievement	Physical health
Fairness	Mental health	Kindness	Recognition	Pleasure
Balance with nature	Family	Creativity	Solitude	Independence
Honesty	Security	Loyalty	Power	Interdependence
Other values?				

Notes to self:

Now that you have identified some of the core values and beliefs that motivate your passion and commitment, the next activity aims to summarize how you use that passion. In Activity 5.3, we ask you to consider social justice issues that arise in your work as it relates to your workplace (or school), the populations you serve, your communities, the nation or world, and to identify what you care about and want to focus on.

Where Do You Focus Your Fire? Issues You Care About

1. Circle all the words that represent issues that you care about.
2. Add any words for issues that are not represented.
3. Place an asterisk (*) by the top three words.

Protecting the environment	Economic justice	Immigration rights	Refugee rights	Religious rights (and freedom from discrimination)
Animal rights	Ending poverty	Education access	Global peace	Access to job training
Civil rights	Employment rights	Healthcare access	Rights of currently and formerly incarcerated	Social justice
Anti-racism	Digital divide and access to technology	Housing access	LGBTQ+ rights	Disability rights
Anti-sexism	Rights of older adults	Victims' rights (sexual assault etc.)	Trans and other gender rights	Rights of undocumented communities
Indigenous people's rights	Reproductive rights	Prison industrial complex	Children's rights	Other?

Our focus on particular issues is sometimes shaped by our observations of privilege and oppression as they play out in systems. It can also be shaped by significant people in our lives.

Muninder's top three issues that guide her work as a faculty member are anti-racism efforts, education access, and social justice. For Muninder, these issues are personal and professional, and they were instilled in her by her family, friends, mentors, and Sikh religious teachings. If these three issues were no longer issues, it would make the world a more equitable, safe, and meaningful place that allowed everyone a chance to flourish. Derrick's top three issues that guide his work as a faculty member and psychologist are anti-racism, social justice, and educational access (and equity). For Derrick, these commitments have strengthened throughout his life and are central to his personal and professional involvements and pursuits.

We cannot all fight for all things all the time. However, through collaboration and solidarity we can work together to make a more equitable society. While Derrick, Muninder, Bryan, and Rebecca might have different areas of focus, we are able to find common ground in order to support one another in achieving our vision of a more just society.

In Activity 5.2, you reflected on what lights your fire for social action, and in Activity 5.3, you reflected on what you are passionate about. For Activity 5.4, you will reflect on who has influenced you and who has shaped this passion for social justice. These three activities have been chosen to tap into different aspects of being: your unspoken sense, your emotional connection to learning from others, and an understanding of what shapes your rules for living.

ACTIVITY 5.4

Heroes and Inspirations

Identify two role models, idols, or heroes that may have influenced your passion for social justice. They could be family, ancestors, people in your community, world leaders, or even fictional characters.

- What kind of social action did they engage in and how did they inspire you?

- What did you learn from them?

- If you don't have a role model or hero for social justice (or can't readily think of one), do some research to find someone you consider inspiring. What did you learn about this person? How do they inspire you?

EXAMPLE

Bryan's Heroes

My family, mentors, and community motivate me. As a first-generation college student, my family always instilled the importance of education. My mentors supported me with the additional knowledge and institutional capital I needed to be able to believe in myself and achieve my dreams. When I think of my family, many people come to mind, but I want to focus on my grandfather, Ovidio Araúz, who didn't have more than an elementary school education and yet was able to create an industry to support the community he lived in. He was a Panamanian man of few words and let his actions speak for themselves. He created the first bus route between Volcan and David, Panama. As a result, people had a way of making it to work or the big city. As an intelligent businessman, he was able to save enough money to buy a small bus to support his community and provide for his family. It was through hard work, dedication, and committed action that he overcame the obstacles that he encountered in the creation of his vision. Being the first and not having a clear path to take was not enough to stop him in trailblazing for others.

Many of my mentors also come to mind, but today I want to focus on Dr. Joseph White. He was a mentor's mentor and a trailblazer within the field of psychology. He would find ways to interact with students at conferences, and I was lucky enough to get invited to talk to him during the first conference I ever attended (Teacher's College Winter Roundtable). At the time, I was starstruck and felt like an impostor among great minds. I asked him, "Will I ever feel like I belong in academia?" His response was something that I would take with me from that moment on. He responded, "Bryan, do not look for validation from your oppressors. Academia was never meant for us, yet we always belonged. Ask the questions of those who truly matter, your family and community and you will find that answer." After that Dr. White and I continued to be in touch via email and saw each other whenever possible at conferences. He taught me to believe in myself, to value my community's opinion more than academia's, and to always remember where I came from in order to help others wanting to ride the "freedom train."

For Bryan, his heroes and role models led to a strong sense of connection and commitment to shared survival, resilience, and community bonds. As you reflect on the next few activities, honor and illuminate those positive forces in your life, whether they be lessons, values, spiritual beliefs, or involvement in a community. What is most important to us, what stokes our fire, and what lights the passion we have often has roots in those who inspired us. Taking a moment to reflect on the people who have influenced, inspired, and guided us can help us to ground our work and purpose. It can also be helpful to revisit these reflections later as we discuss how to sustain our efforts and energy. The activities you have completed thus far in Chapters 4 and 5 are intended to encourage you to connect with important aspects of yourself that can help you shape how you engage in social action and how you sustain that action during difficult times.

Sometimes the most powerful influences on our values and beliefs are those lessons we have been taught through stories, sayings, parables, *dichos*, metaphors, and other ways that wisdom was passed on to us by parents, elders, community members, religious leaders, educators, and others. For example, "do unto others as you would have them do unto you," "*dime con quién andas y te diré quién eres*" (tell me who your friends are and I will tell you who you are), and "walk your talk." Muninder has embraced the Sikhism aspiration to "Live in Chardi Kala"—in eternal optimism even in the face of hardship or oppression. It is a central message that her family passed down to younger generations and the primary principle for her approach to her life and her work. Bryan grew up with dichos in a Latino household, including idioms such as "ponte las pilas" (put on your batteries) as a reminder that hard work and *ganas* (willpower) pay off. Other dichos serve as a reminder of the value of the community and collectivism, such as "*haz el bien y no mires a quién*" (do good no matter who), a reminder to always center community and the importance of taking care of others, no matter who they are.

Initiating Visioning: How We See Ourselves as Social Change Agents

Poet Jamila Lyiscott wrote the poem "2053" to "commemorate" the Presidential Inauguration held January 2017. She states, "The purpose of this piece is to inspire and sustain those of us committed to authoring hope, equity and justice into our immediate future. … My impetus for framing the poem in the future is to remind us that we can claim victory, take ownership of the narrative of democracy and forge a different reality into existence if we can envision it now." If you need a reminder of her beautiful words, we encourage you to read the poem in full (https://ideas.ted.com/5-poems-for-an-inauguration).

Through this poem, we can envision what Lyiscott and so many others yearn for: a vision for healing the pain caused by oppression that our nation and world is historically and currently rooted in. A vision can happen in reaction to others, to events, or they can happen from the inspiration of others.

What Is Visioning? How Can It Frame Our Future?

Using Oxford Languages, Google defines "visioning" as "the development of a plan, goal, or vision for the future." Our ability to envision a more just world becomes fuel to continue our social justice action. In Activity 5.5, you will create a visual or conceptual image representing what is most important to you.

Finding What's Most Important

Consider whether you would like to do this activity as a visual representation or a conceptual one. If you are choosing a visual representation, you will need a sheet of paper at least 8.5″x11″ (used paper is fine), scissors, glue stick or tape, magazines, photos, newspapers, and anything with images. You can also do this activity digitally (e.g., digital images on a PowerPoint slide), if that is a more comfortable medium.

If you are choosing a conceptual representation, you will create your conceptual collage using words, ideas, meaningful moments, and feelings.

Part 1: Creating a collage

Think about what is most important to you in your life and what you value, believe in, and engage in. Bring it to life by creating a collage.

For the visual representation: In the center of the paper, place words, pictures, and photographs that represent what is most important to you in your life, and what you value, believe in, and engage in. Supporting photos, pictures, and words can be placed to surround it.

For the conceptual representation: Arrange the components of your conceptual collage so that the words, ideas, and meaningful moments that are most impactful or evoke the most feeling are the center. Other important, but less impactful ideas surround and support the center.

As an example, let's consider that love is important to you—love of family, community, a partner, and humanity. You would include the word "love" at the center of the paper. Next, you might choose words or images to surround the center and represent ideas that you believe support love. For example, you may believe that civil rights, equality, equity, respect, and certain policies or laws promote love. The collage can also include religious symbols and photos of extended family members and community members of different faiths, sexual orientation, immigrants, justice etc. See a visual of this example below this activity.

Part 2: Reflecting on your initial vision

Now that you have completed the collage, examine it.

- What feelings do the images bring up for you?

- With whom would you feel comfortable sharing this collage and your feelings about it?

- What does this tell you about where you would like to direct your energy?

- What social issues or causes are prompted by the images or feelings?

- Can this collage and the images here serve as an anchor and motivation for you if you feel exhausted or discouraged through your process of creating social change? If not, what images might serve that purpose?

Here is an example of a collage that Rebecca and Muninder put together:

FIGURE 5.1 Visioning collage

For Rebecca and Muninder, the images in the collage above elicit a variety of feelings, including hope, joy, resolve to continue their work, and even sadness and anger that many of the things that are represented have not yet been achieved. The collage helps provide a visual of why they do what they do. Though the four of us (Bryan, Derrick, Muninder, and Rebecca) agree on the importance of family, community, and the fight for social justice that is represented in this collage, each of us might interpret them slightly differently and direct more or less energy into each of these words or symbols.

Thus far, you may have a good sense of what drives you and what you think is important. Now, as a helping professional, you must also take into consideration the collective. Primarily, you must find out what is most important to the individuals and communities you serve (or hope to serve). Secondarily, you need to understand what is important for individuals and groups who serve these communities. As brown (2017) posits, "One of my favorite questions today is: How do we turn our collective full-bodied intelligence towards collaboration, if that is the way we will survive?"

ACTIVITY 5.6

Part 3—The Collective

Reflect on what your collage might be like if you incorporate the collective, the individuals and communities you serve and those who serve them, into your individual vision.

1. Add images or ideas in your initial collage to represent the collective.

2. How has your collage changed?

3. Where do your images/visions overlap between your individual vision and the collective vision?

4. What images reflect your unique vision? Is it valuable for the collective?

5. Are you willing to put the differences between your individual vision and the collective vision aside in the interest of community and in the spirit of collaboration?

Your collage may change depending on whether or not you incorporate a collective into your individual vision and which collective you incorporated. Some areas may become less important and others more important. What may be symbolically important to you individually may not be the symbol that the collective wants to use. For example, Muninder may resonate with the BLM posters as a symbol of the fight for racial justice, while for a group of Black community members, a picture of a raised fist may be more meaningful. And as we seek to move toward action, are we (in this case, Muninder) able to put aside our individual vision for the collective in the spirit of collaboration or work? And are we (again, in this case, Muninder) able to see that as an outsider to the community, it is more important for the communities' vision to be at the forefront?

Toggling between individual vision and collective vision is important to create goals for social action. We must work together for this shared vision. As an example of this sentiment, in a speech in 2013, brown shared: "the *WAY* of flocking: staying separate enough not to crowd each other, aligned enough to maintain a shared direction, and cohesive enough to always move towards each other. destiny is a calling that creates a beautiful journey" (para 5).

Ultimately, we must change our vision based on community input to make that "beautiful journey." Though visioning is a starting point, it is also an evolving activity throughout the book. As we engage in social action, we must consistently and regularly revisit and revise what we are working toward.

PAUSE

Before we begin exploring challenges and barriers, we would like you to take a moment of pause. Take 5 minutes to put the book down, stretch, grab a snack, go outside, or simply sit with yourself and take deep breaths. Take these next 5 minutes to take some time for yourself.

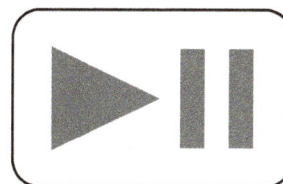

IMG 5.1

Pragmatics: Having Our Work and Vision Talk to Each Other

At times, it may feel (and it may be) that our work is antithetical to social justice (e.g., enforcing bureaucratic oppressive policies of a mental health agency), however, our vision of social action can fit into our work as helping professionals if we can make transformation part of our work. For example, Muninder's top three issues that guide her work as a faculty member are education access, anti-racism, and social justice. She is chair and faculty member in a department of counseling. With the help of her colleagues, she has made social action around these three issues a part of her work. In her roles, there are times when she leads, times when she works together with other faculty colleagues, and other times, she follows the lead of others. An example of this is two counselor educator colleagues, Drs. Michael Hannon and Angela Sheely-Moore, together with Muninder starting a monthly conversation on race and racism for the counseling department community, including faculty, staff, and students, following a summer in which highly publicized (and recorded) acts of violence against Black and Brown men and boys by police officers resulted in a lack of justice. Muninder and her colleagues felt they needed to do something to help with healing and support, particularly for students of color, while also providing a space for everyone to work on anti-racism efforts. This monthly conversation became integrated into the departments work. Social change not only has the capacity to expand our work, but it can transform it. This monthly conversation has added to the array of events and activities the department engages in and has also kept race and racism front and center so that we can work on our programs and department in proactive ways. Of course, there remain barriers/obstacles to achieving social justice in our programs, department, and university. Not everyone is in agreement on what issues we need to focus on, and many times, discussions about racism and anti-racism can feel uncomfortable to some in our department. We have managed to keep on track (mostly) by supporting each other.

Social Justice Action

Social justice can feel large and amorphous. It can be helpful to articulate what represents social justice action for you. For example, Muninder thinks of the photograph of a woman in a flowy dress in Baton Rouge, Louisiana, standing alone protesting the use of excessive force against Black individuals by the police while facing a line of police officers in full riot gear.

The woman in the photograph demonstrated social action in a powerful and concrete way as she used her undefended body to stop heavily geared police. She stood immobile, straight, and directly gazed into the line of police officers. It's as if she knew she was representing something larger than just herself. She seemingly didn't care about the consequences for herself, but rather stood up for the community. Because of this incredible vision of social action, we sometimes feel the smaller steps we make are inconsequential (e.g., taking anti-racism steps in the university system), and we get discouraged. This can then halt our engagement in the work. In the next activity, we ask you to stop and consider a couple of questions.

A protest against excessive police force against the city's Black residents in Baton Rouge. (Jonathan Bachman / Reuters)

FIGURE 5.2 Photo with calm young Black woman facing police in riot gear

ACTIVITY 5.7

Reflection on Action

Take a reflective pause. Then respond to these questions.

1. What represents social justice action for you?

2. What keeps you from engaging in social action?

3. How can you negotiate and align your vision and the work you actually do?

Overcoming Barriers That Prevent Action

Barriers—real and perceived—are important to consider because they often prevent us from engaging, or even trying to engage, in social justice work. However, barriers can be unpacked to understand what lies underneath them and help you decide which barriers are worth the effort to take down or move around.

Depending on who we are and what our social location is (i.e., our identities and how those identities are positioned in society related to access to resources), barriers may be larger or smaller. When we think about our identities (i.e., using the ADDRESSING model), we may notice that we have fewer barriers when we have privilege, and some barriers may be overcome with privilege (i.e., access to money, power, or freedom from harassment, etc.). Additionally, when engaging in social change, privilege can act as a buffer against negative repercussions that might arise. For example, if you are interested in engaging in advocacy that requires money, it is easier to do if you have expendable money and financial flexibility. If your income is essential to your family's survival and well-being, and speaking out might threaten your job, you have a very real barrier to engaging in certain kinds of social justice work.

Other barriers may be more psychological (for example, fear) or interpersonal (for example, objections from family). These can often keep us from taking action. For example, you may not get involved due to a lack of confidence in developing relationships with people in a community different than your own, or a community that you may be new to. Although all barriers are important to consider, it is important to consider how privilege may be stopping us from taking action because of our fear of losing it.

It can be helpful to consider ways around barriers and also recognize when a barrier is unlikely to be overcome, at least for the present time. Most barriers can be transformed to become stepping stones or subgoals, rather than a force that prevents us from moving at all. To use a metaphor of a wall as a barrier, we could come to a wall blocking the path and sit down to say we are done. Or we can sit down and think about whether it is important to get to the other side of the wall, and if so, how might we find ways to go around or over the wall or even take it down entirely.

We encounter numerous barriers in our efforts to work toward social justice. It is important to acknowledge them and then take a look at what we can do about the barriers. Thinking about what you *can* do about barriers, instead of what you can't do, is essential. This next activity is designed to get you started by taking a look at what gets in your way when you move toward action for issues you care about.

Barriers That Make It Hard to Act

Take a minute and close your eyes. Reflect on the issues that you identified in Activity 5.3. Think about the times you wanted to take action but didn't. What kept you from doing it? In the two sections below, consider these barriers. Some may be logistical or circumstantial barriers (for example, you were unable to take time off work), some may be internal (for example, ways of thinking), and some may be interpersonal (for example, conflicts with people we are close to).

Part 1: What makes it difficult to act?

External, logistical, or circumstances
Psychological or internal barriers
Relational or interpersonal barriers

The way you engage with these barriers and challenges is actually a choice. Acknowledging this helps us to begin to be more conscious about the choices we make—and we may decide to act anyway. And it may help us think about alternative approaches to addressing the issue. For the second part of this activity, choose one of the barriers above and answer the following questions.

Part 2: Getting past the barrier

Barrier:
If you ignored this barrier and acted anyway, what would happen?
Are there actions you could take to make this less of a barrier?
Is there an alternative way you could address the injustice or issue you care about?

Now, reflect on how these barriers shape how and whether you take action. What is real about the barriers? What can be changed? Is there another road you can take?

It is important to acknowledge the barriers we face in order to get through or around them. Consider the barriers you most often find in your workplace or school. In the case of private practice, the isolation or lack of built-in professional collaborators can be a barrier to engaging in this work due to competing priorities and the need to be able to wear multiple hats as a business owner and entrepreneur. In some cases, clinical work in community systems makes advocacy feel like an uphill battle in which progress, motivation, and action are derailed by power hierarchies and organizations that want to talk about equity and inclusion without the work and commitment it requires. Additionally, often clinicians of color and clinicians from other marginalized identities are tokenized, overextended, and extracted from, without any additional compensation or recognition.

At a university, the barriers may not be isolation, but rather the inherent structural racism and other "isms" embedded in this system. For example, when people of color are disproportionately not promoted after applying, it can be helpful to secure buy-in from those in power and those with differing identities to investigate and problem-solve. Consider the ways in which you have moved through or around obstacles in the past and how you can continue to do so moving forward. Finally, burnout is common when engaging in social action, and feeling burnt out may affect how and when you confront barriers. We will talk about that and sustainability practices needed to acknowledge and prevent burnout in Chapter 11.

Throughout the rest of the workbook, you may notice that barriers come up in your mind that you hadn't thought about before. We encourage you to acknowledge them, write them down, and then consider the choices you can make about whether those barriers will keep you from acting or may simply shape the way you choose to act. Sometimes it is harder for us to get support when we have difficulty communicating what is important to us and why we are making the choices that we do. In the next section, you will continue creating your messaging about a social justice issue.

Clarity and Creating Your Message

By this point, you have identified and reflected on what you value, what you believe in, and what you care about. You have also explored, in previous chapters, how you are situated professionally, personally, and culturally within your profession, and how your profession is situated in relation to social justice and social change. You can prepare yourself for many of the activities that follow by continuing to develop your elevator pitch to integrate your vision of social action—a succinct description about what you are committed to and what you'd like to see happen.

Our goal is for you to have a concise, clear, and actionable message by the end of this book. This message can help you stay focused on your intent, communicate the importance of your issue, engage others, and even help you overcome barriers you might encounter.

ACTIVITY 5.9

Your Elevator Pitch

Revisit the simple elevator pitch that you drafted at the beginning of the chapter. Now that you have reflected more on what you value, believe in, and care about, what adjustments would you make to this statement? Use the activity below to craft a new elevator pitch. If you have to give an elevator pitch about your work and your vision of social action in your work, what would you say?

1. Introduce yourself, position, and place in one sentence. For example, "I am Maria Davis, a student at Acme University (or a community member in Everytown)."

2. What is the issue, and why is it important to you personally? Why do you care about it? (This should be no more than one or two sentences)

Example:
My name is Derrick Bines, and I am an assistant professor of counseling.
I focus my personal and professional work on creating better academic environments for Black college students. My own experiences navigating college and what I've learned through talking with others and research have impacted my commitment to this work.

Once you have crafted this, try it out on family and friends. What do they think? Do they understand what you are trying to convey about your issue and why you believe it is important?

Now you have your elevator pitch, your concise message about yourself as a social change agent and what social action is important in your work. You will continue to develop this elevator pitch throughout the workbook, integrating your compelling message to engage others and keep yourself focused.

Our intention in creating this workbook is to help you reach your vision through action. The model that forms the framework for this workbook, the S-Quad model, reflects four areas that can help you engage in, and sustain, social action. Now that we know the "what," the next section is the "how." As we work through the model in the next several chapters, you will continue to add to your elevator pitch, as well as to the knowledge, skills, and strategies that will help you to take action and invite others to join you.

Figure Credit

section 2

Introduction of the S-Quad Model and Your Professional Strategic Social Action Plan

Chapter 6

Introduction to the S⁴ (S-Quad)

Strength, Solidarity, Strategy, and Sustainability

FIGURE 6.1 S-Quad image

"You must be bold, brave, and courageous and find a way ... to get in the way."

—John R. Lewis

As mentioned earlier, in the face of increasingly challenging political and social times, many of us struggle to stay positive while living out our values and acting on what we believe is right. No matter how much experience we have as advocates and activists, we still have times when it is difficult to feel anchored, effective, and consistent in our actions. The S-Quad framework is intended as a way to help us stay reflective and active in social action through strength, solidarity, strategy, and sustainability.

In 2016, Rebecca was asked to give a talk in Greece about social justice in counseling psychology. She felt nervous wondering whether the work she had done in the United States would be relevant or culturally sensitive to the complexities that professionals in Greece were facing. She reflected on the lessons she had learned throughout her professional life, as well as the challenges. Four major themes kept coming to mind: (a) strength, (b) solidarity, (c) strategy, and (d) sustainability. We (Muninder, Derrick, Bryan, and Rebecca) have been using some version of these four areas of reflection and action (although it hasn't always been explicit) to help lead us back to our paths and remind us how to continue working effectively toward social justice. This framework provides an anchor for us. We humbly share this with you, hoping that you find it helpful as well.

In the S-Quad approach to social action, the first theme or area of reflection is strength. This emphasizes that we have knowledge, skills, experience, resources, and talents that we bring to social justice work.

The second area, solidarity, reflects the power of our relationships with others. This is important for camaraderie and, more importantly, points to the essential place of partnership, allyship (or accomplicity), and humility in acknowledging and learning from folks who are affected by the issues we are concerned about.

The third area for reflection and action, strategy, embodies the importance of being informed and intentional in confronting injustice. We have sometimes been reminded of this lesson the hard way, after acting quickly without a clear plan or understanding possible consequences. Our mentors teach us that large-scale change requires a multifaceted approach, often over a long span of time.

The fourth area for reflection and action, sustainability, focuses on the importance of balancing our roles in our families, our health, our jobs, and with the time and effort needed to address injustice. Sustainability is about self and community care and acknowledges that if we are to contribute to meaningful and lasting change, we must continue living healthy lives for ourselves, our loved ones, and our communities.

These four areas of reflection and action, S-Quad, work together to help provide focus and strengthen action toward social justice. In the following chapters, you will explore each of these areas and develop a social action plan, as well as identify knowledge and skills that may be helpful in the process. We hope the S-Quad framework stimulates thoughts, ideas, and practices to help you activate in meaningful and sustainable ways, whether you are just starting or have been an activist and advocate for a long time.

Chapter 7

Strengths for Social Action

What You Bring to the Table Personally and Professionally

Strength

FIGURE 7.1 S-Quad image—strength

"You never know how strong you are, until being strong is your only choice."

—Bob Marley

One day, several years ago, Rebecca heard an interview with one of the founders of the Black Lives Movement (BLM) in Oakland, California (she believes it was Alicia Garza). A listener called in and described feeling overwhelmed by all the injustice going on and asked for advice about getting involved. Rebecca recalls that the BLM founder said something like "figure out what you do well, then do it ferociously." Upon hearing this, Rebecca felt a sense of clarity and relief as this seemed to make the task of social action somewhat more manageable—or at least focused. This also fits with what we know about career success and finding a path that builds on what one has to offer. The statement by the BLM founder reminded us (Bryan, Derrick, Muninder and Rebecca) to find and use our strengths to spark and drive our actions.

You can think about strengths—this area of reflection—as the tools you have now that you can use to take action. Taking stock of your strengths is about looking at your toolbox, what you can use to address a social justice issue—whether you are offering it to support a group effort or taking action on your own. Some of these tools have been developed through your professional training, whereas some are unique to your own experience and personhood. We will first explore the skills and knowledge of helping professions and then assess the skills and knowledge that you possess above and beyond your professional training. We will start with individual strengths, then move to strengths in our connections, culture, and community.

Personal Is Political Is Professional

The personal, the professional, and the political are inexorably intertwined in any profession, perhaps uniquely so in wellness professions. Our personal identities shape our lives and influence what is initially important to us. The political nature of issues is connected to our personal and professional lives, yet can be less visible to us with dominant or privileged identities. The political nature is often crystal clear to those of us who have identities as part of minoritized populations. The following is an example of the three arenas coming together.

EXAMPLE

Bryan's Toolbox

From an early age, I learned to give of my time, treasure, or talent. While growing up, my mom was an English teacher and educator, and she taught me the power of education and what it meant to empower others through language. My dad was a businessman and missionary. I remember going with him on many occasions to places deep into the jungles of Costa Rica to work with people who had less than we did. We went to provide them with food, stories, entertainment, and friendship. My dad would tell stories from the Bible that taught us to do unto others as we would like others to do to us, the importance of perseverance, and the power of seeing the best in all people. Although I didn't know it then, this was also shaping me. I would eventually become a wordsmith and storyteller in my own right.

Today I am a slam poet, critical race theorist, and testimonio scholar–activist, trauma therapist, and hip-hop educator. My profession is centered in helping others, and I get to call my acts of kindness "work." I am involved in my community and social justice movements. I try to be mindful of the ways in which I respond to oppression, and I recognize at times that I don't respond like I would like to. Whether I am conscious of it or not, my actions and inactions are political statements. My activism, scholarship, and worldview are a reflection of my experience. My values and political action are connected to my identity as an Afro Latino immigrant man. I've focused my efforts on supporting marginalized communities and increasing their access to mental health and education. My career choice is also a political stand in a field in which men of color are often rare. I can't possibly separate my identities from my activism or professional identity, but instead, I accept one as a part of the other, the summation being greater than its parts. I question notions of objectivity and instead embrace what makes me, me. The moments when I embrace the things that are "less traditional," "less academic," and "too cultural," have served me and helped me stand out, connect, and advocate more effectively. The lessons and tools that I have learned in academia help me better serve my community now. Personal, political, and professional experiences influence each other. Even in personal and professional roles, my existence is political.

In this example from Bryan, we can see that his personal experiences and professional training all work together to provide him with tools, expertise, and resources to take action. Often in our professional education programs we are asked to learn to be objective observers and "blank slates" when working with clients. However, we cannot be "blank slates"; instead, we have subjective experience based on our backgrounds, histories, and identities.

ACTIVITY 7.1

Reflection

Take a moment to reflect on how your personal, political, and professional lives come together or overlap.

1. What personal values, lessons, and experiences guide your professional actions and paths?

2. How does your activism reflect your personal and professional experiences?

3. How is your personal and professional positionality a political act?

For some of us, existing and thriving in spaces that were not made for us and where marginalization of difference is normed becomes a political act within itself (e.g., US institutions of higher education). At the same time, we receive additional power and privileges through our completion of those same educational programs. How we use our earned and unearned power and privilege, as well as our choice to ignore or respond to oppression, also becomes a political act.

Professional Skills and Knowledge

For us, strengths include skills, knowledge, and expertise. We also consider strengths to encompass resources you may access, both material goods as well as relationships with others who bring skills, knowledge, and resources to a project. We will start by focusing on the skills you have now that may be transferable to other spaces and communities. Some skills have been developed in academic and professional spaces and others you have obtained through your personal experiences and identities.

Within counseling, psychology, social work and other helping professions, accreditation standards identify skills and knowledge that professionals must obtain through training. Table 7.1 outlines ethical principles (ACA, 2014; APA, 2017a; NASW, 2021) and competencies (APA, 2011; CACREP, 2024; CSWE, 2022) from professional associations representing psychologists, counselors, and social workers. If your profession is not listed here, we invite you to take a second to look up your association's principles and competencies and add them to the table.

TABLE 7.1 Comparison of Principles and Competencies of Psychologists, Social Workers, and Counselors

Principles			
Psychology (APA)	Social Work (CSWE/NASW)	Counseling (ACA)	Other Helping Profession
Beneficence and nonmaleficence	Service	Beneficence and nonmaleficence	
Fidelity and responsibility	Competence	Fidelity	
Integrity	Integrity	Veracity	
Justice	Social justice	Justice	
Respect for people's rights and dignity	Dignity and worth of the person	Autonomy	

Competencies			
Psychology (APA)	**Social Work (CSWE)**	**Counseling (CACREP)**	**Other Helping Profession**
Professional values and attitudes Ethical legal standards and policy	Demonstrate ethical professional behavior	Professional counseling orientation and ethical practice	
Individual and cultural diversity	Engage in anti-racism, diversity, equity, and inclusion in practice	Social and cultural identities and experiences Lifespan development Career development	
Reflective practice/self-assessment/self-care	(see ethics code)	(see ethics code)	
Relationships	Engage with individuals, families, groups, organizations, and communities	Counseling practice and relationships	
Research/Evaluation Scientific knowledge and methods Evidence-based practice	Evaluate practice individuals, families, groups, organizations, and communities Engage in practice-informed research and research-informed practice	Research and program evaluation	
Assessment	Assess individuals, families, groups, organizations, and communities	Assessment and diagnostic processes	
Intervention	Intervene individuals, families, groups, organizations, and communities	Counseling practice and relationships Group counseling and group work	
Advocacy Interdisciplinary systems Consultation	Advance human rights, and social, racial, economic, and environmental justice Engage in policy practice	(see individual accreditation standards and ethics code)	
Teaching Supervision Management-Administration	(see individual accreditation standards and ethics code)	(see individual accreditation standards and ethics code)	

Understanding the range, similarities, and differences in principles and competencies across helping professions can be useful. The subtle differences in perspective often influence social action that requires collaborative action, interdisciplinary teams, and collective professional efforts. These principles and competencies also influence the training, and thus the strengths, we bring to action, as well as the expectations our professions have of us.

ACTIVITY 7.2

Identifying Points of Connection

Look at the standards and competencies across the helping professions and identify themes or similar concepts.

1. Highlight with the same color each concept that is similar (e.g., across the board, all three organizations require professionalism so this will be highlighted). If it's helpful, you can use different color highlighters (or colored pencils) or another method that helps you to differentiate themes. You may also recognize that different professions label and or define knowledge areas slightly differently, but in related ways. Look for complexities and the different lenses that may be used.

2. Once you are finished highlighting similarities and noticing differences, reflect on what surprised you or was unexpected.

3. How might this knowledge be helpful for collaborating across professions for social change?

Our level of comfort in professional spaces may be influenced by our lived histories, exposure, opportunities (or the lack of opportunities) prior to and during professional training. Maintaining a growth mindset allows us to view strength development as a lifelong process. Next, we would like to shift from looking at your field to focusing more specifically on you and the knowledge and skills you have gained (or will gain) through your professional training.

ACTIVITY 7.3

Assessing Your Professional Skills and Knowledge

You will begin your self-assessment process by reflecting on your professional training using the competencies from your accreditation standards.

Below we have listed some general knowledge and skill areas from counseling and psychology as an example. Indicate your level of confidence in these areas. If you prefer to be very specific in assessing your competencies, you can also do this activity by replacing the lines below with your profession's competencies listed in Table 7.1.

General Competency Area	How Strong is Your Knowledge or Skill?
Developing and maintaining interpersonal relationships	Strong Moderate Weak
Understanding, respecting, and bridging cultural differences	Strong Moderate Weak
Facilitating and understanding group dynamics	Strong Moderate Weak
Understanding and applying methodology and/or generating research	Strong Moderate Weak
Understanding principles of ethical behavior and addressing ethical challenges	Strong Moderate Weak

Understanding and integrating the interaction between individual well-being and environmental forces	Strong Moderate Weak
Understanding human growth and development	Strong Moderate Weak
Understanding social/organizational/ community basis of behavior and applying this in consultation and systems change work	Strong Moderate Weak
Writing for academic audiences	Strong Moderate Weak
Developing awareness and acting on issues of self- in relation to work (including positionality, power, privilege, and cultural issues, as well as self-care)	Strong Moderate Weak

List additional professional skills or knowledge areas that are not reflected (you may need to do this on a separate paper).

1. Identify two areas where you feel strong and would like to continue to develop. Create a plan using SMART (Specific, Measurable, Attainable, Realistic, and Time-limited) goals to guide your development.

2. Identify two areas you feel less confident about, but would like to improve. Create a plan to use SMART goals to guide your development.

In addition to the professional competencies outlined in the accreditation standards, most professional associations have expanded competencies for multicultural and justice-oriented work. For example, in counseling, the ACA has endorsed two sets of multicultural and social justice related competencies for use by all counselors: the Multicultural Social Justice Counseling Competencies (Ratts et al., 2015) and the ACA Social Justice Advocacy Competencies (Lewis et al., 2002; Toporek & Daniels, 2018). Updated guidelines for multicultural practice and research in psychology (APA, 2017b) and in social work (NASW, 2015) also provide resources and guidance for professionals as well as communicate expectations about culturally responsive practice that is also essential for social justice advocacy.

In addition to general professional competencies, many mental health professionals develop areas of expertise or specializations. Specialized training may take place within one's degree program or post-graduation. Some examples of specialized training within the helping professionals include forensic psychology, performance and health psychology, neuropsychology, adventure-based therapy, mindfulness-based stress reduction, and trauma-focused. Additionally, identity-based training and practice guidelines can include competencies related to individuals with disabilities, LGBTQ+ populations, and specific racial or ethnic groups. Below we provide some examples of how Rebecca and Bryan use their specializations as strengths in their social justice work and community involvement.

SPECIALIZATION EXAMPLES

Rebecca in Career Counseling and Bryan in Spanish Language Psychological Services and Research

Rebecca: Specialized training and experience in career counseling provides me with knowledge and skills to help people make career decisions and navigate looking for jobs as well as work through challenges on the job. These strengths are relevant to social action and economic justice issues. For example, holistic career counseling includes understanding oneself in relation to others, contextual and environmental influences on choices (or whether someone even has a choice), and how the larger sociopolitical and economic context influences opportunities and the experience of work. I can speak with some authority about legislative and policy issues that impact the ability for individuals and communities to have safe, meaningful, and livable employment. I can provide support and guidance for individuals who are facing unjust work situations. I can also help communities navigate unfair employment processes and advocate with policy makers.

Bryan: When I was applying to doctoral programs, it was important for me to find a program that specialized in working with immigrants and Spanish-speaking communities. This was in part because of my identities and history, as well as wanting to use my "Latinoness" as a clinical tool to serve my community. Though there were only a few options across the nation, I was able to find a program that fit my needs and prepared me to provide services to Spanish-speaking and immigrant communities. The specialization provided me with training to understand and speak Spanish at a competency level for ethical and responsible provision of psychological services when working with Spanish speaking communities. I obtained a specialized understanding of Latinx/e Spanish speaking populations in the US with respect to sociopolitical history, cultural and linguistic norms, and within-group variation. I became a provider who centered multicultural sensitivity, social justice, and liberatory practices in clinical work and research. I also learned to work with Latinx/e communities in research and the considerations needed when working with vulnerable populations, such as first generation college students, undocumented students, and their families. Today I continue to use those same skills in my private practice where I provide immigration evaluations and trauma and culturally responsive psychological services.

Professional specializations can add unique expertise to the strengths, knowledge, and resources you bring to social action.

ACTIVITY 7.4

Specializations Within Your Profession

If you do not currently have a specialization, try to imagine what you would consider specializing in and how it could change the way you do your work (e.g., counseling, teaching, research).

If you do have a specialization, take a moment to reflect on and answer the following questions:

1. If you have training in a specialty area in your field, describe it.

2. What additional awareness, skills, and knowledge does it provide you with?

3. Why did you pursue a specialization? Why did it matter?

4. What does it mean to you to have this specialized training? What might it mean to your clients or students?

5. How is the specialization regulated (i.e., accrediting body)? Who gets to claim expertise?

6. How can you use your specialization for social action?

Professional and Personal Skills, Knowledge, and Resources: Translating Your Strengths

When we think of the tools that are helpful to have in pursuing social change, it is important to consider all abilities, including those that seemingly have nothing to do with the cause. Consider functional or transferable skills (e.g., possessing people skills, speaking bilingually) and technical skills (e.g., building websites, repairing cars, developing curriculum). Julia Turshen describes in the introduction to her cookbook how she was new to activism and trying to find a way to contribute when she wrote *Feed the Resistance* (2017). She discovered that the expertise she had as a writer and a cook could organize and lead others in preparing meals for large groups during resistance efforts. She also shared her expertise with others so that they could do the same.

Transferable skills are things you do in one setting that could be used in a different setting or a different way. For example, if you are a clinical supervisor, you may be pretty good at helping others find direction, delegating tasks, conceptualizing goals, and leading projects to completion. In the following activities, we ask you to think about the skills and strengths you use currently or have used in the past, regardless of the setting or purpose, and how you have applied these skills. In this first activity, think about your professional skills.

Professional Strengths

Being in academia, clinical settings, or around others with similar training may make us feel like everyone around us has similar skill sets and that we may not have something unique to contribute. We may assume that everyone is able to do what we can do. However, if we intentionally immerse ourselves, build relationships, and gain trust with those who are different from us, we can learn the uniqueness and value of our skill set. We can better appreciate the professional skills and competencies we have, as well as the unique contributions of others and how we can partner and complement one another. For example, as psychologists, our ability to translate academic theories of change into more digestible concepts may be a skill that others in the community do not have and that we can use for the benefit of others. Also note that professional ethical standards can serve as a resource to support social action. For an example, see Flynn and colleagues' (2021) discussion on the connection between APA's code of ethics as a support for psychologists' civil disobedience.

As we develop our professional identities, we gain specialized knowledge and skills both intentionally and unintentionally. Many helping professions have similar competencies, as well as some differences. Take a second to find your profession's competencies document either through your professional association, the appropriate licensing or accrediting organization, or even a general internet search (e.g. "professional social work competencies"). You can also use the references connected with Table 7.1 to find the documents.

As you review these resources, notice that they are organized into different types of knowledge. Think about the skills that you have developed or are developing in relation to these competencies. Identify ways that you might use them in the community and/or in social action. With this in mind, reflect on what it is that you do well.

ACTIVITY 7.5

Professional Strengths for Action: What Do I Do Well?

We all have areas of strength and growth. For this activity, reflect on the strengths set areas in the table below.

1. For each of the strengths areas, identify your comfort level, using a scale of 1–4.

   - I don't feel comfortable and don't want to develop. (1)
   - I don't feel comfortable, but would like to develop. (2)
   - I feel comfortable using, could improve. (3)
   - This is an area of strength. (4)

2. Itemize your strengths by asking these two questions: What strengths have I developed as a professional? How can I translate these skills to my social justice work to benefit the community?
3. Try to identify actionable steps to improve any areas of interest you rated a "2."

If you need help, you can review Bryan's example at the end. In the example, he ranks his comfort with different strengths and then itemizes the strengths by describing how he uses those.

Strengths	Skills Rating	Definition of Strengths	Itemizing Our Strengths
Professional		Professionalism, positionality within organizations, access, cross-cultural communication, and representation.	
Relational		Ability to relate effectively and meaningfully with individuals, groups, and/or communities.	
Scientific		Understanding of research, research methodology, techniques of data collection and analysis, biological bases of behavior, cognitive-affective bases of behavior, and development across the lifespan. Respect for scientifically derived knowledge.	

Strengths	Skills Rating	Definition of Strengths	Itemizing Our Strengths
Applied Skills		Integration of research and clinical expertise for culturally responsive care. Use of skills for individual, community, and societal wellness. The ability to provide expert guidance or professional assistance in response to a client's needs or goals.	
Educational		Ability to provide instruction, disseminate knowledge, and evaluate acquisition of knowledge and skills. Supervise others and pass down academic, community, and healing knowledge to others.	
Systemic		Knowledge of key issues and concepts in related disciplines. Identify and interact with professionals in multiple disciplines. Management and organizational knowledge and skills. Advocacy and systems levels. Understanding of the impact of said advocacy.	
Other:			

EXAMPLE

Sections of Bryan's Activity 7.5: Translating Your Professional Training

Strengths	Strengths Rating	Definition of Strengths	Itemizing Our Strengths
Professional	3 (feel comfortable, could improve)	Professionalism, positionality within organizations, access, cross-cultural communication, and representation.	* Understand professional language and communication * Cross-cultural communication * Member of professional organizations and divisions
Relational	4 (area of strength)	Ability to relate effectively and meaningfully with individuals, groups, and/or communities.	* Collectivistic * Relatable * Approachable * Effective group facilitator * Educator
Systemic	2 (don't feel comfortable, but would like to develop)	Knowledge of key issues and concepts in related disciplines. Identify and interact with professionals in multiple disciplines. Management and organizational knowledge and skills. Advocacy and systems levels understanding of the impact of said advocacy.	* Access to other professionals * Willingness to advocate * Access to leadership **Area of growth:** * New to where I live / work—I need to have a better understanding of this community, their needs, strengths, and power structures
Other: documentary filmmaking	3 (feel comfortable, could improve)	Created documentaries, know processes, ability to integrate psychology and film, access to community	* Creative expression * Use of film editing programs * Access to documents for ethical documentary filming

Personal and Cultural Strengths

As we discussed in Chapter 3, our sociopolitical, historical context determines what knowledge is considered valuable. Colonization dictates what knowledge is valued, defines parameters of professional disciplines, and regulates minds and bodies as a form of control, prescribing what is acceptable. Scholar–activists recognize that most of the methods, perspectives, and systems used in academia and helping professions are rooted in oppressive practices that maintain the status quo (e.g., Kivel, 2017; Prilleltensky, 1989) and White supremacy.

Scholar–activist researchers from historically marginalized communities have identified psychological and cultural strengths challenging perspectives and research that view BIPOC communities only in terms of deficits (Adames & Chavez-Dueñas, 2017; David et al, 2022; Rojas-Araúz, 2021; White, 1984). Such research has emphasized that global majorities possess cultural knowledge, skills, abilities, and contacts that are often undervalued and unrecognized (Yosso, 2005). Yosso (2005) said "various forms of capital nurtured through cultural wealth include aspirational, navigational, social, linguistic, familial, and resistant capital" (p. 69). These forms of capital are learned and passed down in the community, many times in informal settings, through experience, unwritten rules, stories, and cultural ways of being.

Scholar–activists are called increasingly to decolonize their research, practice, and pedagogy (Malherbe et al., 2021). Decolonizing frameworks challenge counselors to actively engage in integrating traditional forms of healing, being, and communicating. It is an invitation to include and honor ancestral wisdom in our work, while being intentional not to appropriate this knowledge. Our positionality and identities may dictate what this looks like for each of us. For example, our connection to communities and/or to histories of oppression may change how we integrate ancestral wisdom into our work. We recognize this may not always be easy and most of us will make mistakes. Still, not being willing to reflect, integrate, and honor traditional healing practices, knowledge, and wisdom would be a form of erasure. These forms of erasure and devaluing of traditional ways of knowing are rooted in White supremacy and in the "othering" of global majorities (Bernal & Villalpando, 2002; Pérez Huber, 2009). As agents of social action, we invite you to reclaim knowledge and find ways to identify and value the healing wisdom that exists and was passed down intergenerationally in communities, with humility and gratitude. We invite you to think about the knowledge you possessed before ever becoming healthcare providers or academics.

Building on Activity 7.5, we move from professional strengths to those you have developed personally in relation to your community.

ACTIVITY 7.6

Community Strengths for Action: Translating Your Strengths of Cultural and Personal Experiences

In the next activity, you will work on identifying your strengths by itemizing them and thinking of ways in which your community knowledge may help you to take action in professional spaces or further facilitate work within your communities.

Take a moment to reflect on the following questions.

1. What strengths did I obtain from my ancestors, elders, and/or community outside of professional spaces?

2. How do I implement them in my work in professional spaces or the community?

As you go through some examples of cultural strengths, identify your comfort level using a scale of 1–4 (similar to Activity 7.5).

- I don't feel comfortable and don't want to develop. (1)
- I don't feel comfortable, but would like to develop. (2)
- I feel comfortable using, could improve. (3)
- This is an area of strength. (4)

After you rank the different areas, try to create bullet points to itemize your strengths. Then try to identify actionable steps to improve any areas you assigned "2." In case an example would be helpful, Bryan has shared an example at the end of this exercise.

Skills	Skills Rating	Definition	Itemizing Our Strengths
Relational		Ability to relate effectively and meaningfully with individuals, groups, and/or communities outside of our profession.	
Cultural Knowledge		Understanding of the community, cross-cultural communication, cultural values, traditional healing practices, etc.	
Applied Skills		Integration of cultural knowledge and community needs to support the profession on creating culturally responsive care. Use of skills for individual, organizational, and societal change. The ability to provide expert guidance or community centered assistance in creating change, etc.	
Educational		Traditional healing methods, cultural knowledge, application of ancestral knowledge / wisdom, etc.	
Systemic		Knowledge of key issues in the community. Bridging community and the field. Identify and interact with community members in multiple roles. Collaborative needs, knowledge, advocacy, and skills. Understanding the impact of said advocacy.	
Other (add any other strengths not named):			

Community Strengths for Action: Translating Your Strengths of Cultural and Personal Experiences

1. What strengths have you learned through experience or from your communities?
2. How can you use these strengths for social action in professional or community spaces?

Skills	Skills Rating	Definition	Itemizing Our Strengths
Relational	3	Ability to relate effectively and meaningfully with individuals, groups, and/or communities outside of our profession.	* Collectivist * Approachable * Connected to the community * From the community
Cultural Knowledge	4	Understanding of the community, cross-cultural communication, cultural values, cultural humility, traditional healing practices.	* Spanish speaking * Personalismo * Familismo * History * Cross-cultural communication * Immigrant identities
Educational	2	Traditional healing methods, cultural knowledge, application of ancestral knowledge.	* Spiritual practices **Area of Growth**: Would like to learn more about traditional healing practices
Systemic	3	Knowledge of key issues in the community. Bridging community and the field. Identify and interact with community members in multiple roles. Collaborative needs, knowledge, advocacy, and skills. Understanding of the impact of said advocacy.	* Understanding of community barriers * Identify as Latino * Bridging community to the field * Contributions to Latinx psychology * DREAM Activist
Other (add any other strengths not named): Bicultural upbringing, Immigrant-American			

Naming the strengths we possess may be difficult to do. It may not be culturally congruent to talk about ourselves or what we do well, and we might take some of our strengths for granted. If that's the case, it might be helpful to recruit those close to us to support us in identifying our strengths. Community can also be supportive in helping us identify our strengths. Ask peers, mentors, and community members to help you identify your strengths or what's needed of you by asking questions such as these: What do you think I do well? What can I do better? What is needed right now? How can I best support the movement?

The two activities you completed (7.5 and 7.6) focused on general areas of strengths professionally and in relation to community. We can dive even deeper and look at specific skills you have developed and those that have made you special your entire life. We will also ask you to consider these as transferable skills—that is, skills you can use in a variety of settings or applications. For example, the skill of "organizing" can refer to organizing people (e.g., activists), things (e.g., resources), events (e.g., protests), etc. Although organizing each of these is different and calls on different sets of knowledge, the general ability to organize involves some level of overseeing and imagining a structure to synthesize multiple parts into a coherent whole. In the next activity, you will consider a range of transferable skills. Although this is not an exhaustive list, it is a good start.

Identifying Our Transferable Skills and Strengths: As Individuals and in Collaboration with Community or Others

Reflect on each skill set and rate your comfort level using this skill set as an individual and in collaboration with community. Use a 1–4 scale (1—a skill I don't have and don't intend to develop; 2—a skill I want or could develop; 3—a skill I feel comfortable using, but could improve; and 4—area of strength).

Skill Set	Skill	How Comfortable I Feel Using this Skill (Skill Rating)	
		Individually (1–4)	In Collaboration with Community (1–4)
Speaking	in person to strangers		
	in person to people I know		
	to legislators or business people		
	to media (e.g., Instagram, Snapchat, news organizations, etc.)		
	by phone to strangers		
	by phone to people I know		
	Conversation / Active listening		
Technical Skills	**Skill**	**Individually (1-4)**	**In Collaboration with Community (1-4)**
	Using social media		
	Creating and maintaining websites, blogs		
	Creating podcasts		
	Setting up and managing sound equipment		
	Video recording		
Working with Information	**Skill**	**Individually (1-4)**	**In Collaboration with Community (1-4)**
	Researching information		
	Budgeting / Accounting		
	Creating talking points		
	Creating training materials		
	Learning systems		
	Understanding professional norms		
	Understanding professional values		
	Marketing		
	Other:		

Artistic Skills	**Skill**	**Individually (1-4)**	**In Collaboration with Community (1-4)**
	Creating posters and banners		
	Painting murals		
	Storytelling		
	Painting		
	Other:		
Writing Skills	**Skill**	**Individually (1-4)**	**In Collaboration with Community (1-4)**
	Writing persuasively		
	Writing letters		
	Writing legal documents		
	Writing technical or academic reports		
	Writing for a specific audience (professional or community)		
	Other:		
Mechanical or Construction Skills	**Skill**	**Individually (1-4)**	**In Collaboration with Community (1-4)**
	Mechanical skills (e.g. fixing machines)		
	Construction		
	Other:		
Language Skills	**Skill**	**Individually (1-4)**	**In Collaboration with Community (1-4)**
	Bilingual or multilingual		
	Code Switching		
	Translating		
	Interpreting		
	Other:		
Other	**Skill**	**Individually (1-4)**	**In Collaboration with Community (1-4)**

Reflect on those skills that you marked as 2s, 3s, and 4s (skills that you have or want to use), and identify the number of skills that you currently have (4s) or could develop (2s or 3s). Add a star next to any skill that you feel comfortable using for social justice issues. In the spaces below, make some notes about patterns you notice and areas where you would like to improve or grow your skill set (identify at least two).

_____

_____

_____

We have covered a lot so far in this chapter. Before going further, we think it's time to take a little break.

PAUSE

Take the next 10 minutes to put the book down and engage in self-care. Perhaps you can take this time to grab a snack, go outside, stretch and move around, or simply sit with yourself and take deep breaths. Whatever feels comfortable for you, take these next 10 minutes to take some time for yourself.

Knowledge

Whereas skills are knowing "how" to do something, knowledge is knowing "about" something— usually some information you have gained over time that may be helpful, sometimes even in unexpected ways. Examples of "knowledge" might include understanding how local elections work, how bail bonds work, the customs of various cultural and religious communities, where to find free or inexpensive art supplies, how to navigate public transportation, etc. Other examples might include having an understanding of human behavior, marketing, public assistance applications, legal processes, local history, zoning processes, economics or financial matters. Some of this knowledge may come from your professional training, occupation, activities you do in your free time, or simply personal experience. It is likely this exercise will not uncover all the areas of knowledge you hold, but we hope it will help you to start thinking about the wealth of knowledge you have acquired that may be useful. In the exercise below, think about the things you learned about in each experience.

ACTIVITY 7.8

Professional Knowledge

1. What have you needed to know about for various jobs and professional roles you have held? The following are some examples: If you have worked as a clinician, you may know about various interventions and forms of healing. If you have worked as an educator, you may know different learning theories or may have experience teaching complex ideas to a large group of people. If you have worked at your synagogue or mosque, you may know cultural nuances and religious practices. If you have worked in politics, you may know policy or knowledge of how to best work with representatives. If you worked as summer camp staff, you might have knowledge about working with young people, development, and icebreakers to help connect strangers. Think about the most recent jobs or professional roles you have held and list as many knowledge areas as come to mind.

Job/Professional Role 1:

Job/Professional Role 2:

Job/Professional Role 3:

Community and Cultural Knowledge

1. What have you learned from your ancestors, culture, or communities? (For example, are you part of any music circles? Do you know of spaces that are trusted by the community or the name of agencies that do the work you want to be involved in? Are you part of a religious organization, nonprofit, or other group with resources?) Think about your roles within the communities you serve or come from and the things you enjoy doing. List as many knowledge areas as you can:

Experience 1:

_____

_____

_____

Experience 2:

_____

_____

_____

Experience 3:

_____

_____

_____

Resources

Beyond skills and knowledge, there are several types of resources, including those that are tangible (e.g., financial, real estate, craft supplies, food, meeting spaces, or access to any of these) and those that are intangible (e.g., time, flexibility, social capital such as relationships with others who might have access to other resources, skills, or knowledge). Inventorying what we have and what we need is a good way to begin, even if we don't know yet that it might be useful or how we would use it. We can think of this like a collective toolbox for social action. When we come together, we can communicate and share these resources for a collective cause.

Rebecca Using Skills and Resources to Support Community Efforts

Rebecca gives an example from her experience. Sogorea Te' Land Trust, an Ohlone organization affiliated with Indians Organizing for Change, was holding a rally to draw attention to efforts to save sacred land and shell mounds from being developed into a shopping mall. The rally was scheduled for Friday the following week, and unfortunately, she was unable to attend due to a previous commitment. However, she learned through the organization's social media page that someone from another organization was holding a sign-making event to prepare signs for the rally. It is important to note here that the sign-making event was put on by an individual associated with Showing Up for Racial Justice (SURJ), a local chapter of a national organization created by White people to facilitate White people to actively support BIPOC organizations to challenge institutional and systemic racism.

Rebecca was thankful that she was able to arrange time that day to help make signs, especially since she couldn't attend the Friday event. She arrived at the house and enjoyed being part of a small group who came to make signs. The organizer provided art supplies, along with some sample signs for inspiration. They probably made about 50 signs, using up most of the supplies. At some point, it occurred to Rebecca that the art supplies had not magically appeared and that they were not cheap. She had craft paint and many markers at home left from years of art projects with her kids, but hadn't thought to bring them. She decided the least she could do was contribute some cash, and she asked the host if that would be okay. The host responded with an emphatic "Oh yes! That would be great!" Then a couple of other volunteers also offered to contribute.

This story illustrates resources that were both tangible and intangible (resources are italicized). The sign-making event was made possible because the organizer took the *time* to create it to support the Sogorea Te' Land Trust using *social media* and her connections with SURJ and the Sogorea Te' Land Trust. The event was held in the *backyard* of a volunteer's rented home. She purchased *art supplies* and *snacks* using her own *money*. As a sign maker, the resources Rebecca had were the *time* and *flexibility* to participate, *transportation* to get to the house, and *cash*. Participants also had access to the *internet* and *social media* accounts to communicate and create awareness about the event.

Resources: "I Have 'X' or Know Where to Get It!"

In the following boxes, brainstorm some ideas about resources you have, or have access to. You may come up with a nice general list now and later, when you are faced with an event or potential action, you may realize that you have even more resources specific to that situation. These can be personal or professional resources and may reflect your positionality, privilege and power, social capital, and/or actual items.

Tangible resources (e.g., computers, furniture, space, information, financial resources, etc.)

_____

_____

_____

Intangible resources (e.g., time, flexibility, connections)

_____

_____

_____

Wrapping Up Strengths

Ultimately, understanding our strengths as well as our areas of growth are important aspects of creating effective and intentional social change. Better understanding our strengths and weaknesses helps us answer the following questions:

1. What are my strengths?
2. What are my areas of growth?
3. What tasks energize me?
4. What tasks drain me?
5. How can I bridge or translate my skills to different settings?

Sometimes getting outside perspectives can help us identify our strengths. When working with clients who feel uncomfortable discussing their strengths in the job search process, Rebecca often will ask them to consider what others would say about them. Asking friends, family, and colleagues to help us reflect on our strengths can be useful. We can also use books or assessments, such as the Myers-Briggs Type Indicator, which measures preferences across four spectrums (extraversion—introversion, sensing—intuition, thinking—feeling, and judging—perceiving) (Myers & Briggs Foundation, 2025), or the StrengthsFinder 2.0 (Rath, 2007), which divides strengths into different themes (strategic thinking, relationship building, influencing, and executing) and subthemes (e.g., under relationship building is adaptability, connectedness, empathy, harmony, include, etc.).

Before going further, it might be helpful to summarize what you have in your toolbox.

SUMMARY OF YOUR STRENGTHS: SKILLS, KNOWLEDGE, AND RESOURCES

Skills	Knowledge	Resources

Reflecting on Strengths in Social Action

Using strengths also entails identifying when to use them and when to let go. Social action does not always look the same. Just because we *can* do a job, does not mean we *should*, or that it is the best use of our strengths or even what the movement needs.

PERSPECTIVE

Bryan

During the second year of my doctoral program, the 45th president of the United States was elected. I had been living in a bubble of San Francisco Bay Area and Eugene, Oregon, politics—participating in activism that made me believe there was no way the election of that particular 45th could happen. After all, everyone I knew seemed to have a clear understanding of what it would cost marginalized communities to have him in office. However, to my surprise, and to the surprise of many Americans, a campaign that was driven by xenophobia, fear mongering, and anti-immigrant sentiment, later known as "Trumpism," had won the election. At the time, I felt stuck and considered dropping out of my doctoral program. Thanks to mentors and peer support, I was reminded that it was important for me to do two things: First, I needed to recognize the new strengths (i.e., skills and resources) I could develop and the impact I could have by staying in academia, graduating, and effecting change. Second, I needed to trust that someone in my community had the strengths needed to take my place in the front line while I developed additional strengths and credentials through academia. I needed to trust the movement and activists I was in solidarity with. Sometimes our persistence is a form of resistance.

We will consider this lesson again when we talk about solidarity, strategy, and even sustainability in the following chapters. Given Bryan's example above, and the evolving political climate, these lessons may be more important than ever. The first step in using our strengths is to recognize, itemize, imagine, and transform our strengths to best support the goals of the movement to which we feel connected. Our connection to our communities as well as our profession provides us with skills and knowledge as well as strength in numbers. Social action is meaningful yet small when it is just one person. In the next chapter, solidarity, we will talk about the value of partnering and collaborating with others who have the skills and knowledge areas that we don't have as well as requesting community members' perspectives about what is needed. Additionally, solidarity and joining with others helps strengthen, protect, and sustain our efforts. As we said at the beginning of this workbook, movements need all kinds of people with all kinds of strengths. Our diversity of perspectives and abilities makes us stronger.

Chapter 8

Solidarity

The Power of Relationships and the Expertise of Communities

FIGURE 8.1 S-Quad image—solidarity

"I didn't always have things, but I had people—I always had people."

—Ta-Nehisi Coates (2015, p. 88)

In Chapter 7, you identified the skills and strengths that will be helpful as you engage in social action. Now we want to spend some time focusing on relationship building. Being in relationship with others is key to sustaining movements. This chapter is intended to introduce (or review for some) concepts related to being in solidarity. Solidarity allows us to combine *strengths* to inform *strategies* and relationships that *sustain* ourselves and the work.

ACTIVITY 8.1

What Is Solidarity?

Before reading this chapter, answer the questions below based on your understanding of solidarity and community.

1. What does solidarity mean to you?

2. What are important factors of solidarity?

3. How do you define community?

4. How do you know if/when you are part of a community?

"Solidarity" is defined by Merriam-Webster Dictionary (n.d.-b) as "unity (as of a group or class) that produces or is based on community of interests, objectives, and standards." Liu and Shange (2018) describe the concept of *thick solidarity* as solidarity that is rooted in empathy, an understanding of cultural histories, recognition of difference, and a willingness to allow those most impacted to lead. As discussed in previous chapters, it is important to understand your personal and professional histories, including that of your profession, while seeking to build relationships with communities. Considering your positionality and proximity to power is integral to being in solidarity. In a video interview, counseling psychologist Dr. Annelise Singh details an example of this in their work with young people.

> It's really easy for me as, you know, an adult to come in and say, 'Oh, this is what I think, what should be happening in schools.' And so I've got to keep a good pulse on my own adultism, right? To make sure that I'm not wielding power in a way that's not cool for young people. So that means, really finding ways to make the coalition, not just culturally responsive, but creating a space that queer and trans folks can empower themselves and that they hold leadership roles. (Toporek & Ahluwalia, 2019)

In the quote above, Dr. Singh not only describes being aware of their own power and position, but also an intention to have others lead. This is similar to adrienne marie brown's concept of interdependence, which she states requires a decentralized way of understanding where solutions come from and how decisions are made (brown, 2017). We seek to develop expertise through our training as helping professionals. However, as we work to be in solidarity with others—community members, students, clients, colleagues, etc.—it is important that we honor their expertise.

Solidarity can be with your own community or group, or it can be with a community outside your own. When you engage in social action related to issues in your own community, solidarity may come easily because unity and trust is already present. For Muninder, advocating on behalf of issues faced by the Sikh community often comes with some ease because she is an insider. However, when advocating for groups or communities where she is an outsider, such as the Black Lives Matter movement, she has to pay greater attention to ways in which power, privilege, and oppression can play out. She has to be more attentive to ways in which she does not know the lived experience of Black community members, and she has to take her cue from them. She has to understand what their experiences are, and then she has to learn when and how to engage.

We believe solidarity is really about the following four factors, which we will explore in this chapter:

- honoring relationships and sustaining community;
- respecting, supporting, and understanding others;
- finding strength in numbers;
- seeking support and camaraderie to help sustain you.

In this section, we will address each of the four solidarity factors and the challenges that sometimes come with relationships. These areas of solidarity apply when working with those you share identities with as well as those you differ from, especially across cultures.

Honoring Relationships and Sustaining Community

As helping professionals, relationships are vital to our work, as well as to our roles as friends, family, and community members. They help us sustain our values and beliefs and help us push beyond our own interests to accomplish larger goals of serving humanity. The people in our lives and their experiences (and our own) are often the impetus for engaging in the causes we choose to champion. The term "community" is often used to describe people who are connected through shared experiences, such as living and working together or having similar identities. As helping professionals, we should not assume that people will automatically consider us part of their communities because we share similar identities. Community is the result of an ongoing process of genuinely connecting with others. The relationships we build allow us to become part of others' communities. Therefore, building and sustaining relationships is an important factor in solidarity.

Our social mosaic is made up of relationships that either create community or are embedded in community. The Sikh concept of *seva*, or community service, can be helpful in understanding how we create a foundation for solidarity through mutually supportive relationships. It is important to realize that mutual support does not mean equal amounts of support or that we support others with the expectation that they support us in return. Rather, when we perceive a need, we help fulfill that need. Through seva, we can promote equity, but more than that, through serving others in ways that are helpful to them at that time, we remain connected by relationships that can create and sustain community.

As helping professionals, we have to be intentional about building and sustaining relationships with those we are serving. These relationships can allow us to learn about the specific needs of those we are supporting and provide the opportunity for the community to ask for specific aid. This may involve entering and engaging in ways different from the way we engage in our own community, which requires us to understand how to do that respectfully. For example, *The Pocket Guide to Ohlone Solidarity for Both Native and Non Native Allies and Accomplices* shares protocol for "the set of societal rules that members and visitors of a community respectfully follow in order to maintain peace and harmony within a nation or territory" as well as guidance for getting involved (Sayers-Roods et al., n.d., p. 1). It is important to note that we cannot assume a community will embrace us immediately (Lovell & Scott-McLaughin, 2023); thus, we must continually show up to build trust in these relationships. In a video interview several years ago, Bryan's description of solidarity illustrated how to integrate ourselves into communities we are working with, rather than being present to fulfill our own needs.

> It's looking at how do we really become part of the community and not just stand in there while we need to, right? So is it going to a cultural event that has absolutely nothing to do with your research. Yes. Is it showing up to graduation because the participants in your program are graduating? It's also that. Is it just standing outside when it's raining while you're waiting for one of the parents to show up and pick up the kids. It's also that, right? And ultimately it's the relationships, the things that we don't get to measure in numbers. (Toporek & Ahluwalia, 2019)

Derrick's experience as a practicum therapist at a university counseling center demonstrates the power of relationship building in addressing community needs.

EXAMPLE

New Therapist on Campus

Derrick was a new therapist on campus and was eager to connect with Black students. Though he had visited the Black student resource center and introduced himself to students and staff there, Derrick noticed that Black students were not engaging with mental health services through the campus counseling center. Acknowledging the history of the Black community and mental health generally, and the lack of representation in the counseling center at this specific institution, Derrick made it a point to begin eating lunch in the resource center regularly. This allowed him to build informal relationships with Black students and learn more about their experiences on campus and beyond. It also allowed students to get to know him outside of the counseling center.

Eventually, Derrick was invited by students to facilitate a workshop on campus focused on Black students and mental health. Through the relationships that were established, Derrick was able to collaborate with students about specific topics that were addressed in the workshop. The workshop was enriched by the relationships that were built, which led to students feeling comfortable to contribute openly and honestly.

Bryan's quote and Derrick's experience exemplify how to build trust, maintain relationships, and change systemic norms about what it means to provide support. Whichever communities we hope to be in solidarity with and/or become connected to, it is important that we put the community first. Similar to the concept of seva, it is not about self-promotion or solely the promotion of one's own community and needs. It is about furthering humanity and working with other communities as if they are our own. Acknowledging and honoring relationships in this way is the first step toward building solidarity.

Respecting, Supporting, and Understanding Others

Liberation, or the act of becoming free or freeing a person or group from oppression, is often the goal of acting in solidarity with others. In Chapter 3, we discussed the interconnectedness of liberation and the importance of recognizing and leveraging power and privilege in solidarity with those who are marginalized. We also introduced liberation psychology (Martín-Baró, 1996) and the perspective that psychologists, and helping professionals generally, are called to be active in changing oppressive systems. In considering how to approach solidarity from our positions as helping professionals, it can be helpful to explore allyship, inclusive language, microaggressions, and cultural humility.

Allyship

One of the central aspects of building solidarity is allyship, or engagement in the process of building relationships and working toward justice on behalf of others in the way that an individual or community directs. Allyship is demonstrated by the actions we take and first considers the people we aim to support. Dr. Bedford Palmer II articulates this point in his description of allyship:

> Allies stand at the side of people and take hits for them. They don't direct things and they don't ask for stuff, right? If you want to ally with me later, then that's great, but right now I'm here for you. (Toporek & Ahluwalia, 2019)

In their sharing about the teachings of Dr. Joseph White, the godfather of Black psychology, Lovell and McLaughlin (2023) describe intersectional allyship, which is based on genuine relationships, considers people's experiences of privilege and marginalization, and uses one's own privilege and power to support others. Using your power and privilege to support others can mean taking risks that would be more detrimental for those with less power. For example, getting arrested at a rally or protest could result in deportation for an undocumented person, whereas the same would be much less likely for someone with citizenship.

Some authors have also talked about the need for different language and understanding of this expression of solidarity. For example, Tiffany Jana suggests "co-conspirators" as a more proactive and collaborative role than ally, which they describe as being less committed and less informed (Jana, 2021). Whether using the term ally, co-conspirator, or accomplice, our point is that when we are in solidarity with others, it is essential that this comes from relationship and understanding, as well as a willingness to use one's position despite the risk or cost. In short, we consider true allyship to be about consistent and committed action.

We have to approach liberation in the way that Lilla Watson refers to it—that is, humanity is tied together and liberation and justice for one is really liberation and justice for all (quoted in Chapter 3). If we don't, we risk approaching our advocacy work from a top-down position (i.e., we are above this group that is experiencing oppression and we will save or rescue them). Jordan Flaherty (2016), in his book, *No More Heroes: Grassroots Challenges to the Savior Mentality*, talks about the harm of "saviorism" on movements. Saviorism is where someone outside an issue who holds little knowledge of that issue imposes their vision of how to fix the problem—usually a person holding privilege, such as a White person in the case of racism. Flaherty describes how this mentality assumes that people need rescuing. The privilege of those attempting to support marginalized communities has led those with a savior mentality to assume that they are more capable than the people who are directly affected by the issue. As helping professionals, it's important that we honor the wisdom of the community and the practices that have been sustaining the communities we seek solidarity with. Many organizations and communities have created resources and information to guide us on the best way to join with them in community and respectfully engage as allies and accomplices.

In the next activity, consider your beliefs about care, support, and solidarity.

ACTIVITY 8.2

On the Receiving End of Support

1. What are the qualities and characteristics of genuine care?

2. Think of a time when you received genuine support or think of someone you consider to be an ally (accomplice or co-conspirator). What about the support offered made it genuine? Think about what support was offered and how it was offered.

3. How did (or does) this support make you feel?

Inclusive Language

Communication can be a powerful tool in relationship building. Further, using inclusive language can show people that we respect and care about them. Inclusive language differs from "political correctness," which is grounded in a dominant narrative. Political correctness uses labels and terms as a surface strategy to avoid being offensive without actually understanding the meaning in context. Engaging in political correctness is also problematic because it elevates the dominant group's definition and labeling of marginalized groups, thereby reifying power structures that keep the dominant group on top and others below. Using inclusive language is not enough. To understand and to be respectful, we must learn about people's identities, contexts, and lives and the impacts of structural oppression similar to the protocol offered in the *Pocket Guide to Ohlone Solidarity*. This is especially true given the power differentials that may exist between helping professionals and those we seek to support.

Microaggressions

If we are not thoughtful about the language we use and intentional about inclusivity, we are more likely to unintentionally commit microaggressions. The term "microaggression" was proposed in 1970 by Chester Pierce to describe dismissals and insults toward Black Americans from others (see the work of Pierce and his colleagues published in 1978). In 2007, Derald Wing Sue and his colleagues, psychologists and scholars of microaggressions, described three types of microaggressions:

- microassaults—conscious and intentional verbal or physical actions such as slurs, aggressive acts, etc.;
- microinsults—rudeness or insensitivity based on race, ethnicity, gender, or other identity; and
- microinvalidations—actions that exclude, ignore, or invalidate based on race, ethnicity or other identity.

The authors described microinsults and microinvalidations as more subtle and thus more difficult to identify, and they suggested that this may leave the person receiving the microaggression to question what just happened, whether it was related to their identity, and whether they should respond. Similarly, for someone who is in the presence of a microaggression but not the target, it may not be clear that something harmful has just happened and the extent of the harm caused. The use of "micro" is not intended to minimize the impact of the offense, but to recognize the often subtle and interpersonal (as opposed to systemic) nature in which the offenses occur. With microaggressions, the intent does not necessarily match the impact. Whether the person who commits the microaggression intended it or not, the impact is often still harmful.

EXAMPLE

Microaggression and Microintervention

The following example reflects a microaggression, likely stemming from unconscious bias.

A group of four people from an agency (a Black woman in a wheelchair and a Latina woman, a Black man and a White man who are standing) are scheduled to meet with a potential funder. As they approach the front desk, the receptionist immediately talks to the White male to inquire about the group. This behavior suggests that the receptionist has assumed that the White man is in charge and more capable of answering than the others in the party. For the other involved people, the extent of harm will be affected by a number of factors such as how often they have experienced being treated as invisible or "less than" others with more able-bodied privilege, racial privilege, or gender privilege, as well the circumstance (for example, whether the White man is actually the boss). In our example, if the Black woman in the wheelchair is actually the head of the agency, she could interrupt and answer the host. Alternatively, the White man, when addressed by the receptionist, could redirect the receptionist's attention to the Black woman, saying something to the effect of "my colleague here is in charge." That would be a subtle way of redirecting the receptionist's action at the time. In addition, if this is a learning opportunity, a member of the party could talk with the receptionist and point out the possible assumption communicated, hopefully making a more lasting change.

Sue and his colleagues provide guidance in the form of "microinterventions," or actions that we might use when encountering microaggressions (see Sue et al., 2019). They suggest four types of strategies:

- make the invisible visible (e.g., name the observation of the biased behavior);
- disarm the microaggression/macroaggression (e.g., disagree with the biased statement);
- educate the offender (e.g., provide information that explains why the statement or behavior was offensive); and
- seek external intervention (e.g., reach out to others for support or intervention; Sue et al., 2019).

In another example example Dr. Joy DeGruy the author of *Post Traumatic Slave Syndrome* (published in 2017) shares a story in which her sister-in-law intervenes and uses her privilege to educate others (DeGruy, 2013). You can see other examples for confronting microaggressions in "Did you really just say that?" a resource from APA (Clay, 2017).

Addressing microaggressions effectively is an important form of everyday action, and yet especially if you are not the target in the situation, you may need practice. In this next activity, consider how you would respond in situations where microaggressions occur. It may seem that a microaggression is not occurring because the individual is not in the room. However, when individuals are being targeted in a microaggression, all representatives of that community are being aggressed. And one can be the target of a microaggression even if the microaggression is not communicated directly to the person or group.

ACTIVITY 8.3

What Would You Do?

Choose one of the two scenarios below. Reflect on the situation and circumstances and then determine how you might respond.

Scenario 1: You are on a search committee for a new director. The search committee includes four White members, one African American member, and one Latinx member. In one meeting discussing the different candidates, a committee member compares several candidates and remarks, "I liked the second candidate [an African American woman], but I wonder if she might be a little too aggressive. I think the third candidate [an Asian American man] didn't really show us his leadership capabilities. The fourth candidate [a White woman] seemed like she would fit our culture best because she has a lot of experience and just seemed to be more comfortable and supportive."

Scenario 2: You are in a case conference with an interdisciplinary team of several other clinicians in a university counseling center. One of the clients being discussed is a young Korean man who has been referred several times for suicidality and has reported a history of significant physical abuse by his parents. One clinician, when describing what the client reported, says, "Well, this is very common for Korean students because extreme physical punishment is a normal part of the culture for Korean families."

Choose one of the above scenarios and consider the following questions:

1. What is the situation and what possible microaggressions are happening?

2. What is your cultural positionality in relation to the people who are being aggressive and in relation to the person who is the target of their aggression?

3. What possible alternative behaviors could you engage in to intervene?

4. What are possible outcomes of the different interventions?

5. How might you follow up? In other words, is there something you can do in your community to reduce the likelihood of this type of thing happening in the future?

The above scenarios exemplify situations where microaggressions and bias have occurred. The next activity is designed to explore the microaggressions you see in your own community.

ACTIVITY 8.4

Becoming and Being Observant

Part 1: Becoming and being observant in your own community

Over the next few days, intentionally observe interactions in your community or organization, and notice interactions that occur between people who have different identities. In particular, pay attention to interactions between people who hold privileged status in relation to others.

You may be very aware of microaggressions that are directed toward you, but for this exercise, we are asking you to pay attention to microaggressions directed toward others. A few examples of microaggressions might include someone not giving up a seat on a bus to a passenger with a disability, a clerk or host serving a White or male customer before an Asian customer or a woman who had been waiting longer, someone clutching their bag or phone more tightly when a man of color passes, a stranger touching a Black person's hair, and many others. The commonality in these examples is reinforcement of stereotypes or power dynamics in a way that ignores, harms, or communicates a subtle message that the person of a marginalized population or targeted identity is not wanted, is dangerous, is less important, or is otherwise demeaned.

Record your observations. Include who was involved? What was the context? Did it seem intentional or unintentional? How did you feel observing this? How did the person targeted seem to react? Would intervention be helpful? How? What might you do if you were to intervene?

Part 2: Being observant of yourself

The second part of the activity is to pay attention to your own activities and, in particular, notice your behaviors, thoughts, and emotions. When you are engaging with others and you have a position of privilege, do your actions communicate that you have more power? Does that perpetuate or act out stereotypes? What do you do when you realize that you have exerted your power or acted on a bias?

Cultural Humility

Our values, beliefs, and behaviors that drive us are rooted in culture. Hook et al. (2013) described cultural humility as "the ability to maintain an interpersonal stance that is other-oriented (or open to the other) in relation to aspects of cultural identity that are most important to [other people]" (p. 2). Cultural humility allows those in solidarity to approach communities from a position of understanding that we (or our values, beliefs, and behaviors) are no more (or less) important or right than others. Our lives are very much driven by our social location or position in society, which is influenced by our identities, histories, and contexts. Our social location influences how we may operate differently and how others may treat us differently. Cultural humility allows us to focus on understanding what is most important to others (as opposed to focusing on what is most important for us) and to work from the frame of the individual or community we are advocating for and with. Cultural humility is a way of being and a way of relating to others that is intangible but essential as a baseline for others to trust us, and ultimately, for effective advocacy.

Consider an example. Imagine that your research is focused on employment opportunities in low-income communities and you have connections to a local city council. You notice that the unemployment rate is high in a neighboring community and believe that increasing the rates of employment would be an important way to help. Though you have a general understanding of factors that might be influencing this unemployment rate, you recognize you do not really understand the barriers that this particular community is experiencing. Thus, you also do not know what might be most helpful in removing those barriers. This awareness and what you do with it are opportunities for cultural humility. Partnering with community members, including those who are currently seeking jobs, will be most helpful. In the video, *Helping Counselors and Psychologists as Advocates and Activists*, Dr. Rita Chi-Ying Chung states, "Who knows the problem? It's the people living in the problem, not necessarily the people studying the problem" (Toporek & Ahluwalia, 2019). That partnership is the beginning, not the end product of cultural humility. You will have to continue working to maintain a stance that you are not the expert on other people's lives.

Using media produced by the groups you are building solidarity with and reading articles written by scholars who are part of these communities can be a great way to learn about other communities, their strengths, and the challenges they face. For example, none of the authors of this text expects others to teach us about their communities from "scratch." We try to learn from community-based media, frame our understanding with humility and acknowledge our limitations, observe and participate, and take cues from the community. Examples of community-based media include radio such as *Latino USA*, newspapers such as *Indian Country Today*, and websites of community-based organizations. Podcasts and other digital media provide a wide range of community-generated perspectives. We are reminded of the TED Talk by Stella Young, who talks about "inspiration porn," referring to media that uses disabled people to inspire others (Young, 2014). She emphasizes how these images objectify one group of people (disabled people) to benefit other people (non-disabled people).

Curated work from members of the community can raise the voices of that community as they are about and from the community. Still, it is important to remember that the voice of one person does not necessarily represent the whole group. That means that we have to be committed to hearing in an ongoing way the voices of many people most affected by an issue.

Cultural humility also helps remind us to reflect on our motivations and intentions for engaging with others. In Activity 8.5, reflect on your experiences as an outsider and how this may impact the ways you engage with communities when working toward social justice.

ACTIVITY 8.5

Reaching in as an Outsider

Reflect on a time when you sought to support a community where you may have been an outsider. Consider the following questions:

1. What was your motivation for joining in solidarity?

2. How did you know what their issues were?

3. What were your issues/concerns and how were they related to those of the community?

4. What were you willing to contribute to the community? What was your investment?

5. Was there anything you needed to give up to partner with the community?

Strength in Numbers: Your Communities and Your Social Mosaic

One of the critical lessons of social action is that big change rarely comes from the efforts of one person. Even when one person is credited with change, it often comes in the context of a movement by larger numbers of people or communities. The kinds of problems we are trying to address require the efforts and strengths of a lot of people with different approaches to the same issue. Perhaps more importantly, as was mentioned in Chapter 7, no one person possesses strengths in all areas, and we cannot possibly understand issues from all viewpoints. Diversification of perspectives is essential in building a strong community and making change. For example, the strengths and knowledge of the people you will identify in Activity 8.6 can enhance your efforts by adding particular skills and resources, or by reinforcing what you already have. We would argue that this is the role of allies and accomplices.

In addition to the individual relationships that provide solidarity, solidarity based in group efforts is necessary for larger scale change. Naomi Klein identifies imagination and coordinated movement across issues as two key elements in responding to deep societal crises with large scale social change. She talks about the challenges and limitations of putting different social issues in separate boxes, for example, climate change as one issue, discrimination as another issue, and poverty in another box (Klein, 2017). These separations or silos may help us feel less overwhelmed, but can lead to us diminishing or ignoring other issues, the connections between these issues, and the potential for working together. Further, the solutions we develop in our silos are limited. Not only is it essential to understand the interconnectedness of these issues, but connecting across issues creates coalitions that are stronger. It can be helpful to identify one social issue that is important to you as an entry point into working in connection with other people and other issues.

Working together multiplies the strengths and resources available as well as amplifies the voice for any cause. It is useful to take an inventory of the people in your microsystem—those who you are connected to and with whom you maintain relationships. This is often called your network, or a social capital map. Many of us have relationships through our involvement in different types of communities, including spiritual or religious groups, social media groups, advocacy groups, parent groups, unions, workplace peers, professional associations, exercise groups, and relationships with our neighbors and people we know in our community. In the following activity, think about all your relationships—close, distant, personal, and professional.

ACTIVITY 8.6

Relationships Connect Us—Your Social Mosaic

With few exceptions, humans are social beings. In the map below, write in the names of the people to whom you are connected. We have created "clusters" to help you think about arenas of your life and the people within those arenas. Fill in names of people you are connected to and then think about the people who are connected to them. It may be helpful to think about this from the perspective of the micro and mesosystem of the ecological model. This represents your social mosaic. Feel free to add clusters that seem to be missing but represent relationships in your life.

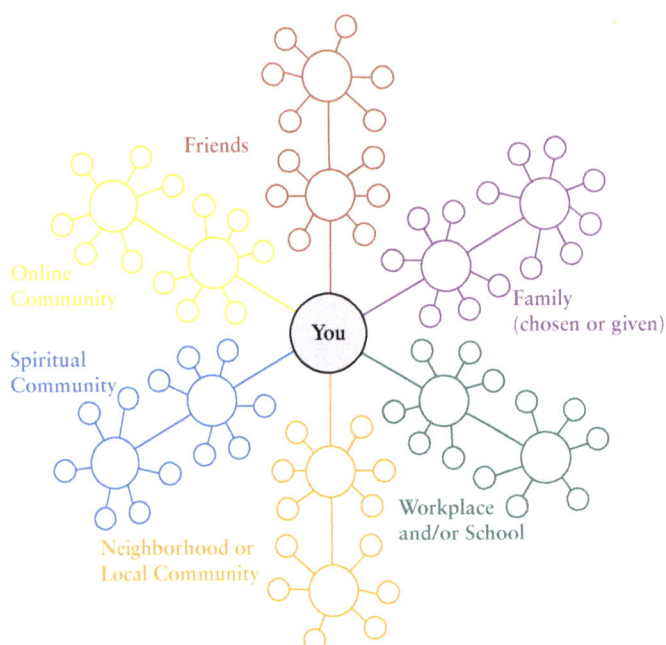

FIGURE 8.2 Social mosaic map

Now reflect on the following questions as you look at your completed map:

1. Are there any overlaps in areas?

2. Are there areas you don't have many people you are connected with (for example, your neighborhood)? Would you like to develop more relationships there?

3. Are there areas where you seem to be connected to a lot of people? What do these relationships add to your life? In what ways do you contribute to those relationships?

4. . Are there issues you are concerned about that others are also concerned about? Are there ways you might work with them to address the concern together?

5. How do you contribute to the well-being of people in your network? What are you able to share with them, and what is needed to sustain healthy relationships with them?

As you look back at your social mosaic, you may notice that you tend to be associated mostly with people who are somewhat like you or have similar values. Who we are and who we spend time with shapes the resources we have access to as well as the way we perceive and experience the world. Often, this also affects how others view us, which, in turn, influences the way we engage in social action.

In Chapters 3 and 7, we focused on reflecting on who you are and who you represent within the larger context of your community and society (your "positionality") in order to help you think through your relational and knowledge strengths, as well as your resources. Expanding your relationships with people who are different from you and people who are connected to the issues you are concerned with in a different way than you are is an important way to build solidarity. A number of resources can be helpful in expanding the ways we connect with others. One example is Southern Poverty Law Center's *Ten Ways to Fight Hate: A Community Response Guide* (2017), which provides a range of strategies for connecting with others to rise up against acts of hate.

Relationships are relevant in all four S-Quad areas of reflection and action—strengths, solidarity, strategy, and sustainability. Our social mosaic contributes to our strengths, including information, expertise, skills, and insights beyond those we hold ourselves. Relationships are central for solidarity, providing both inspiration and partners for strategy. Solidarity and our relationships are also important for our personal and professional sustainability, offering the comfort of human connection and acting as an important reminder of our responsibility to maintain and nurture those relationships.

Working with Others

There are many benefits to working with others on issues you care about, including strength in numbers, camaraderie, shared resources and skills, creative group thinking, and role models, among others. Working together can also present challenges even when people share passion, commitment, and goals for social change. There are strategies and recommendations to help facilitate better interpersonal communication for working together as a team. Think about these strategies in the context of who you are, who your teammates are, and what circumstances your team is dealing with (e.g., how the group came together, what challenge the group is facing). We will focus on two aspects of teamwork: the group process and your work style.

Group process includes the way a group functions together. Setting agreed-upon expectations, also referred to as norms or group agreements, can help to facilitate how a group works together and resolves difficulties that arise. Creating group agreements is essential, particularly as people come from different backgrounds and differ in values, beliefs, and behaviors. A collaborative process for developing these agreements helps to ensure that the group norms reflect the culture and needs of members. Some groups may use Robert's Rules of Order, while others may have a talking stick to facilitate respectful participation. For example, "One diva, one mic" is one of many rules identified by Campus Pride (2012) and refers to taking turns speaking. Many strategies are particularly helpful to facilitate difficult moments or overcome barriers. For example, groups may use "oops," "ouch," and "huh?" as a strategy for flagging misunderstandings or microaggressions. Once established, it is helpful to periodically revisit the agreements and consider modifying them as the group evolves. Alignment of group expectations on different aspects of the work is important prior to engaging in the work itself (e.g., workload), while recognizing that it will be impossible to anticipate all challenges that might arise. Even with group agreements and goals aligned, the reality is that groups are composed of different individuals with different personalities and engagement styles. Just as in other groups of people, challenges may arise within this group. Norms can be used to help decision-making and guide how conflicts are handled. It will be helpful to be mindful of processes as well as members' preferences for how to work. Further, our training in group process can be a useful way to contribute to resolving these conflicts.

Work style refers to the ways you prefer to work—that is, understanding what helps you to work more effectively with others. In other words, there is no one-size-fits-all approach to working together because each member brings unique needs and strengths. It is important to pay attention to your style, your strengths, your challenges, and to how your style can play out in groups. Some things to consider can include introversion/extroversion, high context/ low context communication, and formal/informal communication. For example, extroverts get energy from being around others, while introverts recharge by being alone. We generally have both extroversion and introversion, but to varying degrees. When working with others, this can cause challenges if some individuals want to constantly meet while others want to work completely alone. However, having both extroverts and introverts can be helpful when working with groups—we just have to respect that our work styles are different and equally valuable and find ways to communicate and navigate the needs of all as well as the collective.

Coalition Building

Community organizing is a process where community members come together to address a particular issue. The group can form organically from the community most affected and/or as part of a broader campaign to engage members who may not be aware or involved with the issue. Similarly, coalitions are formed when people come together around a central issue or shared goal. These can be temporary or ongoing groups that evolve over time as they work on the issue. Coalitions may be formal or informal and may be very specific or diverse in terms of expertise and membership.

In addition to establishing the group goals, processes, and working styles, as discussed above, when organizing/forming coalitions it is important to discuss who needs to be represented or who should be "at the table" (i.e., who is most affected by the issue and thus has insight, and also who has power?). Also consider who is not present and why and how to make the group accessible. A coalition can be made up of individuals representing different perspectives or of groups who have shared investment or interest. For example, imagine that you work in a community that has seen an increase in racist graffiti, including on local businesses and on the buildings of the local university. A coalition might form that includes people living in the neighborhood, serving as members of the school board, attending campus as faculty/staff and students, and representing local businesses and local political districts. Perhaps people that live in the neighborhood want to feel safe while a group in the school board and university faculty/staff and students are committed to making the schools a more positive place for all students. The local businesses want the community to be seen as an ideal place to gather and shop, and the local politicians would like to respond to their constituents who are feeling less safe in their district. In your conversations, you might identify a shared commitment to publicly address these acts of hate vandalism and make your community a more welcoming place. Your group is able to bring together different skills, resources, and connections in the community, as well as widen the circle through your respective connections.

In the video, *Helping Counselors and Psychologists as Advocates and Activists* (Toporek & Ahluwalia, 2019), Anneliese Singh describes their coalition building with Georgia Safe Schools (https://gasafeschools.org) to change policies for safety and support of LGBTQ+ students. As a counseling psychologist, Anneliese shares that individual and group counseling support felt like it fell short when kids continued to face bullying, violence, and attacks beyond the school environment. The coalition was a way for Anneliese to contribute to changing the environment that the kids lived in as well as create a web of support for families and community members.

There are many ways to get involved in community coalitions. We may be invited due to our expertise, we may help facilitate a collective to initiate a coalition, we may proactively approach a coalition identifying how we can contribute to their efforts, or we may attend as a member of the public, demonstrate our expertise, and persist as a visible participant. We offer these tips for those who desire to meaningfully contribute to an existing coalition: First, understand the goals of the organization and identify the issues, needs, and gaps in expertise in the coalition. Then, reach out to the person or persons leading the coalition and emphasize how you can address a need the coalition has or a perspective that is missing. You can also ask the group about their specific needs and, based on your capabilities, provide what's needed.

The *Community Toolbox* from the Center for Community Health and Development at the University of Kansas (KU Center for Community Health and Development, n.d.-b) provides more guidance for when and how to establish a coalition, who is important to have represented, barriers or potential problems that might arise, and other essential information. Being thoughtful about bringing together an effective group creates a strong base for achieving coalition goals.

Bill Moyer talks about four different roles needed in social movements: (a) citizen—someone connected to the community; (b) rebel—protester and one who says "no" to injustice; (c) change agent—organizer of people power; and (d) reformer—one who uses existing systems for change. The point is that different types of leaders and different types of skills are needed in concert for more effective action. You can find more discussion about this in his article "The Four Roles of Social Activism" (Moyer, 2019). In Activity 8.7, imagine coalition building focused on an issue you're passionate about.

ACTIVITY 8.7

Who's on the Team?

Choose one of the issues you identified as a priority in Chapter 5. Consider how a coalition might be helpful in addressing some aspect of that issue. If there is already a group working on that issue, think about how to expand or start a local coalition to take action.

1. What is the issue?

2. Who ought to be a part of your coalition?

    a. Who else cares?

    b. Who has needed skills?

    c. Who has intimate knowledge about the issue?

    d. Who has power that may be useful in creating change?

    e. Do you have individuals who can fulfill the roles of citizen, rebel, change agent, and reformer?

3. How might you reach out to them?

4. How could an elevator speech be helpful?

Contributing to Existing Efforts

Knowing your strengths and skills can help you to contribute to work that others are already doing. Investigate organizations that are doing work you believe in and how they are doing that work. For example, what are their goals, their actions, the scope of their work, and how established is the organization? Learn where the gaps are, what might be helpful, and who is in charge of different aspects of the organization's functions. This can be done by paying attention to calls for action and help, speaking with people involved in the organization, and building relationships. In Chapter 7, you assessed your strengths and skills. Consider these strengths and perspectives as a helping professional and how you might offer them to address some of the gaps or support work others are doing. If what you can offer is already being fulfilled and you still want to be involved, talk with the organization about ways to make this possible. Sometimes we feel that we have to be the one in charge, or we come in with ideas about what help is needed and our role. This is not necessarily accurate or attuned with the group's work; their asks may be different than what you expect. Being a contributor only works if what you offer and how you contribute actually helps.

Finding Support and Camaraderie to Sustain You

Working as a professional or student (graduate or undergraduate) can be an isolating experience. When we are engaged in advocacy or social action, being connected with others who join with us can also sustain us. For each of us authors, attending local and national conferences, workshops, and presentations, and being involved in student and/or community organizations have allowed us to form connections with and learn from others engaging in social action. In recent years and especially given the COVID-19 pandemic, communities have formed using online platforms (e.g. social media, websites). These can also be great places to connect with others who are engaged in social action around issues you are also passionate about. An example of such an online community is *Academics for Black Survival and Wellness* (The WELLS Healing Center, n.d.) which launched during summer of 2020 to address anti-Black racism, form community, and educate others.

Receiving and providing mentorship, including peer mentorship, can be a way of sustaining ourselves through connecting, sharing wisdom, and learning from others. Dr. Joseph L. White's establishment of the Freedom Train is an example of how solidarity can exist within professions. Through his mentorship, he provided connection and guidance to generations of counselors and psychologists. See *Practical Social Justice: Diversity, Equity, and Inclusion Strategies Based on the Legacy of Dr. Joseph L. White* (Palmer II, 2023) for accounts of the benefits and lessons learned from this mentorship.

Similarly, mentorship can occur throughout undergraduate and graduate programs as students often rely on each other for internship opportunities, class recommendations, work sites, and other aspects of navigating the academy. At times, lack of trust in the system and living in hidden vulnerable identities may make students become each other's only source of information. For example, undocumented students engage in "patchwork" in order to leverage the strengths of the community to identify financial, social, and emotional resources to overcome systemic barriers (Stuckey & Snodgrass, 2021). In this approach, one student will disclose their identity to an administrator or professor to then share the information given to them with other students who may not feel comfortable outing themselves. One of the psychological strengths of undocumented students is *personalismo,* a quality that provides them the ability to nurture relationships to help them navigate oppressive systems (Rojas-Araúz, 2021). In this way, these students are working in solidarity with each other.

When we work toward social justice, the support and camaraderie of others can sustain our work and add momentum to further the cause. Moreover, sometimes building support and camaraderie *is* social action. We will discuss sustainability in more depth later in the book.

ACTIVITY 8.8

Sustainable Relationships

Refer back to the social mosaic you created in Activity 8.6 to answer the questions below.

1. Which of these relationships helps to sustain you?

2. What about these relationships helps you to stay encouraged?

Solidarity as Social Action

Being in solidarity with others can in and of itself be social advocacy and action. During Rebecca's early years as a community college counselor, she was asked by the Vietnamese Student Association (VSA) to serve as their advisor. She worked with the leadership of VSA, many of whom had been refugees and recent immigrants, and observed several things. First, the number of students who proactively sought counseling increased. Second, she directly witnessed issues the community faced on campus, including discrimination by instructors, exclusion in student government, and application of culturally inappropriate college policies. Third, she gained a greater understanding of the students' cultural values and expectations around managing such conflict. The students taught Rebecca that, although they felt these experiences were problematic, it was culturally incongruent to confront them directly. Rebecca wanted to directly advocate to address those incidents so she sought guidance from other colleagues and the students about culturally congruent approaches for systemic change.

A crucial aspect defining outsider actions as solidarity is the extent to which we do them as directed by, or in partnership with, individuals and communities, as opposed to acting from our own frame of reference. We will discuss strategies for engaging in social action in the next chapters and ask that you keep solidarity in the forefront of your mind as you continue.

Chapter 9

Building a Solid Foundation for Strategic Action

FIGURE 9.1 S-Quad image—strategy

"You begin with a protest, but you have to move on from there. Just being angry, just being resentful, just being outraged does not constitute revolution."

—Grace Lee Boggs, 2013

Where do you want to focus your energy? How do you focus your energy? The first two areas of reflection, strength and solidarity, were about understanding the power that you have and how you are connected to others. *Strategy* is designed to help you think about how you can use that power, along with guidance from decades, even centuries, of others who have taken action. Some strategies are long-term orchestrated efforts, and others are immediate actions we take in response to critical events. In the strategy area of reflection, we consider different approaches, resources, and wisdom that can help address the problem and move us closer to what we—and others—envision for positive change.

Strategy involves decision-making and action, both hefty discussions. In this chapter, we will lay a foundation for strategic action and share a few models that can help you prepare and decide what action may be best for your situation. The next chapter will be a menu of different types of strategies for social change at individual, organizational, and societal levels, and we will share some thoughts and resources for "how-to." We hope that the activities in Chapters 9 and 10 will guide you through evaluating which strategies might make the most sense given the situation, problem, needs of the community, and your strengths and resources.

You will be able to use the work you do in this chapter for your personalized "social action plan" at the end of this workbook. As we said earlier, some parts of these chapters may feel more relevant or informative to you depending on your experience and knowledge. Take what's useful; leave what doesn't fit, but also reflect on why you are leaving it. Is it simply not appropriate for the situation? Are you missing some skills or information that are necessary for using that strategy? Is it outside your comfort zone? Is it something you already know and don't feel the need to expand on? The point is to engage in the process as a reflective and reflexive practice (remember Barrett's distinction in Chapter 1).

Anchoring Your Vision for a Positive Future

Action without vision risks losing focus and power. A vision without action is a fantasy. Action *with* a vision is a powerful force.

ACTIVITY 9.1

Connecting to Your Vision for a Positive Future

Take a minute to look back at the visioning collage you created in Chapter 5 (Activity 5.5).

1. Is there anything you would like to add to the collage?

2. What differences do you see between the world now and your vision for the future?

3. In this vision, what is your work like as a helping professional? What does your day-to-day life look like? What does your family's day-to-day life look like?

4. What would need to happen in order for your vision to become reality?

A vision of a positive future provides us with images and feelings about the way things *could* be. It's dynamic and evolves through solidarity, cultural context, ancestral knowledge, reflexivity, and a deepening understanding of the issues that block that vision from becoming reality. In a discussion at the 2022 conference of the Society of Indian Psychologists, Lali McCubbin, a counseling psychologist, noted the importance of cultural frameworks for moving forward in social action. She shared that her *Kūpuna* (ancestors or elders) taught that when a fish swims, its direction is not determined by its eyes but by its tail. She explained that within that cultural perspective, the past is what moves us forward. Throughout this chapter, think about your cultural frame, the lessons of your elders, and the ways you have found to move most bravely in the direction of social change.

Planning for Strategic Action

Social change is a complex process requiring significant groundwork and coordination. There is rarely one right or perfect action, and action usually doesn't result in immediate resolution of big systemic issues. Any big change needs lots of different people—with different expertise and wisdom—to tackle the issues from many different angles. The exploration you did in the strengths and solidarity chapters helps lay the groundwork for where and how you will contribute.

Take a minute to go back to the work you did on focusing your energy in Chapter 5. We will ask you to narrow your focus. Try to imagine and articulate it in a concrete way. For example, if Rebecca identified "dismantling White supremacy" as the direction she is committed to focusing her energy, she would need to identify more concretely what she actually means by that in her personal and professional life. For example, she could narrow that to protecting access and support for students who have historically been marginalized in education, counseling, and psychology due to White supremacy in all its forms.

Understanding the Issue

As we mentioned in previous chapters, an important step to figuring out where you belong in the change process comes with understanding more deeply the issue and who is already working on the problem. This allows you to better see what strategies make the most sense and where you fit, given the issue, your strengths and resources, and the community. In the next activity, you will work to unpack the issue you have chosen to focus on using the ecological model to consider each level where social action may be happening or may need to happen. If you have difficulty imagining the large-scale issues that may have impact at an individual level, consider looking at Metzl and Hansen's (2014) description of structural competencies. Before you do this activity, it may be helpful to review the activities from Chapter 7 (strengths) and Chapter 8 (solidarity).

ACTIVITY 9.2

Understanding the Issue—Assessing the Situation

The following activity has two parts: First, summarizing your issue or the focus of your energy, and secondly exploring a range of reflection questions. If it is helpful, you can take a look at Rebecca's example just following this activity.

Part 1: Summarize the issue(s) you want to focus on for this activity or the change you want to work toward (if you have trouble narrowing it down, revisit Chapter 5).

Part 2: Fill in as much of the table below as you can by using what you know now and what you can imagine. The point of this activity is to prompt you to reflect, rather than to come up with perfect or complete answers.

	Individual level (you, your clients, your family; colleagues, coworkers, supervisors, etc.)	Organizational or local level (your work arena or your community)	National or societal level
What is the issue or concern (e.g., sexism in your workplace, police violence against communities of color, inadequate healthcare for seniors, harassment of immigrants), and what are the different aspects of this issue?			
How is your positionality connected to this issue? (Review Chapter 3 if you are unsure about this.)			
Who is affected negatively and in what ways? Do you have any concrete information (e.g., statistics etc.)?			
What systems are involved and who has power or influence (specific offices, positions, policies, etc.)?			
Identify and describe allies and potential partners (who else cares about this issue? Who else is working on this issue?) and what is already being done?			
What aspect of this issue do you want to get involved with, change, or have an impact on?			
Other information you've learned about this issue?			
Where can you find more information?			

Part 3: Reflecting on your process.

- What questions were easiest for you to answer?

- What additional information would be helpful?

- Who would be important for you to reach out to?

- Consider asking the people already working on this issue whether there are other strategies that might complement their work.

REBECCA'S EXAMPLE FOR ACTIVITY 9.2

As an example, the following summarizes Rebecca's responses to Part 1 and the first two questions of Part 2 to help illustrate what it might look like when she completes this activity.

Part 1: Issue Rebecca is focusing on: "dismantling White supremacy" and more specifically protecting access and support for students who have historically been marginalized in education, counseling and psychology due to White supremacy in all its forms.

Part 2:

	Individual Level	*Organizational or Local Level*	*National or Societal Level*
What is the issue or concern and what are the different aspects of this issue?	*Individual students from marginalized backgrounds are facing cuts to support services and financial aid.*	*Universities are removing language and services that are specifically designed to support students who have been marginalized historically in higher education.*	*In addition to the history of marginalization of certain populations from higher education, in 2025, the Executive Office at the federal level has targeted all programs and language in universities that are specifically designed to support students who have been marginalized.*
How are you connected to this issue?	*I am a White identified, cis woman and I have benefited from access to higher education however there are aspects of gender that are completely ignored, diminished, and/or problematized. I have also benefited tremendously from learning from and working alongside colleagues and students who have been marginalized in higher education.*	*Throughout my career as a community college counselor and then university staff and faculty, I have worked specifically in programs designed to support and encourage students from marginalized backgrounds. This has required that I engage in re-education, self-reflection and solidarity to ensure that I am supporting efforts at a systems level in ways that minimize oppressive policies and practices and, instead, create liberatory practices.*	*I have the opportunity to contribute to task forces within my national professional associations, voice support for these programs, curriculum and funding through academic writing, public speaking, advocating with legislators, training others in advocacy and collaborating with other organizations that support this goal.*

The purpose of this activity is multifold: Acknowledging and honoring folks already working on this issue; paying attention to who is missing; identifying where more information would be helpful; and thinking about the usefulness of concrete information concerning this issue and the potential of change. Hopefully you reflected back on some of your work in previous chapters around identity, solidarity, and focusing your energies. Ideally, you challenged yourself to think about this issue from multiple angles and levels.

It is important to note that your plan will change over time given circumstances, systemic changes, your growth and other influences. For example, prior to 2025, Rebecca's example above was actually more specifically focused on working to transform counselor education to identify the nuances of how White supremacy was present in admissions, retention and curriculum. With the aggressive and hostile actions of the 2025 US presidential administration, Rebecca shifted her focus to respond more generally to the wide swath of oppressive actions coming from that office directly impacting marginalized students and faculty in counseling as well as across higher education.

> **PAUSE**
>
> Let's pause and take a deep breath. You may be feeling like the tasks we have asked you to do so far in this chapter are really big. Maybe you're feeling like you don't have all the information or clarity about the issue. Maybe you're feeling a little overwhelmed. Take a step back and breathe. Write down some of the emotions you're feeling and some of your thoughts. Maybe take a few minutes away and just let it soak in.

IMG 9.1

Ok, welcome back. We hope you are feeling more grounded. Now, let's move on to discussing the issue and your connection to it.

Communicating the Issue and Your Connection to It

Identifying who is already involved helps to strengthen and deepen your understanding of the situation and how you can communicate the issue to others. You are now going to build on the elevator speech you started in Chapter 5 to communicate the issue. Consider who your audience could be and how they might hear your message. As you work on this, you might realize that you need more information about the issue and its impact in order to give a really powerful elevator speech.

> **ACTIVITY 9.3**
>
> ### Solidifying the Foundation of Your Elevator Speech
>
> Think about what you learned in Activity 9.2. What compelling stories or statistics can be helpful in catching the listener's interest? Personal stories about people who are deeply affected by the issue, combined with statistics that show the issue affects more than just one person or one family, make the speech emotionally and rationally compelling.
>
> Look back at *Activity 5.9* where you began creating your elevator speech. Reflect on what you wrote and then use the following questions to take it to the next level.
>
> 1. Introduce yourself, position, and place (you can use what you wrote in Activity 5.9 or expand on it).
>
> 2. In two to three sentences, summarize the issue and why is it important? (In Activity 5.9, you looked at why it is important to you personally, here we want you to think more broadly. Why is the issue important beyond you? And more specifically, consider why it is important to the audience you are sharing it with?)
>
> The following is an example of a hypothetical elevator speech created in 2018 and we acknowledge that the issue and statistics are much more dramatic now given the current political situation. The information contained in this example was taken from articles in the American Psychological Association's *Monitor* (Stringer, 2018) and an article in the New York Times (Carey, 2018):

> Forced family separation and deportation results in long-term trauma for children … About 2,300 children have been taken from their families by US Immigration and Customs officials. Most of the families were trying to seek asylum in the US due to violence in their home country. These families are not only being torn apart but they are also being prevented from seeking asylum.

Now that you have more clearly defined and articulated the issue, let's focus on the process of deciding what to do about the issue. The following section provides a developmental perspective of the stages for taking action.

The Big Picture: A Flow Chart for Intentional Action

We started our strategy discussion with an activity aimed at reflecting on the context of your chosen issue (Activity 9.2) because there are so many possible social action strategies. Not all of them fit the situation, fit you, or fit you in the situation. The process shown in the flowchart brings together our vision and our goals. It suggests how we can identify subgoals with strategies for action. Important and sometimes neglected steps are evaluating and considering possible outcomes of different strategies and reflecting after taking action.

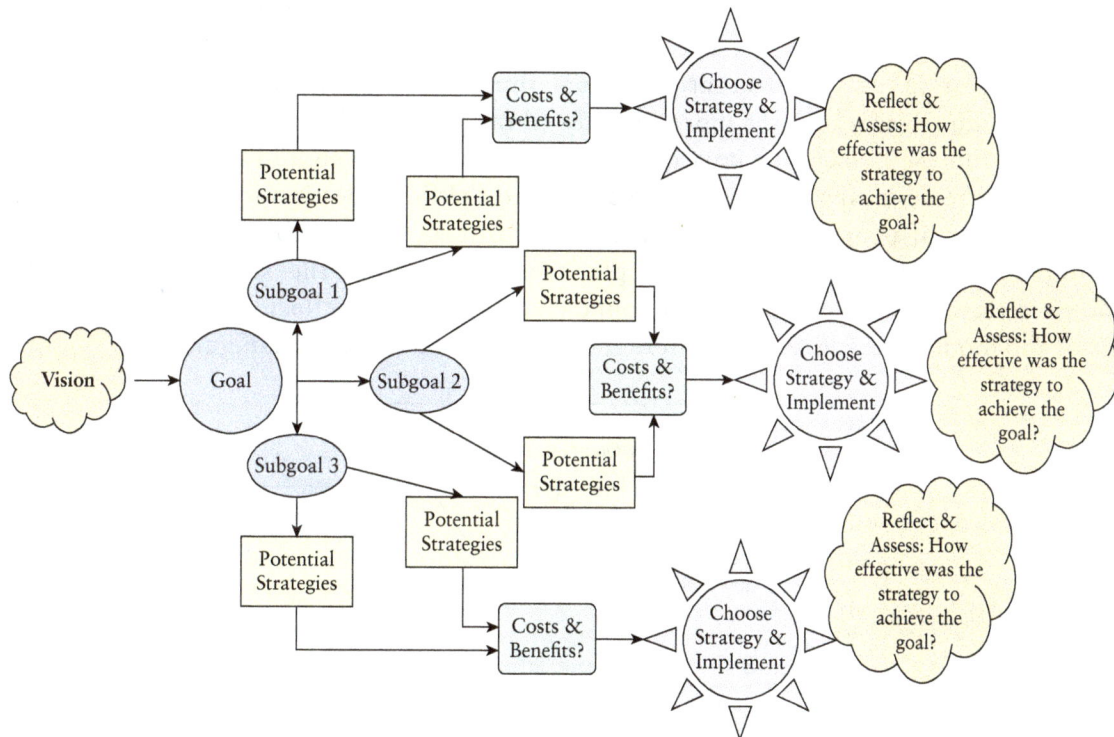

FIGURE 9.2 Strategy flowchart

Your work in Chapters 7 and 8 (assessing your strengths and reflecting on solidarity) are critical when considering strategies. There is such a wide range of different ways we can take action. Knowing what work is already being done by others and who is doing it helps to know where you might contribute to current action or complement existing efforts. In deciding which strategies to use, it's also important to consider the potential benefits and costs to you personally, to your colleagues, and to the overall goal or vision. Your positionality, your strengths and resources, and your relationships with others all influence the benefits and consequences of action. In our conversations, Rebecca has given examples of learning the hard way that some strategies have more negative consequences than others. While there may be negative outcomes for her as an older White woman, she acknowledges that the negative outcomes may be more significant for her colleagues of color. Similarly, Flynn et al. (2021), in their discussion of civil disobedience as psychologists in the face of anti-trans legislation, talk about how each of them take action differently depending on their circumstances and strengths. Be intentional in choosing your actions. What will the consequences be and for whom? Solidarity is critical.

The final part of the strategy flowchart is to reflect on how well your actions and strategies addressed the goal or problem. If your actions helped make progress toward larger systems change, then these may be good strategies to continue. If not, then it may be time to revisit alternative strategies and try a different approach. Your own reflections, as well as those from others, are helpful in this process.

One Decision Tool for Choosing Advocacy and Social Action Strategies

Advocacy is one way that we can think about action for social change and social justice. The American Counseling Association Advocacy Competencies model (also called "Social Justice Advocacy Competencies") gives examples of methods for using advocacy to disrupt, confront barriers, and work toward social change as a counselor or helping professional (Lewis et al., 2002; Toporek & Daniels, 2018). The model suggests that you first identify whether you are trying to address an individual situation or something that affects a larger number of people, either within an organization or more broadly (think back to the ecological framework discussed earlier in the book). The next question is, how involved should or could the client or student be in the advocacy process? If the answer to the first question is that the issue affects a larger number of people either within the organization or more broadly, then the second question is about whether or how the people who are harmed by the issue should or could be involved in the advocacy process. These foundational questions reflect the two central dimensions of the model and suggest six different domains of advocacy (see Figure 9.3).

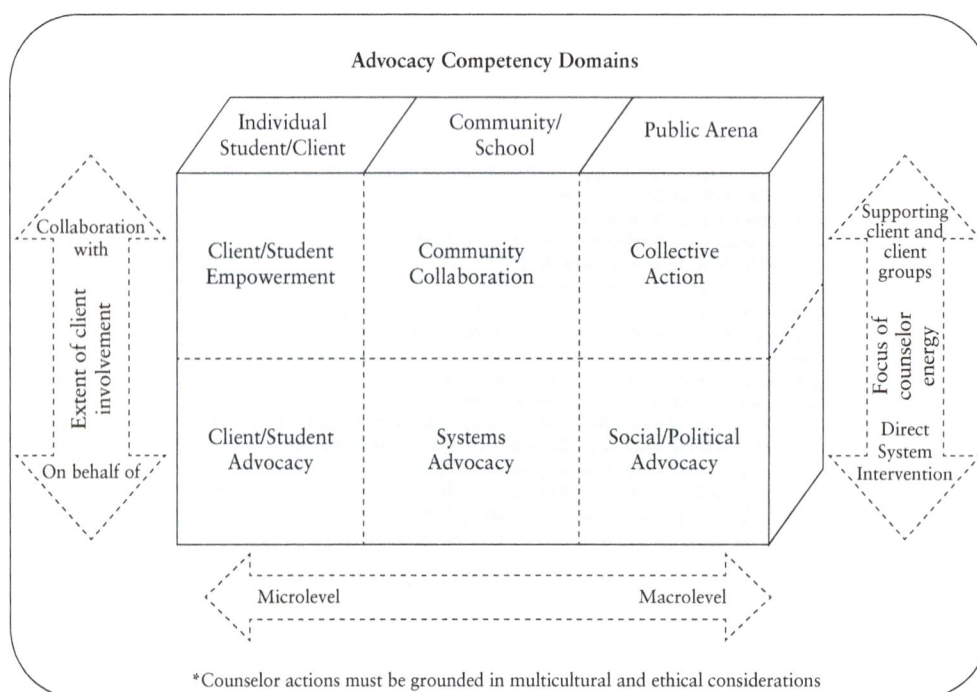

FIGURE 9.3 ACA Advocacy Competency Domains

When you ask the first question about who is impacted by this issue (individual student/client, community/school/organization, public), you are looking to see where you can take action and/or what systems you are working to change. Next, think about your role and the role of the person or people most impacted by the issue. Wherever possible, the role of the helping professional is to facilitate or provide support for people who are directly impacted by the barrier(s) or injustice. One type of action may be to support others in self-advocacy; another action may be to collaborate with others; and other actions may be to advocate on behalf of others. When developing this model, Rebecca and her colleagues (Judy Lewis, Mary Smith Arnold, Reese House, and Judy Daniels) acknowledged that sometimes, given the cost or risk, clients or communities choose not to engage in advocacy. The most ethical thing for a counselor or helping professional to do may be to advocate on behalf of clients or a community, especially if the problem is a systemic issue that will hurt others. At the same time, it is essential to consider the client(s) and how the action the counselor takes might affect them. To illustrate the ACA advocacy model, we use the example Rebecca shared in Chapter 4 about discrimination on campus.

REBECCA'S EXAMPLE

Advocacy on Campus

When I was working as a community college counselor, a student described the distress they were feeling as a senator in student government on campus. They described the experience as discriminatory and hostile. I affirmed their experience, shared information about their rights and resources, and helped them think through what action they wanted to take (individual level empowerment). The student decided not to take action because direct confrontation was culturally incongruent. They also did not want me to intervene directly (client advocacy) on their behalf.

Later, several other students (individually) shared similar stories with me about the same organization, but they were hesitant to make a complaint. I learned from my colleagues that they also had heard similar stories from students. Like my experience, their students didn't want to take action individually, and they did not want to come together collectively (community collaboration). A few students did choose to follow the college's process for filing a complaint with the dean of students. Still, we continued to hear students' complaints of discrimination, despite due process in the college. My colleagues and I met and agreed that this was a systemic issue and reflected serious problems with our organization. We felt we had a responsibility to intervene in the system, while respecting the privacy of the individual students (systems advocacy). Individually, my colleagues and I talked with the staff person in charge of student organizations about what we saw. Despite this, the problems continued. We decided to take action as a group to bring this to the attention of the college, while maintaining the anonymity of the students (systems advocacy).

If you want to dive in, the article by Toporek et al. (2009) and the article from Toporek and Daniels (2018) discuss this model in depth and provide example actions at different levels. We will also refer to the ACA advocacy model in the next chapter as we talk about different strategies. Before jumping to our discussion of strategies, we would like to pause and lay some groundwork for evaluating different types of strategies and approaches based on their potential consequences.

Weighing the Benefits and Costs of Different Approaches and Strategies

If you have been doing social justice work, you probably have stories about lessons you've learned while showing up for justice—sometimes lessons learned the hard way. Understanding the potential benefits and costs of strategies, individually and collectively, is important in terms of effectiveness as well as sustainability and survival. These costs and benefits may differ depending on intersectionality of identities, power, and privilege. We want to emphasize that our intent with this discussion about benefits and costs is to help you take action thoughtfully, not to scare you. Taking action is essential and there are many ways to do it, many choices you can make and resources that can help.

Evaluating Benefits

The most obvious benefits of a particular action are seen in positive change and justice. This is often easier to see with immediate or close-range issues than with large-scale or systemic barriers, oppression, and injustice. Consider the following questions:

- Does the action contribute to accomplishing the goal or part of the goal (subgoal)?
- Who benefits from the change or action?
- Are the people who are most affected by the problem engaged in the solution (either directly or by consultation)?
- Does the action or strategy help lay the groundwork for the next steps in a way that will benefit the people affected and the people working on the action?
- Does the action honor people's strengths?
- Does this action help build community, coalition, or solidarity?
- Is the problem less likely to occur again as a result of the action?
- As a result of this action, will more people care about this issue and join as allies and accomplices?
- Does this strategy align with your values, your integrity, your sense of purpose?

You and your collaborators may not easily see the outcomes of action. It can be challenging to know whether your actions or what you helped to do was the best option. You can gain a sense of whether you are going in the right direction by checking in with trusted others, people affected by the issue and people who are working toward the same goals. The main point is to stop, reflect, and gather information before proceeding.

Evaluating Costs

We can sometimes predict the costs and see them clearly. Other times we can't. Some of these costs may affect us personally, such as our responsibilities, imbalance in our work and life, emotional and physical health, and more. Other costs are professional; for example, risk of job loss, being shunned in our work arena, extra work assigned, and others. Some costs cross over both (e.g., legal or financial costs). Reflect on actions that you've taken (or thought about taking) and what the impact might have been:

- Resources (financial, job, money, time)
- Social (loss or strain of relationships)

- Emotional (isolation, fear, harassment, stress, discomfort)
- Freedom (detainment, incarceration)
- Physical (safety, physical harm)

Some costs may be uncomfortable, while others may threaten our lives and our loved ones. Increasingly, we are feeling the costs of coordinated harassment by networks of well-funded extremist anti-human rights groups that activate individuals to publicly denounce and misrepresent people who are working toward racial justice, trans justice, immigrant justice, reproductive justice, and more. Further, the executive branch of the U.S. government, politicians, and special interest groups that collude with them are targeting entire communities financially, legally, and physically. These aren't costs of specific social action per se, but are actions of direct targeted aggression based on identity or circumstance. Additionally, those of us who take action publicly are increasingly likely to be targeted by harassment. This distinction is important because the actions we take need to be considered within the context of our vulnerability and our privilege. For example, Rebecca, as a White woman, is currently targeted by legislation because she is a woman but not by the color of her skin, her gender identity, her ability status, or her economic situation. She is, however, targeted due to social action and her area of work. At the same time, those who are close to her are targeted because of their identities (trans, gay, Black, Latino, immigrant, economically poor, etc.) even if they are not involved in social action. The action Rebecca takes may have consequences for her as well as for those who are close to her. These consequences may be small but they also can be more extreme such as threats, intimidation, harassment, or discrediting, among other possibilities. We will talk more about resources for dealing with these types of consequences later.

Timing, power, and the larger context all influence the type and severity of costs. The impact of these costs changes depending on our positionality, circumstances, power, and privilege. Power takes many forms. Some of these include the ability to force someone to do something, to give or take away resources or freedom, to allow access, and to influence opinion. When you are allied with large numbers of people who are all working toward the same goal, you have more power (as we discussed in Chapter 8). Obviously, people in decision-making positions who have access to resources or who can withhold resources have power. Within the US, people who have money and ownership have had economic and political power and largely reflect White, male, heterosexual, nondisabled, Christian perspectives. Thus, they have had power to support initiatives that are aligned with their perspectives, and we are seeing a public and vocal insistence on maintaining this power. Raji Hunjan and Jethro Pettit have a great guide for understanding and strategizing power: *Power: A Practical Guide for Facilitating Social Change* (Hunjan & Pettit, 2011).

We face very real differences in treatment based on our identities and risks, depending on whether we are targeted in the situation (refer back to Chapter 3 on identity and intersectionality). The impact of the consequences we experience depends on our history and the specific situation. For example, for most of her life as a White woman, Rebecca has not had to deal with culturally insensitive or racist behavior directed at her or her family. Until she began to understand racism more deeply in her early 20s, she often did not recognize these kinds of situations and thus, did not pay an emotional cost each time they came up. Muninder, Bryan, and Derrick have experienced discriminatory and racist behavior all of their lives. It's exhausting, and each time it comes up, even deciding whether and how to respond adds an additional emotional stressor. Although Rebecca, Muninder, Bryan, and Derrick each experience consequences, the costs are different. Each of us has to consider how harmful the costs will be and decide what to do. Our discussion on solidarity (Chapter 8) is critical as we consider possible benefits and costs of action.

Differential Costs of Speaking Up

Example 1 in a public meeting: If Rebecca speaks up about racism at a community meeting where the crowd is mostly White, there might be a risk that some people won't like what she has to say and will think she is too opinionated or "just trying to be politically correct." Increasingly, they may call her derogatory names and accuse her of many things. The reactions are less likely to be physically dangerous (although that depends on the gun laws in her community and the extent that threats based on gender are used). Alternatively, if Derrick, Bryan, or Muninder speak up in that same meeting, they are more likely to be dismissed, accused of having a personal agenda or grudge, and threatened.

Example 2 in an anti-racism rally: If Rebecca and Derrick are attending a rally, her positionality as a White older woman means that she is generally less likely to meet physical violence than Derrick. To be clear, she may face backlash (and has) both as a woman and as a White woman, but it will likely be different for her than for Derrick. If Rebecca takes more visible action, Derrick may get the brunt of the backlash, even though he may not have been the one to directly confront the injustice. So Rebecca needs to consider that when looking at strategies.

Example 3 in speaking about anti-racism as a White person: In a different example, following a national podcast where Rebecca spoke about anti-racism and White accountability groups, she received numerous emails, social media posts, and letters with insults and graphic pornographic threats of violence and racist messages. Some of those reasonably voiced a different point of view, while others were violent and vile, meant to intimidate based on gender. Many of Rebecca's colleagues of color who talk publicly about anti-racism receive many more, and more violent, hateful messages and threats virtually and in person.

As you consider the issue(s) you have chosen to focus on (in Chapter 5) and think about the possibilities for strategies to address that issue, think about the benefits and costs of each approach. Investigate policies, rules, laws, and practices when weighing the costs for the strategies you consider, as well as resources that you can put into place to reduce the harm to you and your colleagues and clients. In this way, you can make informed choices about how to proceed given what you know about possible consequences. For example, if you (and your collaborators) are considering organizing a public display of resistance through art, maybe an impromptu performance in a public space, look into that community's history of such demonstrations and how they were received by the community, businesses, security, and law enforcement. Are there permit requirements? Are there some spaces where this is allowed and other spaces where it is not allowed? Look into lessons learned by other groups that have done public displays. How do they strategically arrange people, agendas, and art? This information will be helpful to you when deciding what kinds of risks you and your group are willing to take and whether the benefits outweigh the costs. This process can also help you to think about possible ways to plan your strategy to help minimize the costs and maximize the benefits. The wisdom gained by groups and elders who have taken similar action in the past can provide important guidance about things for you to consider.

We want you to pause for a moment and tune into your feelings and physical being. Paying attention to our emotional and physical reactions when preparing for action is important in considering potential actions and costs. Are we feeling uncomfortable, and if so, what is that about? Is the risky feeling an important signal of threat or discomfort, or an unfounded fear? If it is discomfort, do we need to work on being okay with discomfort? Or is the discomfort an indicator of real danger? Once we accurately identify the risk (to the best of our ability with the information available), we can hopefully make a decision about whether the action is worth the risk and then plan accordingly. For example, if Rebecca notices inequity in her university and wants to change that, she calls attention to the injustice, sometimes confronting those in power. Early in her career, she held a part-time temporary teaching job at a different institution, and she depended on that job for her family. If the same situation occurred, she may have felt that the risk of job loss was too great, even though not speaking out might have emotional costs. Additionally, if she lost her job, she may be unable to continue working toward change in the institution. Another person may feel that the same cost of a job is acceptable if they have other job options or other financial resources. Not speaking out may be costly to our well-being, our relationships, and our sense of integrity and fairness, so we may choose to speak out and deal with the consequences or we may choose a different approach that is less likely to be costly. Only you can know whether the benefits outweigh the costs for you, your life, and your family.

Finally, when you are taking public action, we recommend that you consider your professional role and whether that is visible in your action. Are you presenting yourself as a part of your organization or as a private citizen? If your action is not specifically connected to your employment, but your affiliation with your employer is clear in the action you take, it's important to make sure you understand how the organization may react to your involvement. For example, if Muninder writes an op-ed to a national newspaper and signs it "Muninder Kaur Ahluwalia, Professor at Montclair State University," then she is implying that her role at her university is connected to this action. It's helpful for her to think about how the university leaders may react if they do not agree with her position. Alternately, her employer may welcome and even invite her to be a part of advocacy actions. Either way, her expertise as a helping professional, as well as the skills she has developed, can be powerful. This point has become increasingly essential during these first few months of 2025 when universities, public organizations, and even private corporations are being targeted by the presidential administration, state legislation, and anti-human rights special interest groups. In the next chapter, we talk about strategies related to helping your organizations be prepared to support those of us doing work toward ensuring human rights.

It's helpful to periodically circle back to reflecting on strategies, possible benefits, and consequences. Sometimes we don't know the outcomes, benefits and risks until we actually engage in the activity or until new information or opportunities come to light. Policies and legislation change rapidly often affecting the focus of our action as well as the potential consequences. Evaluating and reassessing benefits and costs is an ongoing process because things change and because we learn. Benefits and consequences may also change as action evolves. For example, as a result of our actions, we may have more allies (benefits) or face more backlash (costs), thus changing the path we and our colleagues choose. We aren't saying that if an action has negative consequences you shouldn't do it; we *are* saying that it is important for you to know going in what the possible consequences might be so that you can be clear about your decisions as well as prepare (e.g., make sure your professional liability insurance is up to date, use social media tools that can make you less vulnerable, proactively gain support from your organization).

In the next chapter, we shift to exploring a sample of possible strategies for social action. Throughout our discussion, we will also provide resources that can be helpful in navigating challenges and potential consequences for different strategies and taking action more generally. As a prelude to that, we'd like to revisit wisdom from one of our elders and teachers, Dr. Joseph L. White, as shared by Drs. Thomas and Gerald Parham (2022):

> In the Dr. White school of thought we are most familiar with, giving in to a situation was never an option, and reacting without benefiting from first thinking through and analyzing the situation was never the most appropriate posture for one to assume. He always began with an invitation to look inward, process the hurt, and remind oneself of who you were in your identity. He helped you understand that you were loved, capable of managing the situation, and despite the difficulties of the hour, that there were better days ahead as well as joy, laughter and happiness on the other side of the stormy clouds one was currently experiencing. In those moments where conversations would be intense yet instructive, he would always close with his consistent guidance to "keep the faith." That certainly was a key to healing in the broken places in our lives. (p. 95)

Figure Credit

Chapter 10

A Menu of Strategic Action Approaches

FIGURE 10.1 S-Quad image—strategy

"I am like a drop of water on a rock. After drip, drip, dripping in the same place, I begin to leave a mark, and I leave my mark in many people's hearts."

—Rigoberta Menchú Tum

Some strategies look like quiet action aimed at consistent gradual change, whereas others look big, and demand immediate action. Basically, social change comes from the involvement of all kinds of people who push for change in all kinds of ways. Whether you believe in a gradualist approach or a revolutionary approach, there are strategies that can help make your work more effective. In this chapter, we sample different types of social action strategies and share ideas about how these are relevant in our work as helping professionals as well as personally. Consider using this chapter as a tool and resource to expand your comfort zone and broaden your repertoire of possible approaches. Reflect on your strengths, skills, and resources as well as your education and practice as a helping professional. As we work through and practice some of the strategies in this chapter, we will also heed Dr. Joseph White's wisdom shared at the end of the last chapter and pause. Pay attention to and honor the anger, pain, and trauma we might experience in the oppression we notice, feel, and confront. Simultaneously, honor the potential for joy, hope, and community.

In this chapter, we have organized action strategies loosely using the ecological framework from Bronfenbrenner (1979) and the American Counseling Association (ACA) Advocacy Competencies framework (Lewis et al., 2002; Toporek & Daniels, 2018). We first discuss strategies aimed at large scale, societal level change. Next, we narrow down to local, organizational or community level interventions. Then we narrow even further to individual and interpersonal levels of intervention. Note that some actions may make sense as part of a long-term plan for social change, whereas other actions are more flexible and react to an immediate event. In the moments when you are considering taking action, pay attention to how you are feeling emotionally and physically, honor and acknowledge those feelings, and know that action must live alongside those emotions. Throughout this chapter, we also provide resources to address challenges or consequences related to some of the social action approaches you might be considering. Toward the end of this chapter, we revisit the reflection and evaluation process we discussed in the last chapter and ask you to apply it specifically to your situation and the strategies you are considering.

To help get the conversation started, reflect on your strengths (Chapter 7) and insights about solidarity (Chapter 8). You might find it helpful to go back to some of the activities you completed in those chapters.

ACTIVITY 10.1

Reflecting on Strengths and Solidarity as Your Foundation for Strategic Action

1. What strengths did you identify and what types of actions are you drawn toward (e.g., speaking, writing, developing relationships)?

2. Who are you connected to—in your community and in your organization? What types of relationships do you already have established? Which of those relationships are mutual? Which ones are not mutual (e.g., you hold a higher position of power in relation to them or vice versa, such as a supervisor)?

3. What resources do you have access to?

4. What resources for social action are available in your professional organizations or workplace?

As you read through the following approaches to social action, use these questions to help you identify strategies you feel prepared to use as well as your growth edges.

Public Arena: Macrosystem Including Societal, National, and State Levels

We begin with the largest ecosystem because many of the strategies and skills used at this level can be translated into the local or organizational and individual arenas. As helping professionals, we have a unique and intimate connection to people who are harmed by injustice and we see the oppressive impact of legislation, policies, and practices on clients and communities we care about. We have tools to help us understand social and economic forces that perpetuate oppression and inequity; for example, Ali and Sichel's (2014) application of structural competencies models. We understand and/or conduct research that illuminates the impact of policies on individuals, families and communities (Banks et al., 2019). We have expertise to navigate between communities and power brokers, bringing research and compelling stories to the public and decision-makers. How we use that knowledge and expertise is up to us.

Strength in Numbers: Engaging Through Organizations

Think back to our discussion about solidarity in Chapter 8 and the power of collective action. Professional associations, community groups, advocacy groups, special interest groups, and lobbying groups can be powerful collectives. Whether at international, national, or local levels, taking action through advocacy organizations has many benefits, including built-in infrastructure and momentum, solidarity with others who are committed to similar issues, shared resources and expertise, pursuit and communication of urgent developments and action opportunities, use of social media for rapid mobilization, and more. Many professional associations have gone beyond taking action in the interest of the profession and membership (often called "guild advocacy") to take action on issues that affect individuals and communities. This can take many forms such as legal cases, legislative advocacy, and public letters, to name a few.

When you consider joining a professional association, take a look at whether and how that organization takes stands and/or advocates on issues you care about. Do they have public statements about issues? Do they have a government relations or advocacy group? Do they take a stand and invite members to participate? Many professional associations are very active and invite members to participate in action and/or on advocacy strategy committees, either concerning specific issues or more broadly. For example, the National Association of Social Workers (NASW) provides resources and opportunities for action through their website, events, and planned actions (https://www.socialworkers.org/Advocacy). The American Psychological Association (APA) and the American Counseling Association (ACA) have a government relations branch that provides legislative advocacy training for members and resources for advocacy, coordinates actions, maintains relationships with lobbyists and legislators, and more (https://www.apaservices.org/advocacy; https://www.counseling.org/advocacy/about-our-advocacy).

Within APA, multiple offices focus on different issues; for instance, the Public Interest Directorate addresses issues such as poverty, aging, and housing instability, providing resources for social action, public education, policy briefs, and legislative advocacy. Many of the resources are useful for taking individual action (e.g., writing your legislator) and provide data and information for collective action at local or federal levels. As a member of the organization you can volunteer as an action group member, run to serve on one of the boards focused on a specific issue, or simply use the resources. If you recall the history discussion in Chapter 2, you also know that APA, like many other organizations, also has a problematic human rights history. So another way social action oriented psychologists may choose to be involved is to challenge the organization itself and work toward change (see discussions regarding the Hoffman Report in Chapter 2). Most professional associations, especially those that have been in existence for a while, have oppressive policies and practices in their history. Despite these problems, organizations such as APA, NASW and ACA are demonstrating positive movement forward and provide opportunities and resources for engagement in advocacy. There are more and more examples of action being taken by professional associations especially in the wake of the 2025 actions in the U.S. and state governments to dismantle health services, layoff massive numbers of public workers, delete critical public health databases and records, defund science and education, censor education and public agencies, imprison immigrants and asylum seekers, and eliminate rights for entire communities (e.g., trans, LGBQA+, disabled individuals). Additionally, Flynn et al. (2021) recommend a number of ways that APA, for example, can shift to better support its members in civil disobedience for social justice. When we look at contributing to actions, we can take guidance from our professional organizations and/or join actions they are taking. Alternatively, because these large organizations can also feel daunting, difficult to engage with, and overwhelming, finding colleagues and smaller communities within those large organizations, as well as outside them, can be helpful.

Smaller focused organizations (e.g., state or local branches of professional associations, school boards, local advocacy organizations) can provide more personal connections for action. Organization members and leaders can come together and share their clinical expertise, as well as relational, research, and writing skills to develop comprehensive and compelling statements for educating policymakers and assisting them in becoming stronger advocates for the issue. The increase of digital communication (e.g., video conferencing) has made it much easier to build professional coalitions or work groups at a national level. For example, the National Latinx Psychological Association (NLPA) has increasingly devoted energy toward developing public statements in response to events and issues that affect Latine clients and communities. (For a list of advocacy actions by NLPA see https://www.nlpa.ws/advocacy-in-action.) For those of us working in large organizations, our unions or other employee organizations can also provide opportunities to engage in social action related to the mission of our organization.

There are also great opportunities as an individual to support the work of other types of organizations. For example, participating in public education campaigns can be helpful for those targeted as well as raising awareness for other community members. Additionally, these can help us in our professional work as well, expanding our knowledge of available resources for our students and clients. The National Immigration Law Center's "Know Your Rights" campaign has done an amazing job of creating easy to use and distribute "Red Cards," small red cards that list individual rights and can be used by the holder in situations where their rights may be questioned (https://www.nilc.org/resources/everyone-has-certain-basic-rights/). The cards are available in multiple languages and easy to distribute. For example, Rebecca ordered several hundred and has given them out at her local farmer's market, the staff at the care facility where her mother lives, and anyone she knows who may be in contact with people who are vulnerable to being approached by immigration officials. She is careful not to make assumptions about someone's immigration status and simply says "I'd like to give you these in case you know someone who might need them." On a broader scale, the ACLU provides information about rights related to all kinds of issues including digital discrimination in hiring, police encounters, tribal regalia in schools, health care providers, abortion supporters, LGBTQ rights, voting rights, immigration rights and many more (https://www.aclu.org/know-your-rights). The Disability Rights Education and Defense Fund is a great resource for information and advocacy regarding a range of civil rights of people with disabilities and their children (https://dredf.org). The wide range of organizations providing powerful advocacy, training, and support for social action are too numerous to name here. For Rebecca, this inspires hope and reassurance that we are not alone.

Now it's your turn to think about (and research) the organizations that are working on social justice issues that are important to you.

Who Cares About This Issue and Who Can I Connect With?

Using the issue that you identified in Activity 9.2, find three organizations that care about your issue. You might start by looking at your current professional associations and see if they are advocating on issues you care about. Complete the following questions for each organization:

Name and Contact of Organization	What have they done to advocate for the issue?	How could I use my strengths to contribute? What opportunities do they have to get involved? (e.g., volunteering, letter writing, receiving action alerts, attending rallies)	How do they attend to solidarity? Are communities most impacted by the issue at the table?
Org 1:			
Org 2:			
Org 3:			

For the remainder of this chapter, we dive into the how-to's of specific strategies that can be done collectively or individually. As you read, imagine yourself engaged in these strategies. We will even ask you to try some out as you work through the chapter. As you do, call back to your reflections on your strengths and solidarity. Consider how those can help support or frame the way you engage in these strategies.

Communicating and Working with Legislators, Government, and Policymakers

Legislation and federal, state, and local policies have the potential to address injustice and inquiry, make existing injustices worse, and/or create injustice and inequity as we are seeing now with so many state and Supreme Court decisions that directly harm entire communities. Counselors, psychologists, and other helping professionals are in a unique position to translate the pain and the realities of oppression related to social issues into language that is understandable by people who are removed from the issue. We can also increase the strength of those stories with data and research to emphasize the harmful impact of policies. This combination of data, research, and powerful narratives supports advocacy and can propel and assist policymakers to be necessary allies in the process.

Before we go on, take a minute to reflect on your strengths, your reflections about solidarity, and your connections to others with lived experience or professional experience related to your issue. Professionally, it's likely that you have developed skills in communicating either in writing or in person, developing relationships, navigating systems, researching and understanding data, educating others, conveying compassion and empathy, and more. Think about your own strengths and consider how you might use those in social action at a policy level.

Professional Expertise: White Papers, Amicus Briefs, and Legal Strategies

"White paper" is the term used for a document that provides a concise overview of a complex issue using expert knowledge to help decision and policymakers gain understanding, advocate, or solve a problem. These provide concrete data to support arguments that can be used during legislative debates and decisions. The white paper is a way to help legislative allies bring our professional expertise and experience to impact decisions. For example, Lauren Sneed, a school counselor and a counselor educator in Rebecca's department, worked as a team member on a white paper that has been used by California legislators to argue for greater transparency and accountability from alternative schools (Cobb et al., 2023). In addition to providing critical information about the current problem and its impact, the report also shared questions for advocates and guidelines for filing a formal complaint about schools. Lauren worked alongside representatives from the ACLU, National Center for Youth Law, and the East Bay Community Law Center. As a collaborator, Lauren lent her experience and expertise as a school counselor with system-impacted youth, as well as her understanding of large school districts.

Amicus briefs use professional expertise to provide information or arguments to the court for consideration and may also direct the court to consider the implications of a legal decision (Gilfoyle & Dvoskin, 2017). For example, a Colorado licensed professional counselor, Kaley Chiles, filed for a temporary injunction to bar enforcement of Colorado's Minor Therapy Conversion Law of 2019. The district court denied her motion, and Ms. Chiles appealed the decision. In support of the injunction, the American Psychological Association filed an amicus brief outlining the psychological risks and lack of evidence regarding sexual orientation and gender identity therapy (APA Office of General Counsel, 2023). To put together a brief like this, authors draw on expertise from many different practitioners, other helping professions, research, and often state associations. As of March 2025, Chiles appealed to the Supreme Court and they agreed to hear her case despite firm positions from the state and the lower court that the ban on conversion therapy was harmful and ineffective based on overwhelming evidence. We expect that more advocacy will be needed from counselors, psychologists, and their professional associations. The opportunities for us to contribute to that type of action is greater when we connect with others at local, state, and national levels on issues we care about.

In addition to white papers and amicus briefs, providing consultation to legal advocacy groups and civil rights organizations is another way to engage in social action. One of the best known examples in psychology and education is Mamie Clark's research and Kenneth Clark's subsequent testimony used in *Briggs v. Elliott* (1952), one of the Supreme Court cases in *Brown v. Board of Education* (1954), which resulted in the ruling that racial segregation in public education was unconstitutional. This and other highly visible examples may seem distant and out of reach for many of us. Let's discuss a couple of other examples to better understand how they came to be and what actually happened.

Dr. Janet E. Helms, a counseling psychologist perhaps best known for her contributions related to White and Black racial identity, has also done pivotal research in the area of test bias and assessment. Based on her research and expertise in this area, she was called to provide testimony to Connecticut's Civil Service Commission in the Supreme Court case of *Ricci V. DeStefano* (2009). White firefighters in New Haven, Connecticut, were contesting a decision to remove the civil service test that had been used in the department to determine promotions. The exam had been removed after it was shown to be biased against applicants of color (*Ricci v. DeStefano,* 2009). Helms's testimony was cited by Supreme Court Justice Ruth Bader Ginsberg in an argument to uphold the removal of the exam.

In another example, Dr. Gerald West, a psychologist and a former colleague of Rebecca's, provided testimony regarding the disparate impact of intelligence tests that placed Black students in special education classes in the San Francisco Unified School District (*P. v. Riles*, 1972). The affidavits and testimony of West and several colleagues were used in *P. v. Riles* (1972) in the U.S. District Court for the Northern District of California and supported the claim that placement in those special education classes caused irreparable injury.

How do psychologists and other helping professionals such as Drs. Helms and West elevate voices to have such significant impact? It began with the work each of them did to establish professional credibility and expertise through their research, writing, practice, and public speaking. Rebecca asked Dr. Helms how she became involved in providing testimony. She shared that the Connecticut Civil Service Commission reached out to a former student of Dr. Helms who worked as a consultant. He referred the Commission to her due to her expertise in testing and psychometrics. She provided testimony to the Commission (in the presence of an audience of opposing firefighters) who then transcribed the testimony and submitted it through court hierarchies. Dr. Helms also noted that, "Most people don't realize that there are no witnesses or testimony in Supreme Court cases ... Instead, the Court relies on testimony from other legal entities (e.g., courts, commissions)" (personal communication, December 11, 2022).

In-Person Visits to Legislators and Policymakers

In-person visits to your elected officials can increase the chances of your voice being heard. Visits can also begin to establish ongoing relationships with legislators who can become allies to your issue. In-person visits can be done individually, or, even more powerfully, as a group. If the legislator's actions and opinions are opposite from yours, they need to hear from you (and as many other people as possible), especially if you are one of their constituents. If they are in agreement with your position, they also need to hear from you. They need your voice, expertise, data, narratives, and passion to help them fight for that issue.

> **EXAMPLE**
>
> ### Rebecca's Colleagues Meet with a Senator's Staff
>
> Several years ago, my colleagues, Andres Consoli and Alvin Alvarez, and I were contacted by the APA Public Interest Government Relations Office about pending legislation supporting linguistically appropriate mental health services. We invited several practitioners (alumni from our master's program) to join us in a meeting in our US Senator's office. We used research and statistics to show the human and financial cost of lack of access to linguistically appropriate psychological services, as well as the benefits of culturally relevant treatment. Our practitioner colleagues shared their clinical experiences working with communities and clients who had spent years trying to access linguistically appropriate services. During the meeting, the senator's staff member took extensive notes about the research and data. When the practitioners spoke, the staff member seemed mesmerized by the personal stories. We were all moved to tears when one practitioner shared a letter that a client had asked her to read to

the senator. The senator's staff member forcefully put her fist on the table and said, "I will make sure Senator Boxer understands how important this legislation is." The combined expertise of researchers and practitioners laid the groundwork and provided substance needed for legislative discussion.

In the above example, the APA office had reached out to Rebecca's colleagues because they were constituents of their state senator. Most large professional associations also have an advocacy office that you can reach out to, you don't need to wait for them. You can have the most impact on legislators when you are a part of their constituency because, in theory, they are elected to represent you and your district. Elected officials typically have offices in their local district as well as in Washington, DC (for federal legislators) or in the state capital (for state legislators). The website of the legislator should provide you with information regarding which office they will be in during a specified time, as well as what issues, bills, committees, and voting record they have as it relates to your concerns. This can help you determine whether this legislator will be aligned or opposing the issue you bring to them. The organization Indivisible (2016) has published a guide written by former congressional staffers that provides great insider information and tips about preparing for and meeting with legislators. Additionally, professional associations usually have updated information regarding relevant legislation as well as tips and training for their members.

Rebecca recently provided a day-long training to psychologists in Arizona during a Politics and Psychology Day organized by the Arizona Psychological Association (AzPA). The goal of the session was to prepare attendees for a meet-and-greet that was planned over lunch with state legislators. To help prepare, AzPA legislative committee provided attendees with a list of legislation and talking points before the event. On the day of the event, the lobbyist who worked for AzPA provided an update about current legislation being considered and tips for talking with legislators. Rebecca took the attendees through a process of grounding in their beliefs, their strengths, and their professional lens, and then focused on relationship building. The emphasis on relationship building was intentional because a short lunch meet-and-greet is limited but is a great opportunity to begin establishing an ongoing relationship.

Unsurprisingly, the legislators who attended were invested in sharing with the psychologists at their lunch table both their personal and legislative positions. Somewhat surprising to Rebecca was the extent that the legislators shared fairly intimate and compelling stories and were eager to hear psychologists' perspectives. Of course this was a self-selected group of legislators, but the opportunity for developing important allies was clear.

Now imagine yourself preparing for an in-person visit with a legislator or policymaker. For this activity, choose whether you are engaging as part of a collective or individually and the context in which you are meeting with the legislator.

ACTIVITY 10.3

Laying the Groundwork for an In-Person Visit

For this activity, you will need to do some research. You can use resources from professional associations and advocacy organizations, as well as the ones we have listed below.

Examples of resources specific to the US

Congress.Gov (https://www.congress.gov) has searchable information about legislation (current and past), which committees are involved in specific decisions and bills, and how your representatives have voted.

GovTrack (https://www.govtrack.us) provides an easy way to find out what legislation might be pending regarding issues you are concerned about and the contact information for your senators and representatives. You can also sign up to receive action alerts regarding issues of interest.

5 Calls (https://5calls.org) provides possible actions to address an issue you have indicated interest in as well as scripts that can be used to contact your legislator. They also provide the contact information for the specific legislators involved in those decisions or votes based on your voting district.

Below, follow each step and write in as much information as you can gather.

Step 1: Background

- What is the issue you are focusing on?

- Who do you hope to talk to (legislator and key staff member)?

- When are they in the office? What committees do they serve on? What is their voting record or position on your issue?

Step 2: Talking Points

- Why is your issue important?

- Who does it affect and how?

- Do you have a personal story, research, or some expertise you can include in your talking points? (Be succinct and offer to send additional information if they'd like.)

- What action do you want to see the legislator take?

- How would you like them to follow up with you and how would you like to follow up with them?

Step 3: What will you do to follow up?

Emails, Phone Calls, and Postcards

When communicating in writing or by phone, include the following elements: (a) state your name, whether you are a constituent and location (if you are a constituent); (b) state your issue and your position on it; (c) focus only on your message; (d) customize your message based on what you know about the audience; (e) briefly describe how the issue affects you, your community, or your family directly; (f) offer a compelling story if possible. Most importantly, state what you want your legislator to do about it. Include a brief summary of research in your talking points to make best use of your professional expertise and add credibility. Phone calls tend to be recorded and tallied much more quickly than emails and letters so that is more likely to have an impact.

ACTIVITY 10.4

One Email, One Phone Call

Choose one of your central issues and draft one email and/or make one phone call to at least one of your legislative representatives.

- The resources from Activity 10.3 can help you find a specific decision, legislation, or incident to respond to and narrow the focus of your message. They may even suggest language to use. You can also go directly to advocacy groups already working on the issue to find specific actionable items.
- Your letter or call has more power if you are a constituent and/or if you focus on a legislator who is involved in a committee that has decision-making power.
- Your message should be clear and say what action you want them to take. Examples include continued advocacy on an issue (if they are in favor of your position), voting a particular way, or even providing you with information about a bill whose status is unclear (some bills are referred back to committee and it is unclear whether they are still being considered).

Possible template

Dear (name of legislator or decision-maker),

I am (a constituent, concerned community member) contacting you to express my concern about (issue). This is important to me (or my community) because (summarize in two to three sentences the reasons it is important to you, some research points, the impact, etc., and a personal story or example if possible). I am asking you to vote (or advocate) for (state your position and specific legislation or bill). This issue is of critical importance, and I appreciate the (legislator's name) action on this.

You can adjust this script depending on whether the legislator is opposed, neutral, or supportive of your position, and if there is a specific time frame for legislation. Feel free to use the resources from your professional association or another source such as 5 Calls. They will often provide a sample script for specific issues. If you are a constituent, be sure to provide your zip code or district. If you are calling, you will most likely be connected to a staff member or voicemail that gets tallied and shared with the legislator. Even if you get the legislator's voicemail, be sure to leave all the information and your voice will get counted. For those of who feel awkward with calling, one strategy for practice is to call after hours when you know you will receive a voicemail.

The importance of individuals contacting legislators and elected officials should not be underrated. Additionally, as we've emphasized throughout this book, there is strength in numbers. In the next section, we discuss effective use of media to help coalesce support, awareness, and power for large-scale change, as well as increase individual and community level change.

Communicating with and Through Media

The skill and commitment needed for using media for social action ranges widely from very little to sophisticated. In this section, we will touch on basics for engaging with existing media sources, and in a later section, we will talk about creating media yourself. Engaging with the media is likely new to many of us, and even a little scary. Being prepared and knowing who can support you (e.g., your employer, your professional association) and how they can support makes the process much easier. Practice is also golden.

Media Interviews

Television, print, or internet venues such as podcasts or web series interviews can be great ways to share your professional perspective and knowledge. If you are willing to participate with the media, professional associations often have good resources to help you do this effectively. For example, you can find guidance for working with the media in all kinds of ways on APA's website (APA, 2020a). This resource outlines how psychologists (or any helping professional) can prepare for different opportunities, including television, radio, and print interviews Additionally, Santoro (2022) provides great tips to help get comfortable talking to the media. We have summarized some of the key points below.

When preparing for a media interview, determine which interviews are appropriate and a good fit for your message and intent. Consider the following:

- What is the venue (i.e., what paper, website, podcast, news show, etc.) and who is their audience? Is this source generally supportive or opposed to the types of issues you care about? How did you connect with the media source, and what are they expecting of you (e.g., are you being brought in as an expert, a representative, or are you initiating the contact)?
- What is the interviewer's intention and how will they be using this interview?
- What is the story they hope to get or might care about? Who else are they interviewing for this story?
- Will you have an opportunity to review or amend your comments after the interview is completed?
- Is this an individual interview or will they have a panel? If it is a panel, who else will be on the panel?

Do your research and remember that sometimes an interview is simply for information, other times it is to present opposing views, and other times it is designed to further the news source's agenda. It is your right to request information prior to the interview and hope the information they give you is accurate so that you can make an informed decision about whether and how to participate. Some interviews will involve a preinterview where the interviewer explores some of the questions with you prior to the actual interview. After this short example, we will provide some suggestions.

> **EXAMPLE**
>
> ### Rebecca's Interview for a National Podcast
>
> I was invited for an interview about white racial identity for the *Washington Post's The Lily*. The podcast series focused on racism (Ellis & Sitz, 2021). Because the interview was a planned series, the producers scheduled a preinterview to decide whether I could speak to the issues they wanted to explore. I had a chance to decide if the show was one that would be collaborative or combative. After the preinterview, the producers scheduled a time to record the full interview and provided information about what the interview would include, helpful tips about better audio and recording quality, etc. Because it was a recorded interview, as opposed to a live exchange, I had the opportunity to stop the interview if I wanted to clarify things. After the interview was recorded, the producers edited and then aired the podcast. I didn't have access to review the final podcast before it was aired, so I had to trust that the producers would represent me fairly in the edits. Fortunately, based on my preinterview research, I could see they had produced several powerful anti-racism episodes prior to this one. I felt okay about what I was able to share, and it seemed to have an impact given the White supremacist, racist backlash that I experienced after the episode aired.

Although it is difficult to always be ready for a media appearance, there are some basic things you can do. First, know the scope of your expertise and stick to that. There are a number of ways that you can be identified as "an expert" or "thought leader" on a topic. One way can be through your employer or professional association (make sure you understand their policies regarding public appearances). For example, faculty at universities are sometimes approached by the media to comment on an issue or story using "expert" knowledge. The public relations office of the university keeps a database of faculty and researchers who are willing to talk with the media on specific topics. These requests may be unexpected—often prompted by a traumatic incident (e.g., mass shooting), news event (e.g., court decision)—or planned in advance (e.g., a quote needed for National Counselors' Week). Other ways to be identified as an expert include publicizing your expertise, speaking publicly on a topic, having a vibrant social media presence related to your expertise, writing books, providing training on your area of expertise, or getting involved in community initiatives that will make your expertise more visible to the media.

Second, if you are approached to provide a response (and it is within your expertise), you can choose to tell the inquirer that you would be happy to talk to them at a specific scheduled time and that you would like to have some background information from them. The interviewer may have a very short window in which to get an interview so be aware that you may need to be flexible. Third, prepare some brief talking points about your issue, a poignant story, and brainstorm possible unexpected questions. Ensure you have some basic supporting evidence for your points.

In an interview, stay focused on the issue you wish to address and how you wish to address it. Decide where your boundaries of expertise lay—that is, your knowledge gained through experience and training as well as the position you represent, if speaking on behalf of an organization or issue. Consider how you will handle things if the interview veers into areas you are not ready to respond to or that you feel uncomfortable with. Being caught by surprise and trying to answer without being clear of your position can be a bad recipe. Practice your talking points and illustrations to make sure they are brief, clear, and to the point. It is likely that any interview will be edited into smaller segments and the final product may not have the context that you provided.

Panel interviews can be a great opportunity but can also bring challenges. A media panel may be intended to present different expertise on the same topic or to set up a debate with opposing viewpoints. Consider the following: Who are the other presenters and what are their positions on the issue? In past situations, how has this moderator engaged, and do they have a particular angle? How comfortable are you with politely interrupting people or talking over people if there is a dominating panel member or moderator? How comfortable are you with conflict and heated discussions? Whether the interview is a surprise or you seek it out, being prepared can make a difference in how well you use the opportunity for social action. A great example of a resource that provides guidance for developing talking points about racism and calls to action is The Opportunity Agenda, a social justice communications lab, available at https://opportunityagenda.org/. Even a little preparation can help gather your thoughts and guide you to create a clearer and more intentional message.

Doing your homework is vital. Increasingly, helping professionals are being asked to speak on topics and, unfortunately, there have been some situations where the intentions of the interviewers were not transparent and were sometimes malicious. Sometimes even homework can't prevent a bad situation. You have the right to stop and exit an interview if you feel uneasy, cornered, harassed, or mislead. In the moment, we may feel confused, compelled to continue, or hopeful that we can explain or change minds. Trust your inner sense of the situation.

Interviews and recorded events may raise trepidation for some of us. Fortunately, there lots of other ways we can get the word out. In the following sections we describe how to use talking points when writing for social action.

Op-Eds and Letters to the Editor

Opinion editorials, or op-eds, are often similar to news columns in that they present facts and substantiate their points with data, yet they are different in that they clearly present a point of view. A letter to the editor is usually less formal than an op-ed and can be a way of engaging in a conversation or sending a message. Both op-eds and letters to the editor allow you to have the time to thoughtfully put your words together in a way that conveys a clear and concise message. Op-eds and letters to the editor can express your personal voice or professional voice.

Dr. Kevin Cokley, a counseling psychologist, shares his experience writing op-eds related to African American psychology, racism in public policy, critical race theory, and police violence against Black communities (for some great examples, see http://www.kevincokley.com/op-eds). In an interview in the video *Helping Counselors and Psychologists as Advocates and Activists* (Toporek & Ahluwalia, 2019), Cokley describes how he shifted toward this form of social action.

> Honestly, I had never really thought of myself necessarily as an activist. We think about images of activism, you think of people, you know, being on streets and being

very sort of vocal and ... and I am certainly vocal in my own way. For me, writing interestingly has been one of my forms of activism ... when I had the opportunity to learn how to write op-eds, being trained by professional journalists, it was something that I was very excited about. ... And in many ways I found my voice. I was able to say things that I really had not had an opportunity to say in my normal academic writing. And in doing so, it was very empowering and it was very liberating.

You can see from his experience that the op-ed can make an impact as well as be a fulfilling method to use the skills we are trained in. As you consider writing an op-ed, the following guidelines can help you shape the project.

- Be clear about your purpose in writing the piece. What do you want the reader to come away with?
- Who is the audience you are trying to reach, and what is the best way to reach this audience? What kind of language and structure will be best understood and compelling to this audience? Become familiar with the publications you want to target, the types of articles, letters, and op-eds they publish, their audience, and their instructions for authors (length of article, process for submission, other suggestions or requirements).
- Lead with your conclusion, which differs from journal articles that typically build toward a conclusion. Begin the article with a "hook" that succinctly communicates your purpose so that the reader cares about it enough to keep reading. For op-eds, the Harvard Kennedy School (n.d.) suggests beginning with a "strong claim, a surprising fact, a metaphor, a mystery, or a counter-intuitive observation that entices the reader into reading more." Check out the entire article entitled "How to Write an Op-Ed or Column" at https://shorensteincenter.org/wp-content/uploads/2012/07/HO_NEW_HOW-TO-WRITE-AN-OPED-OR-COLUMN.pdf.
- Make your point and then use the op-ed to succinctly substantiate each aspect of your point with data, research, quotes, and facts that are likely to be perceived by the audience as credible without being excessive. You can help the facts and data come alive by weaving in a compelling narrative or story.
- Create a strong ending that reiterates the main objective, preferably in a way the reader can understand more deeply given the material you shared. Make sure you are clear about what should happen or what action the reader should take.
- Use language and a writing style that is familiar to the audience. Avoid jargon and clichés.

You can find more guidance for op-eds in a 2017 article entitled "Tips for Aspiring Op-Ed Writers" in *The New York Times* (Stephens, 2017). Lee (2018) is also a great source. We would also like to reiterate how important it is to become familiar with the changing editorial policies of various media outlets and sometimes even consider making that a part of your social action. A striking example is the February 2025 decision of Jeff Bezos, owner of the Washington Post, to dictate that the paper only publish opinions that advocate "personal liberties and free markets." His policy also disallowed anything that was viewed as opposing or differing from those topics (Mullin, 2025). Prior to this time, the *Washington Post* had been a media outlet where a wide range of topics could be shared and divergent points and scientific insights could be discussed within the context of op-eds. Knowing these editorial policies and the cultural climate of the media organization will help you strategize and engage with ones that will actually consider your work.

Letters to the editor are typically shorter, more succinct and usually reach a different audience. Unlike op-eds, the information, research or data presented is typically much more brief (if data is even included). For practice, let's write a letter to the editor.

ACTIVITY 10.5

Drafting a Letter to the Editor

For this activity, you will draft a letter to a real news source:

1. Choose the issue you will write about and the purpose of your letter (educate, ask for change, etc.).
2. Choose a news source that fits your purpose and find their guidelines for letters to the editor.
3. Identify the main point you want the audience to take away, and then write out three to four points from your professional expertise that will support your position (use language the audience can relate to).

Dear Editor,

- A powerful sentence or two to let the reader know why you are writing and capture their interest—this is your hook. Is your letter about something that happened recently? Is it in response to another letter to the editor?
- Describe why this issue is important to the reader.
- What information does the reader need to know?
- What should happen? What do you want the reader to do or support?

4. Have someone read the letter and give you feedback: Is your point clear? Is it readable? Does the reader finish the letter knowing what you think should happen? Do they feel energized to take action?

Holding Media Accountable

Media, including television, radio, email, and social media, has the potential to inform or misinform the public. For example, in April 2018, Deadspin exposed that Sinclair media conglomerate required news anchors at all of its local stations around the country to recite an identical speech echoing then US President Donald Trump's perspective that, ironically, mainstream media was not to be trusted. The mandated directive was to make the message sound like it reflected news from the local perspective while it was actually orchestrated nationally (Domonoske, 2018). The company owned 190 stations and was in the process of acquiring dozens more. This proliferation of a specific message to local communities under the guise of independent news illustrates coordinated and strategic efforts of large corporate and political forces. A strategy for social action can be to raise awareness of these calculated and manipulative efforts. More recent examples can be seen in alarming policy shifts in major social media platforms beginning in 2022 and increasing with the federal election in 2024. These have a direct impact on many of our justice efforts and the well-being of marginalized communities in addition to the health of society in general. X (formerly known as Twitter) changed its policies after 2022 when it was purchased by Elon Musk. This change correlated with a 50% increase in hate speech on the media platform over the next year (Hickey et al., 2025). Meta (i.e., Facebook, Instagram, etc.) "scrapped" fact checking and also removed restrictions for hate speech and online abuse (Ortutay, 2025).

Although the actions of large corporations such as social media may feel overwhelming and foreboding, there are important things we can do. Holding media accountable can be done in a variety of ways ranging from writing a letter to the editor, alerting the public to misinformation, conducting and publishing research on the impact of these decisions, boycotting the source, contacting the station or publisher, contacting advertisers, and many others. We can also hold social media platforms accountable. Dr. Bedford Palmer, a counseling psychologist and counselor educator, has talked about the racial profiling that happens on the social media platform, Nextdoor.com, and his involvement in Neighbors for Racial Justice to push the tech company to make changes on the platform (Toporek & Ahluwalia, 2019). He and his colleagues were able to meet with Nextdoor executives and advocate for changes in policies and practices to try to minimize, or at least address, offensive and dangerous posts targeting people of color.

Given the strengths and training we have, and our connection to professional associations, and role models, keeping the media accountable can be an effective social action strategy. Additionally, with our skills and expertise, social media can be a viable platform.

Using Social Media for Effective Action

Social media can help people feel connected in a more personal way through pictures, videos, and stories. This lays the groundwork for action but does not guarantee it and can risk keeping people in a virtual world, sometimes believing they are making change without actually doing it. Alicia Garza, co-founder of Black Lives Matter, noted that engagement in social media doesn't necessarily translate into effective action. She explained, "What it takes to get people from liking and sharing and retweeting to organizing is a hard and long process" (Hunt, 2016). Similarly, research by Kristofferson and colleagues (2014) found that people who "like" a cause on Facebook or similar social media sites are no more likely to take action or support that cause in any other way in their life. So, how can social media be helpful as a tool or strategy for taking action? Nicholas Mirzoeff describes the interaction between a successful "visual activism" approach, such as Black Lives Matter, and social media. He argued that,

> What's so crucial about making visual activism work is that it catalyzes real life social activism through social media. If it's just on social media, then very little will follow from that. But if, by seeing things, people are impelled to take action themselves, and they are helped to find out how to take that action themselves, then change can result. (Funnell, 2017)

The *Youth Activist Toolkit* emphasizes that social media and online actions must be connected and extended beyond the internet (Gasch & Reticker-Flynn, n.d.). For example, online petition signatures can be delivered in person to a legislator with a photo op that is then posted online to publicize that they received the message. Social media is an important way to make activism inclusive by providing different venues for people to participate who may not be able to physically attend events. Social media can also move us to action when it is used to document and share incidents and personal stories of injustice nationally and globally. It can bring awareness, advocacy, and collective action to conflicts that would have historically happened in a vacuum, such as the killing of Black people in the United States, the war in Ukraine, and the killings in Gaza.

Zeitzoff (2017) talked about the advantages of social media in social action, including (a) reducing the "cost of communication"; (b) expediting the sharing of information; and, (c) expanding available information beyond major news sources, which often shapes the conflict itself. In fact, within our professional association listservs and social media circles, we can see clear examples of the potential usefulness for communicating, raising issues and concerns, connecting helping professionals, and quickly spreading information about specific events, concerns and actionable opportunities. Of course there are also examples of miscommunication, conflict, and misinformation so it is always important to be alert and a critical consumer of information, regardless of the source.

As noted in the earlier section, social media companies also provide us with the opportunity to have a voice. For example, when decisions by Meta and X increased hate speech and disinformation, many consumers chose to delete their accounts and shift to an alternative social media platform, Bluesky. Numerous helping professionals who were tech savvy set up "starter kits" on that platform to more easily allow professionals with similar interests to quickly become a part of the online community related to their profession or specific issues. Others became more active on LinkedIn connecting the anti-human rights actions to economic and employment impications.

Blogs, Podcasts, and Other Digital Media

Because digital media is constantly evolving and changing, there are new platforms, apps, blogs, vlogs, podcasts, and websites every day. Through blogs and vlogs, individuals and organizations can present their perspectives on timely topics. One example is the APA's blog *Psychology Benefits Society* featuring varying topics that include discussions such as the "Blog Series on Race, Racism, and Law Enforcement in Communities of Color" (Psychology Benefits Society, n.d.) and "Islamophobia in the US" (Ahluwalia & Ali, 2016). Although APA did not continue producing this blog, the articles produced in the series are still available online.

A growing number of individual counselors, psychologists, and helping professionals are also creating podcasts to share information, interviews, and examine challenging social justice issues. For example, *Cultural Humility* (by Miguel Gallardo, https://drgallardo.com/ch-podcast/) shares interviews with authors, practitioners, scholars, and advocates on issues related to racism, health disparities, settler–colonialism, and more. If you are considering creating this type of media, we recommend guidance from experienced bloggers and organizations. The Peace and Collaborative Development Network provides a great resource for creating and maintaining blogs focused on social issues (Zelizer, 2015). Choosing a platform, theme, name, style, and format are all part of the creation process.

One powerful issue that came into the spotlight in early 2025 is the vulnerability of digital media, digital records, and repositories of critical information created and stored by government agencies, among others. Early in 2025, entire databases with health information were directed by the US presidential administration to be deleted and shut down. Scientists, healthcare professionals, educators and others scrambled to rescue information that was essential for public health, environmental protection, and more. Executive orders directed all organizations that receive federal funding (e.g., schools, universities, federal agencies) to eliminate any programs and language related to diversity, inclusion and equity, including any information published on websites or in print. Thus, entire websites have disappeared losing vast amounts of important information and data. At the same time, a wide range of private and secure information (e.g., tax records, personal health records, social security) became accessible to a newly created department in the US government that also laid off and directed the firing an estimated 100,000 federal employees (Crowley et al., 2025). This, combined with the shifts in privacy policies on social media platforms, raised alarms for individuals and organizations. Several resources have provided some technological guidance and tools. For example, the Electronic Frontier Foundation (EFF) website provides a wide range of resource guides and links for electronic privacy (https://www.eff.org/issues/privacy). The EFF also provides updates on areas for action. The Internet Archive, a non-profit organization, "is building a digital library of internet sites and other cultural artifacts in digital form" (Internet Archive, n.d.). This resource means that even if a website or webpage is deleted, viewers may be able to access it using an online tool called the "Wayback Machine." This is also crowd-sourced so any webpage that an individual wants to ensure can be found, can be entered into the archive so it is accessible in the future (https://archive.org/projects/). The Internet Archive strives to function as a digital library. Here is another social action strategy, help preserve essential social justice digital data and information.

As we shift beyond our focus on macrolevel change, we want to emphasize that many of these strategies can also be useful at a local level. In the next section, we scale our discussion closer to home, our local communities and the organizations where we work.

Acting Locally: Your Community and Organization

For some of us, working toward systems change seems more possible in our neighborhood, community, city, or organization than on a national or international level. In this section, we will talk about getting involved in local and organizational change efforts both as a community member and as a professional.

Working with Local Governments, Boards, and Other Policymakers

Like macrolevel strategies with legislators, we can advocate with our local elected and appointed members of the school board, public utilities board, mayor's office, and others. We can also share important perspectives and expertise for ongoing initiatives and boards by serving as members.

Muninder and ThriveNYC

ThriveNYC was an initiative of the New York City Mayor's Office (under Mayor De Blasio) that brought together individuals, communities, and government officials in response to the local and national mental health crisis. What made this initiative unique was the intentional involvement of cultural and religious communities in the city. The Mayor's office worked with mosques, synagogues, gurdwaras, and churches around the city and their religious leaders, which allowed a bidirectional flow of information to address issues that were unique to each community. I, Muninder, sat on a panel with other Sikh scholars and practitioners and the deputy mayor to inform the Sikh community of the mental health challenges we face, how mental health services could be accessed, and the ways in which mental health services could be used to supplement Sikh methods of healing. Simultaneously, we informed the mayor's office about unique stressors and barriers to mental health care access for the Sikh community, such as Islamophobia, hate crimes, and immigration status.

Keep in mind that many of the resources we provide in this section are helpful whether you engage as a community member or as a professional. You may also want to explore your professional association for additional guides for taking action at state or local levels. For example, *Community Advocacy: A Psychologist's Toolkit for State and Local Advocacy* is a great resource that provides information and a decision guide for selecting strategies, resources, and consideration of consequences for psychologists taking social action at state and local levels (Banks et al., 2019). This easy-to-use toolkit evolved from a joint project between several divisions of the APA.

Running for Office

There are examples of counselors, psychologists, and other helping professionals who serve as national or state elected leaders (e.g., Ted Strickland, Governor of Ohio, 2007–2011 and candidate for US Congress, 2016), but for most of us, local politics feels more approachable and can still have an important impact on issues facing our community. By running for a seat on the school board, development agency, or city council, we can bring our expertise into policy decision-making for social change. Running for office and sharing your concerns, even if you don't get elected, raises awareness and publicizes important issues. There are great resources that provide information about running for office and help you determine whether this is a path you want to pursue. For state-level positions, the secretary of state website for each state lists all of the political offices and provides valuable voter information. For example, the site for the State of California Secretary of State (http://www.sos.ca.gov/elections/) provides information about each elected position, each election and timeline, links for registering to vote, information about lobbying, and much more to help you run for office as well as to be a well-informed participant in the process.

Additionally, many organizations are working to support individuals from groups that have been excluded in politics such as *She Should Run* (https://www.sheshouldrun.org/) and *Emily's List (*https://www.emilyslist.org/run-to-win) encouraging women candidates,

Victory Fund (https://victoryfund.org/) for openly LGBTQ+ elected officials, *Elevate Campaign Training for People with Disabilities (*https://ncil.org/event/elevate-2021-introduction-to-campaigns-self-and-opposition-research-for-candidates/), *The Collective Political Action Committee* (https://collectivepac.org/about/) to increase the number of Black elected officials, *Asian Pacific American Institute for Congressional Studies* (https://www.apaics.org/), and *Latino Victory* (https://latinovictory.org/). Some organizations are partisan, while others are simply focused on increasing representation in government and/or decreasing partisanship.

Finally, if running for office is not appealing, it's still possible to influence local policies and practices by working on task groups and initiatives of elected officials or elected bodies. Even a one-time commitment, for example speaking up at school board meetings, city council meetings, and other governing bodies, can have an impact. Thinking back to the idea of strength in numbers (Chapter 8), local advocacy organizations often publicize when an important decision is being made and how a show of support would be helpful. For example, an initiative in the San Francisco Bay Area to rematriate sacred Indigenous land (Save West Berkeley Shellmound) has a social media page where they share updates as well as periodically call for supporters to attend city council meetings where decisions are being made about the issue.

Getting involved in a sustained way can help develop relationships, collectively move an agenda forward and help increase our understanding of issues, power structures, and the decision process. When we are able to articulate and share our expertise as helping professionals (look back at your strengths assessment), we can make a unique and informed contribution. Reflecting back on the discussion around solidarity in Chapter 8, we can also find many ways to support existing efforts of community groups that advocate with elected officials or governing bodies.

Contributing to Community Coalitions

Community organizing and developing community coalitions are necessary strategies for medium- and large-scale change. Given how integral relationship building and intentional solidarity is to community building, we ask that you take a moment to go back to Chapter 8 and review our discussion of coalition building. Think about how you might engage in this approach to address the issue(s) you have identified. Another way we can contribute to community coalitions and collective action is to offer our expertise in group facilitation and consultation. Groups that are working toward social change are not immune to internal conflict, and our expertise as helping professionals can help. Anneliese Singh, a counseling psychologist, talked about this:

> I think that is another gift we could provide is that, looking out for where that pain lives because often in our movements we have the same goal, but we end up acting out of our wounds. And I think in liberation movements, we don't always take the time or even maybe actually have the time to slow down and see how our internal liberation is so connected to that larger goal of liberation ... I think often in our activist and advocacy movements, we get going and we're moving towards liberation. And then all of a sudden, we're eating each other and taking each other down, and we're losing some idea of the goal. And so I feel like that could be a real gift of counselors to community activist and vice versa. (Toporek & Ahluwalia, 2019)

If you choose to take this avenue, there are important considerations such as understanding the group dynamics and politics within the organization, who is requesting your help, how the members of the group feel about facilitation, what facilitation is needed, what your role and positionality is related to the group, the issue, and the members, etc. Consulting with other colleagues who have experience doing this type of facilitation is important.

Participating in Public Displays of Resistance

Community organizing is relevant for so many different types of social action. Perhaps some of the most obvious are public displays of resistance. Rallies, marches, hunger strikes, sit-ins, and teach-ins are probably the most familiar because they tend to generate large-scale publicity and media attention. There are also quieter and equally powerful public displays of resistance, such as those in visual art, murals, performance art, and craftivism.

Rallies, Marches, and Protests

In the U.S., there has been a resurgence of public demonstrations with greater visibility over the past ten years, including the Peoples March, Black Lives Matter, the Women's March, March for Our Lives, the Nationwide Prison Strike, People's Climate March, March for Science, and many others. During the years when COVID-19 surfaced, there was a sharp decline in these types of events, but also some changes in the ways they happened, for example, protest car caravans replaced crowd marches. Professional events, such as conventions and conferences, also provide opportunities for public displays of resistance. During the 2016 APA Convention in Denver, Colorado, students organized the Black Lives Matter rally and invited psychologists, students, and elected officials to speak and brought media attention (Winerman, 2016).

In the month prior to the 2024 American Counseling Association conference in New Orleans, Louisiana, an email was sent to presenters who were listed in the conference program as presenting on topics related to "decolonizing therapy, refugee and immigrants counseling, racism, diversity, or social justice" and stated, "These topics are remarkably important to the counseling field, but there is a bitterness to seeing them on the schedule while the ACA fails to publicly condemn the violence unfolding in Palestine." The authors, Concerned Mental Health Professionals, called for presenters and attendees to express solidarity by withdrawing their presentation, boycotting the conference, and sharing their actions on social media or, if continuing with the presentation, including a statement in solidarity that "acknowledges the genocide in Gaza, contextualizes it as a decolonization and social justice issue, and calls on the ACA to do the same." One of the recipients shared the email on CESNET (a counselor education listserv of the Counselor Education and Supervision network, along with a summary of the ethical principles of ACA.

For some people, rallies and large public displays of resistance can feel empowering and energizing and provide a sense of solidarity. These events can also come with challenges, including accessibility, unexpected opposition, and threats to safety. Engaging effectively, safely, and with cultural humility requires some preparation. For example, in the event that a demonstration might become chaotic with police presence, safety precautions might include wearing sunglasses and masks (also good for COVID protection), carrying a cellphone with disabled location services, carrying your health insurance card, writing an emergency contact on your arm in semipermanent ink, bringing water and snacks, leaving most valuables at home, etc. For more helpful hints, see Amnesty International's guide for preparing to participate in demonstrations, "Protect the Protest" (n.d.). The Virtual Knowledge Centre to End Violence against Women and Girls (http://www.endvawnow.org), and the American Civil Liberties Union (n.d.) also provide tips regarding your free speech rights while participating in demonstrations. These are especially important as the current US administration is attempting to discourage public displays of resistance that oppose their agenda.

In addition to direct action, a well-organized public display of resistance includes forethought about how to help participants heal and rejuvenate after taking action. Dr. Leah Rouse, a counseling psychologist, shares how elders in her tribal community redirected her energies during the protests at Standing Rock.

> People had really been harmed, physically harmed, spiritually harmed, and certainly emotionally harmed … It was also one of the most difficult things I ever had to do. Because the spiritual community was very clear. The older people, even if you're a licensed psychologist, told me, that wasn't my role to be out there, that was the young people's. So my role was to be there when they come home and to support their family while they're gone. And that was really difficult for me, but I know it was what I was supposed to be doing. And it was really important that there was someone there clinically, but also as an advocate for families … who could help connect them and provide resources, and recommendations, and food for thought. "When you go to court, you might want to consider this" and, you know, that kind of thing. (Toporek & Ahluwalia, 2019)

The *Healing in Action* toolkit from Black Lives Matter (n.d.) also suggests that an important part of organizing includes reaching out to healers in the community who may be willing to provide support during or after actions. Healers who are willing to coordinate other folks from their network can be extremely helpful, especially when public action is large scale and requires intense emotional and/or physical engagement. Some examples of services include counselors on-site or on call, food drop offs, legal support, medical support, acupuncture, massage, foot care, and others.

Community Events

Bringing people together for joy, mutual empowerment, and sharing resources can be a powerful contribution to solidarity, as well as building coalitions or preparing for public demonstrations. Some examples include fundraisers, celebrations, art or sign-making events, teach-ins, community gatherings, and more. When organizing a community event, the process of determining who should be involved as leaders, planners, and decision-makers is critical. This may be easier if you are a part of the community. If you are not, the principle of solidarity resurfaces again as communities who care about the issue and those most impacted should be important contributors as planners, consultants, and participants. Assessing and appreciating the range of skills, strengths, interests, assets, and resources people bring to the table is essential, as is being sensitive to their capacity and the impact of the issue on them (e.g., such as whether they have experienced, or are currently experiencing, trauma related to the issue). Guidance for planning events, including those focused on social action, is provided by the *Youth Activist Toolkit* (Gasch & Reticker-Flynn, n.d.), Beautiful Trouble (https://beautifultrouble.org), Virtual Knowledge Centre to End Violence against Women and Girls (2012), and the Community Toolbox (KU Center for Community Health and Development, n.d.-b).

Art as Resistance

Art can send a message, provoke feelings, and make the invisible visible in ways that words do not. The process of making resistance art can also function to bring people together, build solidarity, and provide a platform for people who are most impacted by an issue to raise awareness and amplify excluded voices. For example, the land rematriation efforts mentioned earlier in this chapter included persistently painting (and repainting) a mural on the city street in front of the parking lot that was under dispute between the owner and Land Back activists (the city gave approval). Murals have been used extensively to bring communities together to express their concerns, love, and pain. Like many other urban communities, the San Francisco Bay Area is home to incredible murals that portray resilience and resistance. The Mission District, a historically Latine community in San Francisco, is well known for murals and their place in activism, as well as the dramatic threat to this community through gentrification and economic inequity (Flores, 2017).

Across the bay, the Oakland Super Heroes Mural Project is a development effort by Attitudinal Healing Connection that "cultivates, educates and engages youth in community issues and solutions through the power of public art" (**Center for ArtEsteem, n.d.**). This project engages community artists and youth to envision a vibrant community beyond the violence that is prevalent there.

Like murals, photovoice projects also provide venues for individuals and communities to document their reality and share it. Louvenia Jackson, a licensed MFT and registered, board-certified art therapist, initiated a photovoice project in the youth detention facility where she worked. Many of the youth felt discarded, ostracized, unwanted, and unseen. The facility, and its youth were stigmatized by other staff and the community at large. As both a clinical intervention and organizational change response, she engaged the youth in a collaborative photovoice project where the youth chose to take photos that represented who they were and how they wanted to be seen by others. Using those photos, she and the youth created an exhibit that was shared with the community and staff to tell a different story and change how the youth and this specific facility were viewed (L. Jackson, personal communication, January 5, 2023).

Documentary making can also be a powerful way of raising awareness about an issue and guiding viewers to take action. As one example, check out the documentary entitled "DREAMless" that Bryan and his partner Dr. Darien Combs (another counseling psychologist) created in 2017 while they were doctoral students, featuring the experience of being undocumented in the United States: https://vimeo.com/221658847. Documentaries such as these can be shared and used in a wide range of strategies, including community education, building solidarity and support, affirming the experiences of other undocumented community members, and providing powerful messages that can be used for legislation, funding, and other purposes.

Art as activism can also be heard through spoken word, poetry, song, storytelling, theater, and performance art. *Theater of the Oppressed* is an approach developed by Augusto Boal in Brazil in the 1970s as a method for people to engage with the theater process in a way that facilitates them in critically analyzing the oppressive structures and systems that impact their lives, and then envisioning a desired future. Based on the work of a number of other scholars, educators, and community organizers, most notably Paulo Freire, this approach is meant to subvert and make visible the systems that shape and constrain communities that are harmed by forces such as poverty, oppression, discrimination, unemployment, and other results of inequity. The process of engaging in the theater is meant to draw spectators into action, to help them to see how they are also affected by these forces, and to encourage them to become active in addressing issues that are important to them as well as the powers that shape their life.

A number of artists share their perspectives on the use of spoken art as resistance. Marcus Ellsworth, a spoken word artist, described in a TED talk the power of art in activism to bring people together and raise awareness (Ellsworth, 2014). Marquese McFerguson, in his TED Talk on art, social change, and uncomfortable conversations, describes the power of storytelling to help people shift their perspective and better understand experiences of people who are different from themselves. He emphasizes the power of storytelling in building bridges and leading to being better allies (McFerguson, 2016).

There are thousands of examples of art as activism globally that have impacted social change. Some of these can be seen in the Design Museum's 2018 exhibit, "Hope to Nope: Graphics and Politics 2008–2018," which chronicles resistance art globally (https://designmuseum.org/exhibitions/hope-to-nope-graphics-and-politics-2008-18).

For our next activity, look beyond the sources listed above and find inspiration through activist art to help communicate about issues you care about.

ACTIVITY 10.6

Discovering the Art of Activism

Option 1: Find three pieces of art (visual, spoken, or performance) that relate to one of the issues you prioritized. Examine each piece with the following questions:

1. How do you feel when you sit with this piece? How might others feel?

2. What is the message the artist is trying to share?

3. What is the desired outcome of the piece?

4. How might this piece move someone to take action?

Option 2: Create a poster or poem regarding your issue to inform or activate. Consider how your piece can tap into the viewer's emotion (or listener's) to trigger action or thought. What is the central message or feeling you want them to take away? What do you want them to do with that feeling, message, and activation?

Working for Systems Level Change in Your Local Work Arena or Organization

> We are trying to alter the destiny of Higher Education in this country ... and I feel it is about time that the power structure in this country gets off this gun smoke game and comes to grips with the changing order of the times. (White, 1969)

This quote is taken from a 1968 television interview with Dr. White while he was an administrator on the San Francisco State University campus during a 5-months protest by Black students and supporters. As one of only a few Black faculty on campus at the time, he was vocal in supporting student activism and challenging his own campus, particularly around diminished funding for students of color and the statewide equal opportunity program. We chose this quote from Dr. White because, although the statement was in reaction to his institution's lack of responsiveness, it highlights the connection between social action in the work arena and larger scale impact.

The strategies described early in this chapter are largely framed as public action yet can also be effective in our work systems. When we think of our responsibility to address injustice from within the systems we work, Paul Kivel's (2012) discussion of the "buffer zone" is a powerful frame. Kivel asserts that we (social services, education, and policing) are funded and supported specifically to maintain the status quo and maintain distance between the very wealthy and the large portion of the population without access to the majority of the wealth. Most of us did not become helping professionals for this purpose, so challenging systems is critical. As an agent for change working within the systems that employ us, we have unique access and power to make change. In many ways, we are insiders in the system. Because we are paid by this system, the consequences we face may be more direct for challenging that system—magnified for some of us given power, intersectionality, and historical legacy of white supremacy in our organizations and systems. For those of us who experience oppression within the workplace, especially historical oppression based on identity discrimination, speaking up and taking action may take a different form than for those of us who represent identities that have historically held power. Forming alliances where people have a range of roles and vulnerability to consequences can help deal with those disparities while continuing to work toward change. It's worth taking time to explore what this might mean for you and how you can apply what you've learned so far.

For this next activity, we'd like you to think about an issue that presents itself and/ or where you would consider (or are already) taking action in your workplace, organization, or work arena. If you are in private practice, this could be local, state, or national organizations or policies. Reflecting on strength and solidarity is an important frame for our conversation about strategies for social action in your workplace or adjacent organizations.

ACTIVITY 10.7

A Reflective Frame for Taking Action in Your Organization or Work Arena

For this activity, choose one issue or concern within your organization or work arena then consider the following questions:

1. What is the issue within your workplace and who does it affect?

2. What is your paid job and your role? In what type of organization or system does the issue exist?

3. How are you included or excluded from decision-making, voluntarily or involuntarily? Are there ways you can change that?

4. What are your strengths?

    a. Professional expertise

    b. Personal strengths

    c. Assets (access to resources, power within the organization, etc.)

5. Who are you connected to, and how are you connected?

    a. Who cares about this issue (both inside and outside the system)?

    b. Who holds positions of power, and what have they done related to this issue?

    c. Who is (or has) worked on addressing this issue, and what did they do (or are they doing)?

    d. What's your role in all this?

    e. Who can support you or join you in action?

6. What are some strategies you might use to address this issue?

7. What strategies have the best potential for positive outcomes and minimal negative consequences?

8. What ways can you prepare or minimize the impact of those consequences?

9. Where can you build in joy and a sense of community within your work arena (or outside)?

EXAMPLE

Muninder's Experiences Working Within Organizations

As professors, many of us work toward systemic change to try to make our workplace more socially just. I have worked within organizations on issues of Islamophobia, racism, and power differentials. For example, in our college, I worked with staff and faculty who were interested in working on issues of race and racism. Together, we brought light to the ways in which racism is embedded in our system, and we were committed to enact change. We organized large-scale activities that engaged everyone and small-scale events that brought together smaller groups of staff, faculty, students, and administrators to address ways in which racism was problematizing certain processes. For example, we worked on issues related to faculty of color retention and differential rates of tenure and promotions compared to white faculty; faculty encountering racism with the Institutional Review Board when they submitted their research with racial and minoritized ethnic groups; and microaggressions against women of color staff.

The strategies you choose should be influenced by what you know about the issue, who is involved, what has been tried, and the change you and your community wants to see. Some strategies may be more appropriate for gradual long-term systems change, whereas other strategies may be immediate responses to incidents or decisions. The strategies and skills described in the ACA Advocacy Competencies (Lewis et al., 2002; Toporek & Daniels, 2018) for community collaboration and systems advocacy are worth reviewing and thinking about how they relate to your role as a change agent and insider.

There are more examples of helping professionals who have worked toward change within their organizations than we can talk about here. Instead, we will briefly list a few and describe some of the strategies used. As you look through these, notice the range of different approaches and consider your own organization.

Issue	Strategies
Political violence, mass atrocities, and genocide internationally, for example, in Gaza, Sudan and the Ukraine. Students' call for faculty and the institution to make a formal statement and take action	• Meeting with students and faculty to hear their perspectives on the issue • Researching a range of diverse news sources to understand the history and current context • Investigating institution's policies regarding formal statements (e.g., can it come from the department, does it have to be from individual faculty members, etc.) • Considering possible consequences for different courses of action interpersonally, institutionally, legally, etc., including consequences to different communities on campus (e.g., Palestinian and Jewish faculty and students) • Reaching out to other academic departments, and/or counselor education or psychology programs that may have written similar statements • Collectively deciding whether and what to write, as well as any additional action that might be outlined
Layoffs and program cuts disproportionately affecting students and employees of color in a community college	• Organizing staff, faculty and students for teach-ins and demonstrations • Letter writing campaigns and appearances at administrative offices and trustee meetings • Writing letters to the editor in the city paper • Emailing community members • Collaborating with the union and academic senate • Researching and providing statements regarding impact of decisions on success and retention of students of color
Agency policies regarding session limits	• Identifying where the policy originates and identifying where the agency has wiggle room vs. outside funder policies • Sharing with clients "know your rights" information about services they have access to as well as appeals processes
Limited cultural and linguistic awareness of staff and administrators in an agency	• Establishing a staff biweekly bilingual reading and reflection group • Advocating for agency self-study on how it is meeting needs of bilingual clients and communities • Sharing research regarding the efficacy of linguistically and culturally appropriate services • Ensuring that contributions to reports accurately reflect agency reality
Disparities in tenure and promotion rates for faculty of color in a university	• Raising the issue with academic senate, union, and administrators • Using, or conducting, research illustrating this issue beyond the institution and within the institution • Identifying points of intervention (e.g., problematic student evaluation instruments and processes, tenure and promotion policies, bias in tenure and promotion process) • Raising awareness about unpaid labor by faculty of color (e.g., higher advising loads, expectations for additional service related to diversity)
Burnout, retention issues, high caseloads with insufficient time for follow-up and necessary paperwork, and unsafe therapist-to-client ratios in large healthcare institution	• Raising issue with administration • If working conditions don't change, union intervention (for example, see Kaiser mental health worker's strike [Green, 2022])

Being a force for justice within the systems that we rely on for our economic survival is tough, with possible negative consequences, and we usually do it on top of our regular workload. For some of us, there is already a lot of uncompensated labor given our positionality and the needs of the communities we are serving. When we do this work alone, we are more vulnerable to the consequences, to burnout, and to tunnel vision. Solidarity within your organization (i.e., allies, coconspirators, and accomplices) as well as outside your organization is essential. In Chapter 4, Rebecca shared action that she and her colleagues took in response to discrimination on her campus that not only involved the 10 to 15 faculty and staff who signed on to the action, but also included reaching out and receiving support from the NAACP and ACLU. One area for social action within one's organization is to advocate and participate in creating systems of transparency for how your organization will respond to or support an employees' social action. Although the response may vary considerably depending on the situation, knowing what is in place (e.g., legal counsel, protocol for who would be involved to support, what boundaries are expected of the employee) can be very helpful for organizational change as well as acting as an individual. The National Center for Institutional Diversity at the University of Michigan has been doing some great work to help faculty and institutions create better structures and plans for responding. The panel discussion *Envisioning Institutional Responses to Supporting Scholar Safety* presents a powerful discussion from faculty who have been targeted because of their work as well as administrators navigating better systems for responding (National Center for Institutional Diversity, 2023).

Individual and Interpersonal Level

At the most intimate level of the ecological framework is the individual and interpersonal level of action. Individual acts of injustice include exclusion from services, mistreatment, harassment, hostile or derogatory language or behavior (including "humor"), and other examples where someone uses their power over another in an unjust way. There are so many individual acts of injustice that we can't possibly address them all here. Although they are individual acts, they are rooted in larger systems of oppression. In Chapter 3 and Chapter 8, we explored individual level identity-based injustice at the personal level. In this section, we touch on it again within the context of action and spend more time focused on strategies related to overt hostility and harassment.

Before going forward, we'd like you to take a moment to bring awareness to your emotional, physical, and cognitive experience.

FIGURE 10.2 Your body, mind, heart and spirit

ACTIVITY 10.8

How Do You Feel?

Identify a situation where you were struck by inequity or an injustice you observed or experienced related to your workplace. As you consider the following questions, it may be helpful to refer back to some of the activities from Chapter 3 about intersectionality and identity as well as the section on positionality in Chapter 8.

Awareness

1. Close your eyes and reach inside to bring awareness to your physical, emotional, and cognitive self. Open your eyes and write or draw on the head, heart, body, or sun (spirit) in the figure above (or on a separate paper) as you bring your awareness to the surface.

    a. When you think about the situation you identified, what do you feel in your body (e.g., your stomach, your shoulders, your chest, your jaw)? Are you experiencing an urge to fight, flee, or freeze? How is your breathing?
    b. What emotions are you aware of (e.g., anger, fear, frustration, anxiousness, indignation, despair, nothing)?
    c. What thoughts are going through your mind?

2. Now, try to answer the following questions:

    a. What experiences have you had in the past that shape how you perceive or experience this situation?

    b. Have you, or others you love, experienced trauma, hurt, harm, and pain in situations similar to this?

    c. What biases might you hold about the situation or people involved?

    d. What feelings do you have about intervening?

    e. How does your experience or your biases influence your understanding of the situation?

Take a minute to reflect on your responses to these questions and reflect on Dr. Joseph White's wisdom (shared at the end of the last chapter) about processing your emotions before moving to action.

Knowledge

With clarity in your heart and mind, let's continue to focus on the issue you identified in Activity 10.7 and shift from awareness of yourself in relation to the situation to knowledge about the specific situation you are encountering.

1. What do you know about the situation, including background or history, the immediate context, and possible outcomes.

2. How much do you know about what is happening?

3. What is the historical context for what is happening now? Who is involved, directly or indirectly? How much do you need to know?

Awareness, skills, and knowledge lead to us being more effective in the third part of individual action, strategy and intervention.

PAUSE

The work you have done just now can bring up a lot of feelings. Before moving on to the next section, we would like you to pause. Take the next 10 minutes to put the book down and engage in self-care. Perhaps you take this time to grab a snack, go outside, watch a funny video, or simply sit with yourself and take deep breaths. Whatever feels comfortable for you, take these next 10 minutes to take some time for yourself. We promise we'll be here waiting for you the moment you are done.

IMG 10.1

Acting at an Individual Level as Helping Professionals

In addition to working toward organizational change that will benefit the clients and communities we serve, we often encounter specific client situations where advocacy or strategic action is necessary. At this point, you may want to take a quick break and do a little investigation into your own field. Perhaps review the work you did in relation to the code of ethics for your field in Chapter 4. Are there any guidelines or resources that can help you navigate social action addressing individual level concerns? For example, in Chapter 9, we talked about the ACA competencies model (Lewis et al., 2002; Toporek & Daniels, 2018). That model identifies two individual level advocacy domains for counselors: client empowerment and client advocacy.

Client empowerment includes strategies related to collaborating with the client to support them as they self-advocate. This might include helping them to understand their rights, recognize their strengths and capabilities to address injustice, practice taking action on their own or their loved one's behalf, facilitate them in connecting with other supportive identity based communities, and more. Alternatively, client advocacy is action that a counselor takes on behalf of their client. In the ACA advocacy competencies model, this is listed as an individual level intervention because it is in response to an individual client situation. Advocacy on behalf of the client may happen simultaneously with client empowerment (i.e., the client advocates for themselves in the ways they have access to while the counselor also advocates within the arenas they have access to). Client advocacy may also be important when the client is unable to advocate on their own behalf. For example, when a client doesn't have the language or cognitive capacity for self-advocacy or doesn't feel safe in self-advocacy. This may also be appropriate in situations where the client does not have access to places where advocacy can take place (e.g., staff meetings or case conferences). It is best, even in these situations, to find a way for the client's voice to be heard. The advocacy competencies model suggests that advocacy is best when multiple domains are used simultaneously.

The opportunities we make for advocacy are influenced by the situation, as well as our position within that situation. In the example below, one of our colleagues (who prefers to remain anonymous) talks about the delicate line she walks in her workplace as a "double agent." Her experience and position as a Black female school counselor supporting students within an oppressive system can have sharp consequences if she directly confronts the system.

EXAMPLE

Hearing from "Jordan"—Experience as a School Counselor Court School Settings

[The carceral school setting] is a cross-agency operation involving the court system, school system, and other providers as co-agents in maintaining the coloniality of power [in the school to prison pipeline] … In my role as the school counselor, I am uniquely positioned to act as a double agent in the system. Hence, I engage in systems advocacy, with a cultural emphasis that embraces my intentional role as a middle leadership school counselor to ultimately assist students by providing sustainable agency outside of the criminal justice system … The social justice principles of access, equity, and human rights are daily double-agent areas of action in the carceral school setting. As a school counselor/advocate, I operate quietly, similar to a ninja, without creating personal conflict or white supremacy attacks in my role as a double agent. It requires a mindset of professionalism, cultural humility, and balance, which in the end creates positive change for students who are impacted by the school to prison pipeline.

Acting at an Individual or Interpersonal Level in Your Community

There are multiple ways we engage in social action at an individual level. The example earlier about Rebecca distributing the Red Cards regarding immigrant rights to her community members is one form of action. Many of the strategies shared earlier in this chapter can apply to individual and interpersonal social action in terms of developing relationships, supporting others, facilitating discussion, creating art, and more. Other situations may involve injustices we observe at an individual level in our daily life. In this section of the chapter, we will focus on individual and interpersonal challenges and discuss possible ways of responding.

Lack of Awareness, Differing Perspectives and Microaggressions

Opportunities for individual and interpersonal action arise throughout our daily lives, with people in our community, colleagues, family members, students, clients, and more. Although we don't have space to talk about all of the considerations and strategies for having difficult conversations, we will touch on a few things briefly.

Over the past several decades, polarization has increased across political parties, within families, and in communities. With social media and fragmentation of information, disinformation and misinformation, many of us struggle to communicate with those who embrace a reality that does not reflect our own. Further, the climate in the U.S. and across the globe has seen a resurgence of openly White supremacist, anti-immigration, anti-trans and LGBQA+

rhetoric. Although much of this rhetoric is extreme, there are those in our communities who are struggling with their conflicted views. For some of us, one of the ways we can engage in social action is to have those difficult conversations to find common ground, raise awareness and rekindle a sense of compassion, empathy and understanding about the harms that marginalized and targeted communities face. There are many resources that can be helpful for those of us who chose to engage in these difficult conversations (e.g., Israel, 2020; Nam, 2023). There are a plethora of resources and organizations working to bring people together who have very different political, social, and religious beliefs. Yet, when our identities and people we love are being threatened or disrespected, those conversations are complicated and sometimes harmful. Everyone needs to make the choice about how and when to engage. As we noted earlier, given our identities and lived experience, the costs and benefits of engaging in these conversations vary especially when microaggressions (and outright aggression) are part of the dynamic.

"Microaggression" and related terms are used when the act of aggression is subtle (such as ignoring or making stereotypical assumptions based on race, gender, disability, or other identities). We will refer to actions that are more visible and aggressive as overt hostility and harassment (such as racial slurs). Whether microaggression or overt hostility, the impact we feel varies depending on whether it is targeting us or someone we love, what similar experiences we've had before, and the power and relationship we have with the person violating us. Sometimes the impact feels different depending on the intent of the aggression. In Chapter 8, Solidarity, we presented you with two workplace scenarios of microaggressions and asked you to consider how you might respond given the framework of microaggressions (Sue, 2010) and microinterventions (Sue et al., 2019). These two scenarios illustrated the impact of microaggressions and discrimination. Overt hostility, harassment, and verbal, emotional or physical violence often require a different kind of response.

Overt Hostility and Harassment

Whether and how we take action in the face of overt hostility and harassment often depends on the circumstances, our positionality, and our resources. When we observe someone being targeted, we have choices about how to respond either by intervening or witnessing. This choice needs to be made thoughtfully with awareness of the situation so that we understand the level of danger and choose whether and how to become involved. Thinking through how we might respond ahead of time, before situations arise, allows us to think more clearly and act more quickly when we are in the situation, as well as to proactively develop skills and knowledge that can help us respond more effectively.

The central intention of taking action as an accomplice or witness of harassment is practical—to support the person being harassed and help preserve their safety as well as your own. Ultimately, intervening in harassment situations also demonstrates a commitment to your values. There are great resources to help us think through and prepare for these roles. Right To Be (n.d.) describes five methods for supporting someone who is being targeted with physical or verbal threats: (a) direct, (b) distract, (c) delegate, (d) delay, and (e) document. Their training resources illustrate specific actions and provide guidance for making decisions about what type of action might be best, given the situation and context. Right To Be also provides a space for people to share their stories of harassment and intervention as well as offering free workshops for the public at https://righttobe.org/what-we-do/.

The increased attention to incidents of police and other public officials harassing and using unnecessary force has also resulted in more resources for reporting, witnessing, and documenting such incidents. Organizations such as CopWatch (https://www.berkeleycopwatch.org; http://wecopwatch.org) provide training about community members' rights, how to be an effective observer and witness, and how to document what you notice. Until just recently, Mobile Justice CA, an app that was offered free from the ACLU, allowed a cell phone user to record and upload interactions with law enforcement to local ACLU representatives in real time. The advantage of this tool was that the record of the incident was no longer only held on an individual's cell phone, which would be vulnerable if the phone is seized, for example during a protest. Unfortunately, in February 2025, the ACLU announced that they would be discontinuing the app to "ensure compliance with a growing number of consumer privacy laws and the ACLU's own privacy policies and to minimize risk with surveillance technologies currently used by law enforcement" (ACLU, 2025). More information about this decision and links to other resources can be found at https://www.aclu.org/mobilejustice.

In addition to monitoring community policing, airport security is another area where individuals have found a way to respond to bias and incidents of harassment. FlyRights tool, an app developed by the Sikh Coalition in 2012, allows travelers to complete a brief survey and report experiences of being profiled or harassed while traveling, especially in encounters with airport security. These reports are automatically sent as official complaints directly to TSA. See Sikh Coalition (2021) for more information.

For additional examples of guidelines and bystander training be sure to check out Southern Poverty Law Center (2017b), New Tactics in Human Rights (2012), and Resolution Northwest (n.d.). These resources can also be helpful if you are the one being harassed or threatened. Although most of the aggressive or hostile responses to our social action happens online, there are situations where it hits closer to home or our workplace. As you engage in social action, an important part of planning ahead is to know the local and online resources that can help.

Online Harassment and Aggression

Online harassment is increasingly problematic and according to a 2017 study by the Pew Research Center, 66% of US adults have observed harassing behavior toward others online and 40% reported being the target of online hostility (Duggan, 2017). This type of harassment and bullying is difficult to address, particularly because law enforcement has limited understanding of this as a problem and may minimize it. Further, because laws are generally defined state by state, but online activity is global, there is often a lack of concrete legal action available. As we mentioned earlier, the two largest social media conglomerates (X and Meta) have rolled back their protections for harassment and online aggression. Holding them accountable for this is one way to address harassment. More immediate situations may come up as well: confronting aggression you observe aimed at others (whole groups or individuals) and dealing with harassment and aggression directed at you. There are several great resources that you can use for both of these situations. The National Sexual Violence Resource Center provides key resources for digital and online safety that are very useful for anyone trying to maintain their own safety and are especially useful for survivors of sexual abuse (Heinze, 2022). PEN America's "Online Harassment Field Manual" provides guidance for situations where the reader is directly being targeted, where they are a witness or ally, and guidance for employers (https://onlineharassmentfieldmanual.pen.org). Other guide, created for writers and journalists, Brown et al. (2021)

and Ray et al. (2021) provide useful discussions about responding to cyberbullying and racism in social media including strategies for bystander intervention. What happens online can, although rarely, result in a cross over to your physical location. Doxing is the term used when your private information has been breached including your phone number, address, etc. The resources above provide guidance about how to minimize this threat and how to respond if it does happen. One of the most important strategies is to reach out and maintain your connection to healthy support and community. We are in this together!

Using What You've Learned for Strategic Action

Before we close our reflections on strategies, we'd like you to take a few minutes to explore one of the issues where you would like to take action or strengthen your action.

ACTIVITY 10.9

Review and Reflection

Take a minute to think about the issue you identified early in this workbook.

1. What are your goals (or your community's goals)?

2. What are your strengths and assets?

3. What does, or would, solidarity look like?

4. What strategies are already being used to address your issue? Which strategies are you already involved in?

5. Which strategies make the most of your skills and strengths?

6. What are some of the benefits, costs, and potential consequences of different strategies for addressing your issue?

7. If you anticipate challenges or consequences, how might you prepare for that?

This reflection will be helpful to you in Chapter 12 when you create a more detailed action plan. A quote from Ed Roberts, the great disability rights activist, comes to mind as we begin to close our discussion of evaluating strategies, consequences, and potential change.

> And when there's maximum danger, and when our programs are in the most jeopardy, there's also maximum opportunity. To make changes in them, to fight for what we know we need, to make them more responsible for the needs of our people too. Let's take advantage of that. Let's figure out some alternatives. Let's not just be naysayers. (University of Kansas Research and Training Center on Independent Living, 2003)

Closing

Although we have taken a how-to approach throughout this chapter on strategies, one of the biggest challenges we often face is how to sustain our energy, commitment, and ourselves as we fight for justice. Taking action has so many benefits—a sense of agency, living with integrity and solidarity, using our strengths with purpose—and it is also hard. Large scale change is slow and can be exhausting. We also may be the target of those who don't want positive change and will aggressively attempt to block our work, sometimes in ways that are toxic, threatening, and hostile. We have provided strategies for addressing some of directly and now we want to shift our focus to attending to your wellness. Sustainability, the fourth S, is a critical area of reflection and one that we often take for granted. This will be the focus of the next chapter.

Figure Credit

Chapter 11

Sustainability

Self-Care, Ensuring Resilience, and Preventing Burnout

FIGURE 11.1 S-Quad image

"Caring for myself is not self-indulgence, it is self-preservation and that is an act of political warfare."

—Audre Lorde

The term "self-care" has become synonymous with indulgence of self in the face of tiredness or overwork. It is often, but not always, a material reward, such as eating a special treat, playing video games, going to a movie, getting one's nails done, or going shopping. While these types of activities may feel like a break, Lorde is referring to the deepest sense of care for ourselves and our communities. For her, as a queer Black woman, self-care was about preserving herself as she engaged with systems of oppression. Here we consider self-care to be about social justice action and the sustainability of social change.

Thus far, we have discussed and worked through the first three S's in this book: strength, solidarity, and strategies, but we have yet to discuss how the movement continues—how **we** move forward in our work, how **the community** moves forward, and how **the work** moves forward, with or without us. We use the term "sustainability" to capture maintaining movement while maintaining health for ourselves and our communities in the process. Remember in previous chapters that we suggested you step back, breathe, and take note of how you are feeling? This is an example of sustainability—taking the time away to be able to continue to devote time to the work and maintain perspective.

Merriam-Webster (n.d.-b) describes the essential meaning of "sustainable" in the following three ways:

1. "able to be used without being completely used up or destroyed" (*sustainable* energy resources, a *sustainable* water supply);

2. "involving methods that do not completely use up or destroy natural resources" (*sustainable* agriculture/farming/techniques);
3. "able to last or continue for a long time" (*sustainable* development/growth).

Although Merriam-Webster isn't directly speaking of social justice work when defining sustainability, the definition fits well. We want to use ourselves to forward the work, and we want the work to continue for a long time—all without destroying us or wearing ourselves out. We'd like to go a step further and look at how different aspects of the definition can be applied to social justice (see Table 11.1).

TABLE 11.1 Sustainability Definitions and Social Justice

Aspects of Sustainability	Dictionary Definition	Dictionary Examples	Social Action Examples
Resources are plentiful	Able to be used without being completely used up or destroyed	*Sustainable* energy resources, a *sustainable* water supply	Restorative practice for the individual
Methods are healthy	Involves methods that do not completely use up or destroy natural resources	*Sustainable* agriculture/ farming/ techniques	Relationships with community are in healthy solidarity
Engagement lasts	Able to last or continue for a long time	*Sustainable* development/ growth	The work continues with or without the individual

(Merriam-Webster, n.d.-b, para. 1)

We have talked about the importance of people and relationships throughout our discussions on solidarity, strength, and strategy. Sustainability has a nuanced difference. For example, a central goal of solidarity is to do the work *right* (in solidarity with others), whereas sustainability is about healthy *continuity* of the person, their relationships, the work, and the communities they serve and fight for. It is all connected, and for many of us, being in solidarity with others is an important part of our sustainability.

Positionality and What It Means for Sustainability

Most systems don't encourage or provide support and resources for sustainability practices. The schools, colleges, and universities we train within are about productivity and seeking excellence, sometimes at any cost. Mental health organizations may talk about self-care, but these same facilities are understaffed, with heavy workloads helping clients and students with trauma-filled lives. If self-care is discussed, it is often about what works for dominant groups—not what works for marginalized populations. Even then it is not a practice embedded in the work. In fact, some systems may present barriers to sustainability of minoritized groups with inequitable workloads, hostile environments, lack of support, and more.

Positionality

To discuss sustainability in a meaningful way, we believe it is important to root ourselves in our own positionality. Reflect back to what you know about us as authors. You can see that we have differing identities and positionalities. We come from different communities and, in turn, have different ideas about how to engage in self-care. Consider what self-care or renewal looks like in the different communities you are part of (e.g., personal, helping profession). How do those practices relate to what you do for self-care?

PAUSE FOR A MINDFULNESS BREAK

Before moving on to the next activities, we would like you to pause a moment. Take a few minutes to put the book down and engage in self-care. Sit with yourself and take deep breaths. Whatever feels comfortable for you, take these moments to center yourself.

Prioritizing Self-Care

Reflecting on personal values and priorities is generally encouraged in the training that helping professionals receive. Yet, the way we actually use our resources (e.g., time, energy, money) may not reflect these priorities for a variety of reasons. The key to sustainability is to consider not only what our priorities are, but also whether we spend our resources including those activities and people who sustain and renew us. This way we can live with intentionality, consciously aligning our actions with the priorities that restore and fulfill us.

ACTIVITY 11.1

Prioritizing

Make a list of your priorities by answering the following questions:

1. What different aspects of my life are important to me?

2. What do I love to do?

3. To what extent are my priorities actualized in my life?

4. Do I show up on the list of my own priorities? If so, how? If not, why not?

Next, draw a circle and create a pie chart. What takes up the most time? What takes the least, and what is not even on the chart in terms of time spent?

1. Now reimagine and draw an ideal pie chart.

2. How can we take a mindful approach to reprioritizing our lives?

Using a SMART goal approach, set a goal for yourself to reinvest in your well-being. (Reminder: SMART is specific, measurable, achievable, realistic, and timely.)

Muninder's Priorities

Muninder loves to dance salsa and bachata, sing shabads, engage in seva, work with her students at the university, engage in social justice work, take care of her parents, do frivolous things with her friends, and spend meaningful time with her fiancée. Right now, those items may or may not be an actualized priority. And she never mentions herself directly as a priority because she thinks in terms of "we" or the relational collective and secretly thinks it is selfish (now you all know!). When she puts this on a pie chart, she is surprised that some items have very little of her time and energy dedicated toward them right now. In fact, the things that she would characterize as self-care are often overlooked in service of others. At what cost?

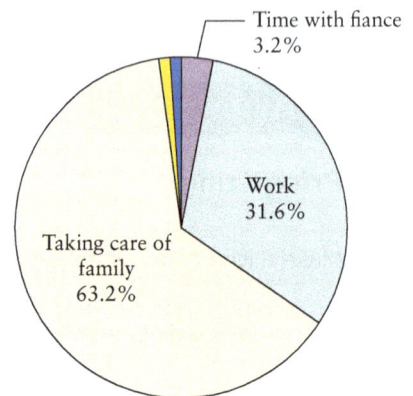

FIGURE 11.2 Muninder's pie chart of priorities

Looking at this chart is a way for Muninder, and all of us, to assess, potentially reprioritize, or reallocate our time and energy. If Muninder reimagines her pie chart, she may create bigger pieces of the pie for dancing, family, and friends. Using a SMART goals approach, she might identify a specific, measurable, attainable, relevant, timely goal such as, "I will call my best friend once per week for 30 minutes on my drive home." Where the ideal pie chart might not be attainable given life circumstances, a phone call once per week that would help refill her cup might be attainable.

Thinking Ecologically

We want you to think back to the first part of the workbook where we introduced Bronfenbrenner's (1979) ecological model. Consider how the model acknowledges the interplay between the individual, community, and societal factors. This interplay also becomes important when we think about sustainability.

Sustaining the Self Through Self-Care

Sustainability is essential to continue moving toward positive change, to thrive in the face of challenges, even to simply survive. Being engaged in action about issues we care about can be good for our health, yet that work can also challenge our health, responsibilities, and relationships. To impact issues we care about, *we* are one of the most important tools. Personal sustainability means that part of social action requires that you, your well-being, and your life, matter. Part of the social justice work that needs to be done is to keep you thriving, joyful, and effective. Personal sustainability helps us to live our lives, keep healthy, and honor our priorities, such as family, community, and spirituality. Sustainability is critical for effective social action, not just so we can be more effective in our work, but also because the harmful effects of not taking care of ourselves often result in us quitting the fight altogether—taking our potential and our contributions with us. Even worse, we may actually become harmful to others and the causes we care about when we are not doing well. These are things most of us already know, but few of us actually act on the knowledge.

In this chapter, we acknowledge the challenges of sustaining ourselves and our work, we explore what sustainability might be like in action, and we discuss ways to move forward in social action while maintaining or recovering from challenges to our well-being. In the second half of the chapter, we provide activities to help you think about and make space for your life in the midst of your social action.

Challenges of Sustaining Ourselves

There are many challenges experienced by people engaged in social action and activism. If you feel stress, anger, alarm, grief, or challenges, you are not alone! We have designed the following activity to begin to explore the current state of your well-being and sustainability needs. We will come back to this throughout the chapter to acknowledge challenges to well-being and to focus on moving toward health and wellness.

ACTIVITY 11.2

How Am I Doing?

In this activity, reflect on your beliefs and behaviors. Be honest with yourself. This is your opportunity to consider the path you're on and make adjustments that could help you stay healthy. Please know that it is ok to have seemingly conflicting emotions and actions. You will be able to use these results later when we focus on your health and wellness.

In the following questions, reflect on the past 3 months and mark an "X" in the box relating to how often this describes you. The tables below contain six different areas that affect wellness: mental (M), emotional (E), social or relational (S), physical (P), spiritual (Sp), and contextual (C).

1. **How am I doing mentally?**

	Never	Rarely	Sometimes	Often	Always
I feel overwhelmed thinking about all the ways I should be involved. (M)					
It seems like if I don't step up, no one else will. (M)					
I end up taking on more than I can really handle. (M)					
I feel that I shouldn't burden other people with my worries. (M)					
I feel distracted thinking about injustice and what I should be doing. (M)					

As you reflect on your responses above, if you notice a lot of "often" or "always" answers, attending to your wellness in terms of your thinking processes and mental energy may be helpful. Sometimes we get caught up in thought patterns that are stressful or don't allow ourselves a mental rest, sometimes not being compassionate with ourselves.

2. How am I doing emotionally?

	Never	Rarely	Sometimes	Often	Always
I feel guilty when I don't stand up for what I know is right. (E)					
I feel a level of anxiety, sadness, grief, anger, sometimes without a clear reason. (E)					
It seems like no matter what we do, we can't stop the injustice; it feels hopeless. (E)					
I get frustrated because I don't get recognized for the work I do. (E)					
I feel like so many people suffer so much that it's not right for me to feel sad, tired, or like I want a break. (E)					

As you reflect on your responses above, if you notice a lot of "often" or "always" answers, attending to your emotional health may be helpful, including giving special attention to the emotional health discussion in this chapter.

3. How am I doing socially or in my relationships?

	Never	Rarely	Sometimes	Often	Always
It seems like there are few people who care about the issues that I care about. (S)					
Other activists in my group expect too much from me. (S)					
I have trouble saying "no" when I'm working with a group. (S)					
I am torn between spending time with family or friends and engaging in activism. (S)					
When I am around other activists, I feel disconnected or disrespected. (S)					

As you reflect on your responses above, if you notice a lot of "often" or "always" answers, attending to your wellness in terms of social engagements and relationships may be helpful. Are you feeling stress or tension in your social connections and relationships related to your time or effort to address injustice?

4. How am I doing physically?

	Never	Rarely	Sometimes	Often	Always
I am physically exhausted. (P)					
I'm so busy that I don't get much exercise or take care of myself very well. (P)					

I have trouble sleeping because I am distressed or thinking about what I should do. (P)					
I overeat, drink too much, or use other drugs to deal with the stress, grief, anger. (P)					
I have physical pains (e.g., headaches, stomach aches) or get sick a lot. (P)					

As you reflect on your responses above, if you notice a lot of "often" or "always" answers, attending to your physical health may be helpful. These physical stressors may reflect general health issues or may be exacerbated by stress.

5. How am I doing spiritually?

If you clearly identify as a person who is not spiritual or religious (e.g., atheist) this section may not apply to you.

	Never	Rarely	Sometimes	Often	Always
It seems like none of it really means anything in the long run. (Sp)					
I feel like my beliefs about spirituality (or religion) are not helpful to me. (Sp)					
I feel like I'm missing something or lost and disconnected spiritually. (Sp)					
I feel like my spiritual beliefs and community are not respected or valued by others who are doing social action work. (Sp)					
I feel conflicts between my religious beliefs and the issues that come up in my social action. (Sp)					

As you reflect on your responses above, if you notice a lot of "often" or "always" answers, attending to your wellness in terms of your spiritual life may be helpful. Perhaps consider if you are feeling some discomfort, stress, or disconnection related to your spiritual or religious beliefs. Everyone has their own set of beliefs, whether belief in a higher power or belief that there is no higher power. This category refers more about how you feel about the beliefs you hold rather than the beliefs themselves.

6. What context do I live in?

	Never	Rarely	Sometimes	Often	Always
In my community or neighborhood, or in my social action circles, it seems like there are very few people who share important aspects of my identity (ethnicity, sexual orientation, etc.). (C)					
Legislation or practices prevent people from my racial group, sexual orientation, gender, ability status, religion, or other identity from having the same rights as other people. (C)					
If I speak out against injustice, I often get called "too sensitive." (C)					

There are higher rates of violence toward people like me than other groups (e.g., gender, sexual orientation, race, etc.). (C)					
There are documented hate crimes and/or discrimination against my communities/identities. (C)					

As you reflect on your responses above, if you notice a lot of "often" or "always" answers, it may be helpful to acknowledge the impact of your context on your health and wellness. You may often encounter systemic hostility in your environment or in society regarding your identity. This may, in fact, be an area where you are doing social change work. Or, it may not be. Regardless, as we discussed earlier in this workbook, sometimes just holding a targeted identity means that we may end up having to deal with situations and hostility. We end up having to choose whether to react—"did they really just say that?"—how to stay safe, and what the consequences might be for anything we do

7. **Are there any additional areas that were missed?** Where are you struggling for personal sustainability?

As you reflect on the areas above, some questions may resonate with you and others might not. This is certainly not an exhaustive list and you may have a better sense of how you are doing than what you notice here. This activity is meant to stimulate your thinking and alert you to areas that might need attention. Ultimately, the goal is to help build up our resilience and support systems in all aspects of our lives. How can you care for your community if you are not healthy?

Community Care as Part of Self-Care and Sustainability

Now, let's shift to a different sustainability question—how can you be healthy if your community is not? When we look at injustice and the trauma related to it, we can see how communities come together and take care of each other in culturally driven ways. We also see individuals do this for their community. For example, when André Leon Talley (amongst other titles, the first Black editor at Vogue) passed away in 2022, he had many designer items that he could have leveraged to leave a personal mark on fashion history. And yet, as explained in the *New York Times* article, that wasn't his goal:

> "André was very, very specific," said Alexis E. Thomas, the executor of his estate. "He left a very clear will." And that was: Sell. Sell it (almost) all. The proceeds to be split between the Abyssinian Baptist Church in Harlem and the Mt. Sinai Missionary Baptist Church in Durham, where he grew up. Communities that represented his private life, where he had been an active (and activist) member for decades, and where he marched for change alongside … "Basically what André did was monetize his fashion assets to secure the financial sustainability of two very important Black institutions of faith," said Darren Walker, the president of the Ford Foundation and a friend of Mr. Talley's since 1995. (Friedman, 2023)

The important social changes that we have seen over the past decades could not have been possible without enormous effort on the part of many people working for many years.

We often see the outcomes but not the costs, psychological and physical, that can be felt as a result of such big efforts. Despite the positive effects of collective action, activism, and other social change efforts, we may also experience exhaustion, anxiety, withdrawal, broken relationships, and burnout, among others consequences. In the next few paragraphs, we dive into what is known about burnout and risks, and then turn to explore the healthy ways we can work to maximize the benefits of our social action and minimize the "wear and tear."

Burnout

Research on activism burnout helps us understand the toll that social action can take, as well as how to prevent and recover from burnout. Additionally, helping professionals tend to be at high risk for burnout given the nature of their work. The term "burnout" was coined in the early 1970s by Herbert Freudenberger (Freudenberger & Richelson, 1980) and was expanded later as a cluster of symptoms resulting from chronic and long-term stress related to one's work (Maslach, 2003; Maslach & Jackson, 1981). According to Maslach and colleagues, an essential aspect of burnout is that the stressor is relatively unrelenting over time and has no clear resolution. We may feel the effects of burnout emotionally (e.g., numbness, sadness, anxiety, despair, etc.), mentally (e.g., mental exhaustion, thoughts of worthlessness, feelings of helplessness, etc.), physically (e.g., physical exhaustion, chronic illness, etc.), behaviorally (e.g., self-defeating behaviors, substance abuse), and motivationally (e.g., apathy, disillusionment). These effects often appear gradually so we don't recognize that it is happening until we are already suffering and unable to easily fix the problem. In fact, one of the most difficult challenges of burnout is becoming exhausted and feeling powerless or too overwhelmed to do anything about it. Sometimes we believe that it is our fault. For this reason, it is often hard for us to shift to a more positive place. For example, if you experience burnout in your job, the symptoms of burnout may make it hard for you to be energetic and confident in searching for a new job.

Burnout in activism can have a similar pattern. Ongoing stress related to the systems we are challenging, our limited ability to create immediate change, the hostility of those who oppose the work we are doing (or us individually), and the tension even within the working group can result in similar symptoms, making it difficult for us to continue as effective change agents.

A number of other forces contribute to burnout in activism, given assumptions and beliefs that sometimes go along with social justice work. For example, we may feel that we should be working tirelessly because the communities we are fighting for have faced so much; the privilege of taking a break feels selfish. It's hard to view self-care as an integral part of community care, even if it is. In addition, we may feel a constant sense of urgency and hypervigilance (always having to pay attention) because incidents of injustice arise constantly and so do opportunities to take action. It can feel overwhelming and dizzying to keep up with all of the everyday social actions, not to mention the big collective actions.

Our positionality in relation to oppression and the issues we care about is also an important factor. As conscious people of color in a racist society, there may be daily challenges to our integrity, sense of belonging, and worth. "Persistence is our resistance" is a mantra to recognize that sometimes the act of persisting is the most important thing to do, especially for people who face marginalization. For others of us, we have identities that are not targeted regularly with oppressive acts, thus we are not subjected daily to personal affronts and we have more choices about when to fight. Still, we may feel assaulted by the harm that is done to those who we love and the issues we care about. We may also feel a sense of guilt and a responsibility to work toward justice unceasingly because we are not subjected to injustice in the same way others might be. In both cases, the risk of burnout, exhaustion, and fatigue can interfere with us being able to effectively act.

Finally, activism is fraught with trolls and institutional surveillance. As we are writing this book, we see an attack on everything we are fighting for. For example, the intentional targeting of critical race theory as a framework to understand our country's oppressive systems also targets the individuals using this theory, the increasing number of states and court decisions directly harming trans individuals, censorship and erasure of truth in history, and even supreme court decisions and state legislation that threaten the right to come together in protest. As we do this work with an understanding of race and power structures, we are constantly aware of the possibility of becoming, or remaining a target.

Activist Trauma Support (https://www.activist-trauma.net/), an organization that was dedicated to helping activists recognize and recover from burnout from 2004–2014, argued that often we believe that burnout is just part of the process and the toll to be paid, but it doesn't need to be that way. They suggested that a more helpful way is to use symptoms of burnout as warning signs, alerting us to the need to step back and reflect on how we are working, how we are relating to others, and how we are caring (or not caring) for ourselves. Are we being true to the goal of justice?

Toxicity

Throughout the book we have talked a little about the ways that oppressive forces and status quo resist change and, more specifically, social action. That resistance may be directed toward us and can be overt or covert, mild or harsh. When people disagree with our beliefs, values, and action, there may be an opportunity for productive dialogue and building stronger communities. Other times, resistance can be in the form of backlash, harassment, and toxic environments. For now, we will refer to the range of negative responses that are intended to silence or threaten social action as toxicity. Throughout Chapters 9 and 10, we included some discussion and resources for preparing for, recognizing and responding to these types of threats. This toxicity can be a threat to our health, our relationships, our communities and our work. On a panel discussion about how organizations can better support faculty, Patrick Grzanka talks about his experience being targeted for his research supporting LGBTQ individuals and communities (National Center for Institutional Diversity, 2023). In the recorded session, he describes the strategies that were used to harass him, the impact on his health and well-being as well as what he found helpful and supportive. The American Association of University Professors (n.d.) also provides information and guidance for faculty who receive targeted harassment. Additionally, resources we presented in the section on burnout as well as resources we provided throughout Chapter 10 related to different social action strategies can be very helpful. For the past several years, Rebecca and her colleague, Amy Reynolds, facilitated discussions at annual conferences and invited psychologists and students to come together to talk about what resources and supports they found helpful in the face of harassment and backlash for their anti-oppression work. It was clear from those who attended that these types of toxic experiences are often very isolating and the impact is very complex. It can be powerfully healing to be in community with others who help to filter out the hate as well as to listen, validate and support the person being targeted. Burnout, toxicity, and threats to our well-being require specific strategies and resources as well as ongoing practice of sustainability.

We argue that it is unhealthy and ineffective to approach social justice work without also regularly engaging in practices that sustain you. There is danger in being "too woke to sleep" and it can be helpful to remember that all social change doesn't need to be big things all the time, there are resources to help us, and that there are other people pushing for change too. As Bryan often says, "I can be woke and still have this cup of tea" meaning we have to continue to live as we fight to maintain awareness, gain knowledge, and use our skills for social change.

Healthy Mind, Heart, Body, and Spirit: Focusing on Our Wellness

Despite the challenges of participating in social action, there is also plenty of evidence that being engaged and active around issues we care about can be good for us. Some research has shown that being involved in collective action can actually help reduce feelings of stress and other negative psychological effects felt by people who are in targeted groups. For example, in a 2014 study by DeBlaere and their colleagues, sexual minority women of color who were engaged in collective action seemed to experience lower psychological stress than those who were not. Szymanski and Owens, in their 2009 study of women of color involved in feminist collective action found that high levels of involvement seemed to buffer the negative effects of sexism. Helen Neville, the 2023 president of the Society of Counseling Psychology chose her presidential initiative to focus on "Justice and Joy" and a means of transforming healing within the context of justice and well-being (Neville, 2024).

In the next few sections, we will guide you through activities designed around your well-being, both within and beyond your social action. First, we'd like you to take a moment for a break.

PAUSE FOR A MINDFULNESS BREAK

Take a step away from the book for a moment before you come back to the next section.

Whole Body Sustainability

Working to eliminate injustice and working toward social change can challenge our health and relationships despite the positive effects noted in the research above. We will organize our discussion of some of these challenges and wellness opportunities relating to the head (your mind and mental well-being), heart (your emotional health and your relationships), body (your physical well-being), and spirit (your sense of connection to something greater than yourself or the thing that anchors you to your beliefs and values). As you explore each of these areas, we will also offer examples of the gems and resources shared by research and organizations aimed at helping to sustain us in social action.

FIGURE 11.3 Whole body sustainability

Before going on, reflect on your responses to Activity 11.2, "How Am I Doing?" and consider where you may need a little extra attention. These realms are all connected, and although we talk about each area separately, the overlap and stress in one area affects other areas. Similarly, when we care for one area, we care for all.

The Head: Our Mental Well-Being

Ideally, there is a balance between being mentally active and mentally at rest. We may find that engaging with other people who share our interests and concerns is inspiring and energizing mentally. Staying engaged with information and current events related to the issues we care about can be stimulating (especially when the news is good) and also overwhelming. Still, it is essential to give yourself a break, an opportunity to reflect or even an opportunity to let your mind get lost in something completely unrelated (e.g., watching an insect, a sunset, or a movie). Inspiration and mental stimulation can foster an engaged mind through laughter, nature, art, poetry, or any healthy activation.

FIGURE 11.4 Your head and mind

When our minds are overly engaged, especially in stressful ways, we may develop mental fatigue that can spread to physical fatigue or illness, as well as unhelpful thinking patterns. For example, mental stability is essential for our ability to maintain a clear and grounded perspective of events and distress around us. Many of the issues we care about can trigger our own distress, which can lead to difficulty recognizing and dealing with forces or actions that oppose the work we are trying to do. Sometimes we end up feeling like everything is so urgent that we have trouble prioritizing the work and think we have to work on it all the time.

A number of studies have noted common themes around mental well-being and activist sustainability. They have also shared recommendations for healthy mind and mental coping. Rosales and Davis (2023) offered the following four key practices for individuals and collectives in their discussion of the need to attend to mental health and wellness in social change efforts:

- Reimagine yourself as a member of the mental health ecosystem and build a community of mutual support.
- Honor the emotional and mental impact of the difficult realities we face.
- Provide opportunities for connection and support rooted in shared experiences.
- Foster a shared language around mental and emotional experiences to build a culture of empathy.

Further, empirical research with activists also provides useful insights. In a qualitative study of LGBTQ+ communities of color, participants cited advocacy, collective action, and community potential as community strengths (Hudson & Romanelli, 2020). Similarly, Watson et al. (2018), in a study of bisexual women's discrimination and mental health, found that resilience and collective action were positively related to psychological well-being. And Downton and Wehr (1998) found that activists who were able to learn how to manage criticism and negativity were better able to sustain their involvement. They described several strategies used to deal with critics, especially those with opposing beliefs: "They [the activists] discounted them [the critics] knowing they were based on irreconcilable differences of belief; they insulated themselves by limiting their contact with the critics; and they employed humor to remove the sting from harsh words" (p. 543). Although their study was done many years ago, the insights feel very relevant today. We want to add that it is helpful to distinguish between criticism that is malicious and disagreeable and criticism that may actually be helpful in reflecting on the approaches we have taken. When we feel healthy and stable, we are better able to hear criticism that could be helpful in assessing whether we are meeting our objectives in the best way possible and buffer ourselves from criticism that is meant to harm us.

Among different strategies for dealing with burnout, Gorski and Chen (2015) explored the usefulness of mindful techniques. In their qualitative study, participant activists described three ways they felt mindfulness was helpful. First, they shared that they were better able to find a balance between activism and self-care without blame or guilt. Second, they reported that mindfulness helped them slow down or step back to "see the big picture and letting go of the pressure to eliminate injustice instantaneously" (p. 706). Third, participants believed that mindfulness helped them manage stress and anxiety.

Mindfulness practice, rooted in Buddhist philosophy, integrates breathing with attention to the present moment and release from judgment and preoccupation. There are many different forms and guides for using mindfulness, some of which are applied in everyday activities such as walking meditation, eating meditation, or sitting meditation. Interestingly, the activists that Gorski and Chen (2015) interviewed also described several ways that their mindfulness practice improved the effectiveness of their activism. It helped them "become clearer and more thoughtful—more mindful—about their activism" (p. 709); better able to integrate a peaceful nonviolent approach to their work; and able to maintain a greater sense of compassion for others.

Quieting one's mind is one way to provide space and time for mental rejuvenation. Before going on, we want to acknowledge the centuries of cultural and religious practices related to meditation and mindfulness that have become widely used, often in ways that have resulted in appropriation and colonization of the practice. We offer the following guided meditation along with our thanks and gratitude for the mindfulness teachings that have been built through centuries of knowledge and oppression. Some of us may be really good at finding a quiet mind and already use practices regularly to help us. Some of us may be able to do that well when we aren't stressed or distressed, but when we feel stressed or upset, our minds may replay scenarios, prepare for difficult conversations over and over, or just continue to plan and dwell on things that are hard. Activity 11.3 is designed to guide you in experiencing a few minutes of a more quiet mind. You can choose an alternative activity if you prefer. For example, some people find that prayer, poetry, chanting, or music are good tools to quiet the mind. Find what works for you.

ACTIVITY 11.3

Clearing Our Mind

1. Choose a time and place where you can have 10 to 20 minutes undisturbed (5 minutes may be a good starting point if you are new to this practice).
2. Find a comfortable place to sit, put on music if you choose (quiet without lyrics is best), and find something to gaze at that doesn't require mental energy (a design, a flower or plant, an object, etc.). Set a timer for 5 minutes to start. A periodic gentle bell or ringtone can help bring your mind back to a clear state.

3. Have some water nearby in case you get thirsty.
4. Breathe slowly (in through your nose and out through your mouth as though you are blowing through a straw), paying attention to your breath, the rising and lowering of your chest and stomach.
5. Focus on your breath, the object, or the music. If you find your mind preoccupied, or the wheels turning, gently return your attention back to the original focus, your breath. Thich Nhat Hanh, a Vietnamese Buddhist Monk and peace activist, suggests thinking about the intruding thoughts as gentle clouds that you observe and let float away, not fighting them but noticing them and imagining them float on. He also suggests that it is important to be compassionate with ourselves in that process.
6. When the timer goes off, slowly bring your attention back to the room and your surroundings. Reflect on how that experience was for you and jot down a few notes. If you found you had some difficulty staying focused, no worries. That often happens, and you will find that it will generally become easier as you continue to practice.

The activity above focuses on body, breath, and attention to help release persistent thoughts. It takes practice though, so if you are new to it, you may not see results until after you have practiced for a while. This type of activity integrates physical and emotional calm in addition to mental calming. For Derrick, the practice involves putting on a lo-fi music playlist or a favorite album while washing dishes or relaxing after finishing a workday. There are a number of other resources and techniques that you might try, depending on your interests. Two great resources we can suggest include the Black Lives Matter Meditation for Racial Healing shared by Dr. Candice Nicole, a counseling psychologist (https://soundcloud.com/drcandicenicole/black-lives-matter-meditation-for-healing-racial-trauma), and a wealth of resources and tools for mindfulness and meditation shared by Thich Nhat Hanh and Plum Village (https://plumvillage.org/mindfulness-practice/).

In addition to the distortion that mental fatigue can create in our emotional lives, it can also affect our social or relational well-being. When we are mentally "on" all the time, we may miss out on other lived experiences as well as important relationships with people. When we are so focused on our own issues, we sometimes don't let go long enough to notice what is important to other loved ones in our lives. We need to find ways to stimulate our mind in healthy ways. A healthy mind can contribute to healthy relationships.

The Heart: Our Emotional and Relational Well-Being

We have chosen the metaphor of the heart to represent the importance of emotions in our well-being as well as the role that relationships have in sustaining or draining us. The emotional aspect is the heart focused within and the relational aspect is our heart extended out toward others. These two aspects of the heart are very interconnected, just as the heart is interconnected with the head, body, and spirit.

FIGURE 11.5 Your heart

Emotional Well-Being

As a helping professional, you know that there are whole books written on emotional health from a wide range of perspectives. We will focus on just two aspects in relation to social action and sustainability: the role of emotions as an alert system, and emotions as healthy tools in social action. For our discussion, we will consider emotions as the range of feelings we experience such as joy, love, happiness, anger, fear, sadness, loneliness, frustration, apathy, and excitement, among others.

When we think about emotions as an alert system, we consider how paying attention to the range of emotions we feel can help us identify and decide how to proceed in a given situation. For example, when we feel fear or discomfort, that signals us that there might be possible danger. As discussed earlier, it's a good opportunity for us to discern whether the fear or discomfort actually reflects real or imagined danger. Feelings of isolation, loneliness, and disconnection signal that there is something going on in our social and relational life that we may need to attend to. Frustration and anger may signal that there is an injustice happening right now and/or a previous experience is being triggered again. Of course, it is not that simple. We often feel multiple, seemingly conflicting, emotions at the same time. Tracey Michae'l Lewis-Giggetts (2022) emphasizes that rage, grief, joy, and pleasure can coexist, and she shares her journey of embracing this complexity in an article in *Yes! Magazine*.

Most of us are raised being taught that certain emotions are more acceptable than others, and we learn patterns of responding based on our gender, cultural background, and/or family socialization. For example, in U.S. dominant society, it is deemed acceptable for girls and women to cry, but not for boys and men. And it is acceptable for boys and men to display anger, but not for women. How we are allowed to express emotion is closely tied to how society interacts with our identities, particularly for minoritized people.

In addition to the role of emotions as warning signs, emotions can also play an important role in our social action. Scilla Elworthy (2012) talks about the positive power of anger in her TED Talk on nonviolence in peace activism . Similarly, research has found many positive results of anger (DeAngelis, 2003). If we think about emotions as energy, they can be destructive or constructive. If not channeled or used effectively, anger can end in frustration and a sense of helplessness or harming others. Channeling active emotions, such as anger, can motivate and energize us, increasing our adrenaline and stamina. When we are fueled by energetic emotions that create adrenaline, we may be more likely to take action and take risks. In this process, we may want to enlist someone we can check in with to help us make sure that the action we are taking is actually what we intend and to support us in using that energy. We also want to reiterate that the ways we are able to express emotions, such as anger, are impacted by our positionality and how we are perceived. The freedom to express emotions publicly (e.g., anger, fear, sadness) is influenced by power and privilege. Fear and anxiety can also be powerful emotions, yet can also drain energy or redirect our efforts and make us hesitant to act. In contrast to anger, Scilla Elworthy noted that it can be helpful to imagine embracing those emotions like a child that needs comforting to learn what we need during that time of fear.

We know that everyone has different circumstances and contexts and that there are very real power differences in societies and communities. Yet, commitment, control, and challenge attitudes can be helpful in thinking about how we relate to difficult circumstances and social action. For a general resource for considering the interaction of our emotions, physical and relational well-being, take a look at APA's resource guide "Building your Resilience": https://www.apa.org/topics/resilience/building-your-resilience.

Relational Well-Being

The second aspect of the heart, our connections with others, is as important as our emotional well-being. One strategy for sustaining us emotionally and socially is maintaining relationships, both chosen and familial. Relationships support our emotional well-being and help us to feel connected and accompanied, even in the most challenging of times. In the video *Helping Counselors and Psychologists as Advocates and Activists*, Kevin Cokley explained,

> You need to surround yourself with like-minded social justice warriors, if you will. And you need allies across racial, and ethnic and cultural sort of boundaries, that's critically important. We can't do this work in isolation. And we need to always have people, who have our backs, who will, you know, when the going gets rough who will say, "You know, fight the good fight and that was hard, but we're here for you." (Toporek & Ahluwalia, 2019)

Downton and Wehr (1998) found in their classic study that peace activists were likely to have created close relationships with other peace activists and, to a lesser extent, leaders. The activists described the importance of mutual respect and shared experiences, as well as caring for each other and sharing feelings of hope. When we are able to find colleagues with similar concerns and energies, relationships can provide fuel for ourselves as we engage in this work. These relationships can be established or maintained in different ways—professional gatherings within conferences and spaces within professional associations, meetings of therapists, professors, research teams, racial healing circles, and even writing groups. This is especially important as the political and social climate becomes more and more hostile. Finding communities that support each other through the pain and outrage is important but also finding communities that can experience radical joy together is essential.

EXAMPLE

Rebecca and the Importance of Values, Relationships, and Accountability

My immediate family (my partner, two grown children, and my siblings) are at the core of my daily sustenance. Beyond that, as a White person doing anti-racism work, it has been really important for me to develop long-standing relationships with others who are also engaged in and understand anti-racism work, especially in counseling and psychology. As I described earlier, my relationship with Muninder has spanned more than 20 years and provides support beyond words. Other long-term relationships provide mutual support and camaraderie for the personal and emotional challenges of being an evolving White person striving toward anti-racism. For example, in 2020, I participated in the first Academics 4 Black Survival and Wellness. As a part of that experience, a small group of other attendees and I came together as an anti-racism accountability group and met every other week for 4 years, providing support and challenging each other in relation to dismantling anti-Black racism.

From Rebecca's example, we can see that the warmth of shared values and beliefs can help us to feel a sense of belonging, while diversity of opinions can help us to see issues from different perspectives. While professional relationships can be sustaining and strategic, it is also important for us to consider how to stay connected with the communities that we came from and which were originally the impetus for our action. The following activity is designed to help you explore with whom you share values and issues you care about. Following the activity, we will talk a little about possible strategies you could consider if you find conflicts between your values and the values of those around you.

ACTIVITY 11.4

Where Do You Stand and Who Stands With You?

1. Before you start this activity, take a look at the values you identified in the values exercises in Chapter 5 (especially Activities 5.2 and 5.3).
2. Then, in the table below, list in the first column eight of the values or issues you chose as most important to you.
3. For each value, think about how much the people around you hold and demonstrate the same value: **you; your family; your community; your coworkers; society.** List each group in the boxes according to how much they share that value. For example, if one of my values is harmony, I think about my family, my community (however I define that), my coworkers, and society and decide whether and how much they value harmony. If I think my family values it somewhat, my community somewhat, coworkers somewhat, and society only a little, then I write that in the boxes below (see example).
4. Now that you have placed everyone on the values table, take a look at who seems to hold similar values.

Example	Does not Value	Values a Little	Somewhat Values	Highly Values
Harmony		Society	My community, my family, my coworkers	Me

Your Values:

Top 8 Values	Does not Value	Values a Little	Somewhat Values	Highly Values
1.				
2.				
3.				
4.				
5.				
6.				
7.				
8.				

In reflecting on this activity, if you find that you have company—in other words, your family, community, coworkers, and society seem to value the same things you do—then you may feel less of a need to explain your motivations for actions. This may help you feel like you have people you can vent to, brainstorm with, or simply spend time with enjoyably. If you find that there are strong differences and very few people who share that value, then you may want to think about some steps to care for yourself and manage those relationships in a way that doesn't feel too costly or stressful. We may change our expectations and how we engage with them. For sustaining our emotional health, it may be important to actively seek out other friends, family members, and community members with whom we feel a shared sense of values and can provide and gain support.

For many of us, finding solidarity with others who care about similar issues is a major act of self-care and sustainability. In this way, participating in demonstrations and social forms of action with others can help break isolation and feelings of being overwhelmed. Sometimes, we adjust our expectations and acknowledge that not every relationship can fulfill all our needs. Sometimes those relationships still fulfill some need, while other times we may choose to discontinue relationships that work against our well-being. For people who engage in activism, it is often helpful to have connections with others who can relate to that experience, even more specifically the social issue of focus. Support groups, activism resource centers, online interest groups, and chat groups can all provide that sense of camaraderie. Interhelp is one resource that provides guidance on developing and engaging in support groups specifically oriented for folks engaged in social change (https://interhelpnetwork.org/).

With our training as helping professionals, we may bring skills to help facilitate the positive role these groups can play. If you engage in such a group, be mindful of your role. Are you there to facilitate as a helping professional, or are you there to be a part of collective care? Both are valid, while requiring different inputs from you. It is also important to develop the skills to recognize when groups (or individuals in these groups) may not be helpful and how to disengage if we find them toxic and unhealthy.

One challenge that can arise in relationships is a sense of isolation when we feel like we are alone in our beliefs or that the people we care about don't share the same values as we do. Not everyone needs to agree with us, and a diversity of viewpoints makes for richer and broader opportunities for expanding our understanding of the world. The challenge comes when we have very few people who we share our perspective with or when people we spend a lot of time with have such different viewpoints about things that are important to us. One of the striking things that has been increasingly reported over the past couple of years is the disruption in personal relationships due to political differences. Conflicts within families, workplaces, and friendships due to political viewpoints have resulted in fractures in relationships and, in some cases, searching for ways to bridge these challenging divides (Israel, 2020). We don't always need to agree with the people we care about, yet when we talk about sustainability, we may need to actively work to surround ourselves with people who share our worldview and feel passionate about the issues we care about. In a previous chapter, we spoke about solidarity as a way to engage in social change. Solidarity is also important as a means to sustainability.

There is a lot we can do to help ourselves maintain balance, care for ourselves to repair hurt, and invest in healthy relationships. As individuals in human services, we sometimes forget to care for ourselves as we care for others. It is often important to reach out beyond ourselves for help from those who are trained and have expertise to provide support. Depending on your economic resources, availability of health insurance, and where you live or work, you may even have access to mental health professionals who specialize in providing support for activists and community organizers. With increased availability of telehealth, it may be easier to find providers who specialize in or understand your activism and/or the issues you are committed to.

The Body: Our Physical Well-Being

Sustainability in terms of physical health is both obvious and elusive. We will address two related but slightly separate aspects of physical care: caring for our physical self and being compassionate with our physical self. The first refers to actions we can take to maintain healthy

FIGURE 11.6 Your body

physical functioning, and the second refers to knowing when we just need to rest (see The Nap Ministry https://thenapministry.wordpress.com).

Care for Our Physical Self

In spite of an abundance of advice on physical health and exercise, we often find it difficult to do the things we know are good for us: paying attention to what we what we eat, drink, or ingest that has positive or negative effects on our physical health and stamina (including caffeine, nicotine, alcohol, cannabis, and other drugs), engaging in ongoing physical exercise, and getting regular and sufficient sleep. We know that opportunities for basic healthy lifestyle choices are affected by economic privilege or oppression. For example, barriers to physical health can include underfunded neighborhoods that limit outdoor activity, lack of clean water, lack of access to affordable healthy food, and necessity of multiple jobs to afford housing, among other barriers. For some of us, these barriers may impact us directly and be a target for our activism. In other words, the social action issues we focus on will hopefully help create more equitable access to these basic building blocks for health.

For others of us, it is not these real barriers that limit us, but rather our own choices that lead us toward less healthy ways of living. Our choices often get poorer when we are feeling stressed or overcommitted. It can be a vicious circle: We get stressed and feel like we have too much to do so we keep working; then we get less sleep, we don't exercise, and our meals become irregular and less healthy. All of this results in us becoming even less healthy and feeling even less energetic and able to do the things we want to do. Some of us have chronic illnesses, vulnerable health, and physical or sensory challenges, so there may be added complexities to what we need to maintain our health. We know that everyone's situation is different and can be impacted by our positionality and privileges. We also know that as life changes, healthy habits we may have had can fall to the side. Still, within our unique situation, we can consider the options we have, the choices we make, and possibilities we have not yet contemplated. We may need to reorient ourselves to a healthy path.

The recommendations for maintaining our physical health are probably not surprising to anyone reading this. Although additional evidence can help propel us to healthier behaviors, at least temporarily (e.g., the health benefits of at least 30 minutes of exercise per day, the negative impact of sleep deprivation), we may still struggle to maintain healthy patterns. Challenges to maintaining physical health are both individual (i.e., what we control in our own lives) and systemic (i.e., how our environment and society supports or interferes in healthy living).

Remembering our strength-based approach, let's start at the individual level and build on the times and ways that we have been able to take care of our physical self.

ACTIVITY 11.5

Good Times and Challenging Times

This activity is focused on increasing how well you are able to take care of your physical health. Sometimes when we become stressed at work, everything seems urgent. Thus, we may work longer hours and we may be preoccupied with work even when we're not working. It doesn't feel like we have *any* time to take a break—not even 30 minutes to take a walk. This activity will guide you in finding out what helps you take care of yourself, what interferes, and what small changes you can make to integrate care more consistently.

1. **The Good Times:** Think about a recent time when you had at least 1 week of taking good care of your physical self. Try to recall some details:

    a. How were you "taking good care" of your physical self? (e.g., eating, exercising, sleeping)

    b. What was happening in your life during that time? (e.g., Where were you? Who were you with? What demands were placed on you?)

    c. What made it easier to take care of your physical self? (e.g., routine, buddy)

2. **The Challenging Times:** Now think about a time in the recent past when you were not taking good care of your physical self for at least 1 week. Try to recall some details:

    a. How were you **not** "taking good care" of your physical self? (e.g., not eating healthfully, not exercising, not sleeping enough hours)

    b. What was happening in your life during that time? (e.g., Where were you? Who were you with? What demands were placed on you?)

    c. What made it harder to take care of your physical self? (e.g., no routine, too busy, prioritized other needs)

3. What were some of the differences between the good times and the challenging times?

4. Now think about three small things you can put in an imaginary "emergency box" to pull out during those challenging times. For example, 15 minutes to stretch, drink an extra glass of water, etc.

5. For one week, track the three "emergency box" things you did. Every day, write down how difficult it was to do those three things. What did you notice when you were doing each thing and after you did it? If it was difficult, think about three other things that might be easier to introduce during stressful times. Then try again.

6. Each evening, write three words to describe how you feel.

	Sun	Mon	Tues	Wed	Thurs	Fri	Sat
Thing 1:							
Thing 2:							
Thing 3:							
Reflections at night: Three words to describe how you feel							

This activity is just a start. One week of something new is really not enough time to draw conclusions. However, it may give you the opportunity to get started and see some small successes—or at least loosen patterns that may not be healthy. We might start off intending to follow through, but then something comes up, or we forget, or just don't do it. If that's the case, try again, with no blame and no judgment. Consider what interfered with you doing the three things. Sometimes it's that we start too big or just haven't shifted our patterns. If you can, try it for 3 weeks and see what a new pattern might look like.

Compassion for Our Physical Self

In addition to maintaining our physical health and well-being, we also need to acknowledge that sometimes we may be physically at our limit. The sustainability section of the S-Quad model is intended to remind us that it's okay to pause, maybe because we have other demands in our life or because our health needs attention. In her contribution to *The Impossible Will Take a Little While*, Danusha Veronica Goska (2004) shared the following insights regarding the challenges of her physical condition and her connection to social action:

On some days I was functional. On others, and I could never predict when those days would strike, I was literally, not metaphorically, paralyzed … that paralysis has taught me something. It has taught me that my protestations of my own powerlessness are bogus. Yes, some days I can't move or see. And the difference between being able to walk across the room and not being able to walk across the room is epic … The problem is not that we have so little power. The problem is that we don't use the power that we have. (p. 47–48)

The Spirit: Our Essence or Our Connection to Something Greater Than Ourselves

Nourishing your heart can involve giving and receiving love. Taking care of your mind may relate to mental stimulation, growth, and quiet. Taking care of your body can include physical exercise and rest. And part of spirituality is paying attention to your soul and taking care of your spirit. The *spirit* represents our sense of connection to something greater than ourselves, whether it is our principles, values, belief in a higher power or a greater being, connection to a shared history, or other aspects of life. This

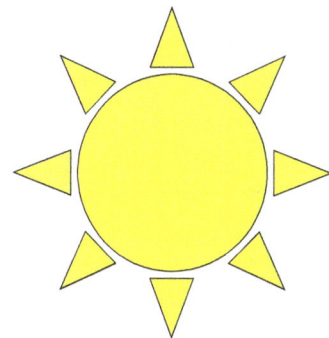

FIGURE 11.7 Your spirit

is different for everyone, and we all have varying degrees to which this is present, conscious, and meaningful in our lives. For some people, the spirit is the core of their lives, while others feel spirituality differently.

Spirituality can be many things: a belief in the teachings of a shared religious or spiritual practice; beliefs about the nature of life, the universe, human and animal kind; our connection to living beings and nature; or other ways that we are deeply rooted. Cultural traditions and beliefs can shape, support, and connect us to a spiritual life, for example through meditation, prayer, art, and song. Or spiritual practices may involve engaging with nature. Even for those of us who don't identify with a greater being, religious practice, or spirituality per se, we may have some connection to a sense of meaning and a purpose. It is that sense that we refer to as "spirit."

EXAMPLE

Muninder

For me, spirituality is in the context of religion and means being connected to something bigger than myself, in particular with my community, with humanity, and with God. I become in flow with something meaningful outside myself, but I also pay attention to how it resonates within myself. I can engage in religious practice on my own, but being in gurdwara allows me to be immersed in the Sikh community, pray with others, sing shabads (hymns) in unison, engage in seva, hear the lessons of our 10 Gurus, be in the presence of the Guru Granth Sahib (the Sikh holy book), and share a meal prepared by the congregation for all who wish to partake. For Sikhs, religion allows us a venue by which to ask for guidance and support, celebrate joyous occasions by expressing gratitude, receive and provide solace in times of distress, and promote social justice.

There is a belief in Sikhism, and in many religions, that if you are not in the community of people who are like yourself, you can become spiritually bereft. Muninder takes a practical view of this that goes beyond religion. For racial, ethnic, and religious minorities, nourishing the spirit involves being with people who look like you and people who share your values and beliefs, particularly if you live and work in places where you don't regularly see people like yourself. It allows a coming together for people of color and of minority faiths to fight against "isms" (e.g., racism, anti-Semitism, Islamophobia). For many immigrants, religion and spirituality can offer a consistent sense of home, a naturally existing community to connect with after moving to a new country, and a place to hear one's language spoken as a means of connection.

Though religion is a powerful tool that nourishes and develops Muninder's spirit, we acknowledge that for some people, religion is the antithesis of spirituality. It can be even more complicated for many people because both positive spirituality and oppression coexists in religion. Religious systems have been used to oppress different groups over time (e.g., women, LGBTQ+ individuals), and religion has been used as a politically divisive tool. When understanding how your spirit may or may not be connected to religion, it is important to pay attention to ways in which religion or spirituality has been used to promote and/or block social justice for you, for your community, and for others.

The next activity is intended to help us notice what is sometimes unnoticeable. We ask you to imagine your spiritual well-being.

ACTIVITY 11.6

Imagining Your Spiritual Well-Being—A Collage

The purpose of this collage is to create a representation of your spiritual well-being and to reflect on whether you allow yourself the time and space to attend to this in your daily life. Get a large piece of paper, a board, or use digital tools on the computer. Select words, quotes, images, songs, and/ or photos that help you define your spirit and what nourishes your spiritual well-being. Once you are finished, reflect on these questions:

1. What do the representations (words, pictures, images) mean to you?

2. How do you feel as you take in what's on this board?

3. Is there something missing that you would like to add in the future?

4. What activities do you currently engage in that develop and support the well-being of your spirit (e.g., spiritual or religious)? What activities could you add?

5. How do these things help to bring balance and well-being to your life?

Your Big Picture of Sustainability

There is no one right way to work toward health and wellness in the face of challenges. As we wrap up this chapter, we will guide you through an activity to reflect on your own experience, personality, and spirit to help you create a sustainability plan that includes resources and strategies.

ACTIVITY 11.7

Sustainability Menu

Part 1: In the table below, list as many feasible sustainability activities as you can think of. For each one, include symbols to indicate what might be required in order to engage in that activity. Then mark an "X" to indicate which aspect of your well-being might be nurtured by that activity.

Symbols:
$ - Requires money
T - Time
C - Collaboration
P - Planning

Activity	Mind	Heart: Emotions	Heart: Relational	Body	Spirit
Example: Go dancing with friends requires $, T, C, P	x	x	x	x	x

Part 2: Choose two activities that you can put into practice this week. Try to incorporate these into your regular routine.

Part 3: Create two surprise boxes. On an index card, write each of the activities from the table in Part 1. Separate the cards into two piles: one with activities that require little time, money, or planning; and the other pile with activities that require more time, money, or planning. Each pile will have its own box: "easy" and "extended" (you can make up your own names). If you'd like, you can decorate each box with photos or pictures that represent the activities in the box.

Part 4: At least once a week, choose two cards from the "easy" box and do the activities on them. Decide how often to choose a card from the "extended" box and plan when you might do it.

There are times when we believe we are the ideal person to do the necessary work and we successfully do it. While that may be true, a part of that narrative is also limiting. Often, someone else can also do it. While they may not do things the way we do or accomplish what we may accomplish, the very fact that someone else is doing it nourishes our personal sustainability and nourishes the sustainability of the work. Sometimes they do it better! It is our responsibility—and important collaboration and succession planning—to share the work and, when needed, pass the torch. Sustainability involves mentorship of others and encouraging others to take on parts or even the whole from us.

As a final note about your sustainability plan, we would like to advocate for the idea of a "sustainability buddy." This is someone who helps to let you know when you seem to be slipping away from healthy practices, who can join you in joyful activities, and who can sit with you when you're feeling sad. Of course, this buddy relationship works both ways—to have a buddy, you need to be a buddy. Rebecca and Muninder have been sustainability buddies for each other for 20+ years and have supported each other through challenging times in their work and personal life (e.g, from predoctoral internship and dissertations to illnesses and caregiving) and even through everyday hiccups. In fact, for them, having each other as a sustainability buddy has been a wellness strategy in and of itself. For Bryan and Derrick, supporting each other has included anything from exercising together, processing experiences of graduate school and personal and professional life, providing peer mentorship, and enjoying meals together.

Additional Sustainability Resources

As noted throughout this workbook, our experiences and identities influence our work and the way others respond to us. When we are working toward justice in areas that affect us and/or our community, we feel the toll that it takes even more personally. We may be retriggered, we may be targeted, our trauma response may get activated, and we may feel the pain of others. Seek wisdom shared by leaders, artists, and others who have felt trauma and who have persisted.

- A beautiful resource for people who have experienced racial trauma is *Healing in Action* from Black Lives Matter (https://blacklivesmatter.com/wp-content/uploads/2024/05/blm-healing-action-r1.pdf). This guide integrates awareness about the unique costs experienced by folks who experience racial trauma when they engage in activism, especially given the intensity and frequency of anti-Black, anti-LGBTQ+ anti-immigrant, and anti-People of Color rhetoric and opposition they may face.
- Another resource is the Psychology of Radical Healing, from the Radical Healing Collective (https://psychologyofradicalhealing.com/). It rose from a Division 45 APA presidential task group with Helen Neville and shares podcasts, resources, and toolkits for clinicians, scholars and self.
- Psychologists Isaac Prilleltensky and his colleagues have developed a comprehensive online wellness assessment and activities tool entitled "Fun for Wellness" (https://www.funforwellness.com). This resource is designed to reduce stress and increase feelings of wellness.
- Esther Brownsmith's (2018) online op ed provides great links to a range of useful websites and tools for self-care (https://medium.com/@esther.brownsmith/new-to-activism-grow-your-practices-of-self-care-56c95cec1a32).

While the resources above tend to focus on helping us care for ourselves at an individual or personal level, Christine Maslach and Michael Leiter (2005), two researchers who have extensively studied burnout in many occupations, suggest that preventing burnout in activism needs to be done at a personal and institutional level. Rosales and Davis (2023) describe the ways that our mental health may be challenged or can be strengthened, depending on the ways social change organizations ignore, or integrate, attention to the wellness and mental health of their members. They emphasize the necessity of embedding attention to mental health within social change efforts and organizations, writing, "Integrating positive mental health practices is the only way for social change leaders to maximize the incredible potential of their organizations and the communities they serve."

In other words, it is important that we find ways to cope and prevent burnout while we engage in activism and social action, individually as well as within organizations and larger efforts. If we think about an automobile as a metaphor for a movement or social change organization, we consider that it needs fuel and has many moving parts that depend on each other. Maintenance is required to keep each part functioning and it is also necessary for them to function well together. Lubricating, cleaning, and preventing wear and tear all require attention. Sometimes we need to retire parts when they become worn out; otherwise they can potentially damage other parts or the whole system. Some elements discussed in the earlier strategies and solidarity sections, especially regarding working with groups, can be helpful in thinking about the dynamics that can arise. adrienne maree brown, in *Emergent Strategy*, talks about understanding our role within social movements and how we can contribute in ways that support movements, as well as what to do when we feel critical (brown, 2017). The Community Toolbox also describes user-friendly strategies for maintaining coalitions (KU Center for Community Health and Development, n.d.-a).

Creating a routine for everyday action can help with sustainability in that it can help you make social action a part of your life, rather than an add-on. When we are exhausted or burned out, we may be ineffective, or worse, harmful to others or to the cause we care about. When we integrate sustainability practices, we can not only keep moving forward in a positive direction, but also help others do the same. Self-care becomes community care, and self-care is a form of resistance.

We end this chapter with a quote from Tracey Michae'l Lewis-Giggetts (2022):

> I know that my joy stands defiant in the faces of those who try to dehumanize me. I know that my joy makes my oppressor big mad. Because more than stealing our rights, stealing our joy is their greatest, albeit subtlest, evil. Ensuring that we can't access our joy or that we have a fear or guilt around expressing it is probably the most insidious form White supremacy takes. Black joy is a kind of currency, and when we learn to spend it recklessly, the results are glorious.

Figure Credits

Fig. 11.3: Rebecca L. Toporek and Muninder Kaur Ahluwalia, *Taking Action: Creating Social Change Through Strength, Solidarity, Strategy, and Sustainability*, p. 159. Copyright © 2021 by Cognella, Inc. Reprinted with permission.

Fig. 11.4: Rebecca L. Toporek and Muninder Kaur Ahluwalia, *Taking Action: Creating Social Change Through Strength, Solidarity, Strategy, and Sustainability*, p. 160. Copyright © 2021 by Cognella, Inc. Reprinted with permission.

Fig. 11.5: Rebecca L. Toporek and Muninder Kaur Ahluwalia, *Taking Action: Creating Social Change Through Strength, Solidarity, Strategy, and Sustainability*, p. 163. Copyright © 2021 by Cognella, Inc. Reprinted with permission.

Fig. 11.6: Rebecca L. Toporek and Muninder Kaur Ahluwalia, *Taking Action: Creating Social Change Through Strength, Solidarity, Strategy, and Sustainability*, p. 169. Copyright © 2021 by Cognella, Inc. Reprinted with permission.

Fig. 11.7: Rebecca L. Toporek and Muninder Kaur Ahluwalia, *Taking Action: Creating Social Change Through Strength, Solidarity, Strategy, and Sustainability*, p. 173. Copyright © 2021 by Cognella, Inc. Reprinted with permission.

section 3

Synthesizing and Articulating a Professional Social Action Strategic Plan

Chapter 12

Your Strategic Professional and Personal Social Action Plan

With contributions by Sunanda M. Sharma

FIGURE 12.1 S-Quad image

*"Without leaps of imagination or dreaming, we lose the excitement of possibilities.
Dreaming, after all, is a form of planning."*

—Gloria E. Anzaldúa

This chapter is all about creating your social action plan. Before we get to that, we want to briefly summarize what we've covered to get to this point.

The first section of the book was intended to help you situate yourself and your profession in the context of social action. In Chapter 2, we described the history of social action within the helping professions by highlighting efforts of some people and organizations that have challenged our fields to be more equitable and just. We also asked you to reflect on your own history and the experiences that have influenced your interest in your current field and in social action. In Chapter 3, we introduced and reflected on concepts of intersectionality (Crenshaw, 1989), identity development, the importance of multicultural sensitivity in our society, and its role in increasing awareness of power dynamics and privilege across diverse lived experiences. We also discussed the importance of taking action and what it means to take a liberatory stance in the work we do. Chapter 4 focused on the relationships between personal, community, and professional values, lessons, and ethics. You considered how professional ethical codes are aligned or misaligned with your cultural self and community and how they may support or hinder social action. We ended the first section of the book by discussing the importance of finding your focus for social action. In Chapter 5, we wanted to help you share the work you do, articulate your ideas of your desires for your work, the barriers you face, and how to work through these barriers.

In Section II, we focused on the four areas of reflection that make up the S-Quad model: (a) strength, (b) solidarity, (c) strategy, and (d) sustainability. Chapter 7 reflected on ways to transfer the strengths, resources, and knowledge we have developed in our personal life to professional advocacy and use for the good of the community. We also reflected on the ways in which the personal, political, and professional interweave and impact our advocacy. In Chapter 8 we discussed ways to be in solidarity with others, including considering positionality as a helping professional who may be an insider or outsider to the community you hope to support. You explored your social mosaic and identified those with whom you are or can be in solidarity. We focused on the third "S"—strategy—in Chapters 9 and 10. First, in Chapter 9, we discussed tools to assess which strategies might be useful for different situations, your strengths, involvement of others, and what is already being done. We also explored ways to assess potential consequences and benefits of different strategies for you and for others. Chapter 10 provided a menu of strategies for impacting different spheres of influence—personal, organizational, local, state, or national. We ended this section with a focus on sustainability for both personal and the work—how we move forward in our work, how the community moves forward, and how the work moves forward, with or without us (Chapter 11). Without sustainability, we stop and the work stops, so we share some ideas for you to find what works for you in terms of self-care, ensuring resilience, and preventing burnout.

So far in this book you've reflected a lot about yourself and the issues you care about. Now that you have some understanding on the context for social action and the S-Quad model, let's put it all together to create your social action plan.

Creating an Action Plan

Now let's create your action plan. As you create your action plan, make sure to revisit context (Chapters 1–5) and reflection areas (Chapters 6–11). We suggest you review the activities as they might be helpful in bringing your plan together. In addition, take note of what you think might be missing from what we have shared with you. You may expand or create new activities that better support your and your community's goals and context. Use your personal and professional experiences to help guide you. In the following pages, we present some general frameworks that will aid you in creating your action plan and provide a template that you can use to bring the highlights together.

Mind Your Ecology

As we plan to take action, it is important for us to be intentional and consider what level of the ecological model our action impacts, as well as the cost of said action for ourselves and others. We encourage you to reflect back on the ecological model we discussed in Chapter 2. This model, described by Urie Bronfenbrenner (1979), was designed to help us better understand the complexity of human experience, and it focuses on different "systems," or levels, in which people interact: centering the individual, encapsulated by the microsystem, mesosystem, exosystem, macrosystem, and chronosystem. In this book, we have roughly followed this with a focus on individual or interpersonal, organizational or local, and societal levels. More recently, Stern and colleagues (2021) included a racial cultural lens that considers both challenges and strengths at different levels. Understanding the workings of each level can help us to better support individuals, families, and communities in their interactions with one another and create change at multiple levels of said ecology (Bronfenbrenner, 1979).

Tool 1: Timeliness, Steps, and SMART Goals

Employing a timeline and stepwise approach alongside SMART goals can significantly enhance your effectiveness and success. As Malcolm X (1964) said, "Tomorrow belongs only to the people who prepare for it today." Therefore, preparation needs to be mindful and intentional.

Using a timeline and stepwise approach can help you in multiple ways, including providing you with a clear path and a structured framework to allow you to identify the resources, knowledge, needs, responsibilities, and tasks taken on by you and the collective. It allows you and the movement to have a better understanding of the resources available and when to use them. Such a plan can help identify needs, prioritize activities, and optimize the use of time, energy, and available resources. Additionally, a timeline and stepwise approach can help with greater accountability and progress checks along the way.

Tools such as SMART goals (specific, measurable, achievable, relevant, and time-bound) provide one way to help you go from ideas and discussion into action. SMART goals provide a framework for setting clear and actionable objectives that are more likely to be accomplished.

Specific: Goals should be specific, well-defined, and focused. They should answer the questions, What needs to be achieved? Why is it important?

Measurable: Goals should be measurable to track progress and determine success. They should include concrete criteria or indicators to gauge achievement.

Achievable: Goals should be realistic and attainable, considering available resources, skills, and external constraints. They should stretch individuals and groups to strive for growth while remaining within practical boundaries.

Relevant: Goals should align with the broader social issue or cause at hand. They should be relevant and contribute directly to the desired change or impact.

Time-bound: Goals should have a specific time frame or deadline. A defined timeline creates a sense of urgency, provides focus, and helps in allocating resources effectively.

EXAMPLE

Let's say you are passionate about supporting immigrant communities, and you want to improve the services available to them.

Timeline and Stepwise Approach

- Week 1: Identify key stakeholders, including local organizations, community leaders, and volunteers who can contribute to the initiative. Assess what is already being done.
- Week 2: Conduct a community needs assessment and research the challenges faced by immigrants in accessing resources and services.

- Week 3: Establish partnerships with local service providers, government agencies, and nonprofit organizations to enhance support networks for immigrants.
- Week 4: Based on needs assessment, begin to plan action. For example, plan and design outreach materials, such as brochures or flyers, websites such as FindHello, or bilingual radio programs such as Radiobilingue, to provide information about available resources and support for immigrants.
- Week 5–8: Conduct workshops and informational sessions to provide guidance on navigating immigration processes, accessing education, healthcare, and employment opportunities.
- Week 9: Organize community events to celebrate and showcase the cultural diversity and contributions of immigrants.
- Week 10: Evaluate the impact of the initiative by collecting feedback from immigrants and stakeholders and identifying areas for improvement.

SMART Goals

Specific: Enhance access to resources and support for immigrants in the community, addressing key challenges they face in integration, inclusion, and access.

Measurable: Reach and support at least 100 immigrant individuals/families, providing them with essential information and connecting them to services.

Achievable: Leverage existing community networks, partner with local organizations and volunteers, and secure funding or in-kind support to facilitate the initiative's activities.

Relevant: Based on a needs assessment, address the needs of immigrants in the community, promote their well-being, and contribute to fostering a more inclusive and welcoming environment.

Time-bound: Implement the initiative within a 10-week time frame, from conducting needs assessment to evaluating the impact, ensuring timely and efficient execution.

By employing a timeline and stepwise approach and setting SMART goals, you can effectively identify your (and your community's) strengths, solidarity, strategy, and sustainability plan. This comprehensive approach allows for structured planning, clear objectives, and strategic execution in your efforts to support your movement.

Tool 2: My Social Justice Action Plan Template

Based on the S-Quad model and the activities in this workbook, Sunanda M. Sharma developed a tool and template titled "My Social Justice Action Plan" to help bring together and summarize the work described in this book. You may want to get some blank sheets of paper, start a computer document, or a notebook so you can expand on each of the sections below and come back to it periodically. We encourage you to try this out in the following pages and refer back to previous chapters as necessary. Consider some of the activities you did earlier in the book, and you may find that you'd like to make some changes, add some things, or rethink how you approached the activity.

MY SOCIAL JUSTICE ACTION PLAN

Strength   Solidarity

Sustainability   Strategy

FIGURE 12.2 S-Quad image

Your Name and Your Focus

Begin by choosing *one* cause or issue that you feel strongly about. Being as specific as possible about the issue will make it easier to be specific about your four S's, which in turn will make it more likely for you to take action.

Elevator Pitch. My name is …, I am (position and place). I am working on or concerned about … (the issue) because (why it is important). I am (what are you doing about the issue). I am working with … (organization you have joined forces with—how would you concisely describe them and their mission statement?) I am asking for you to … (what do you want from the listener?).

My Strengths

I have strengths that I know will come into play as I engage in social action. They include my professional and personal skills and knowledge, and my positionality, which reflects my lived experience.

Use this space in 12.1 to include images, media, quotes, etc. that speak to you about your strengths and/or about what

Professional skills and knowledge   Personal skills and knowledge

FIGURE 12.3 Your strengths

you find most important. Look back at your work in Chapter 5 (Activity 5.5) and Chapter 7 (Activity 7.5, 7.6, and 7.7).

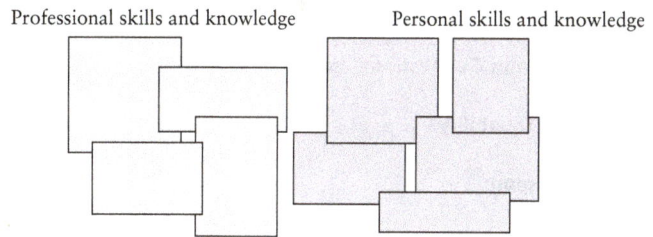

Next, elaborate on each strength. You do not have to include each category that is listed; use the categories that make the most sense to you! Be sure to specify how you intend to use your strengths toward your identified cause.

> **Example from Sunanda:** As mental health practitioners, we are trained empathic listeners, which is a strength I think we can leverage in justice work. Listening respectfully was listed under "working with groups" in Toporek and Ahluwalia (2020), but I think it is important to include it as a category of its own.

Strength or skill I have or would like to develop	Details about my strength or skill	I intend to use this strength toward my identified cause in this way…
Listening		

Working with Groups		
Technical Skills		
Organizational Skills		
Working with Information		
Artistic Skills		
Writing Skills		
Mechanical or Construction Skills		
Language Skills		
Other Skills?		

My Positionality. Knowing ourselves is crucial to engaging in social justice advocacy. This is how my identities show up in the ADDRESSING framework (Hays, 2008). Please indicate, with asterisks, the categories in which you have privileged status. Elaborate on how these identities will come into play with respect to the social justice cause that you are interested in working on. You may want to look back at Chapter 3, Table 3.1, as a reminder.

Age and Generational Influences:
D + Disability:
Religion:
Ethnicity and Race:
Socioeconomic Status:
Sexual Orientation:
Indigenous Heritage:
National Origin:
Gender:

How others perceive us makes a difference. Look back at Chapter 3, Activity 3.5. What stood out? What might be relevant in social action work?

Point of Reflection: Strengths and Positionality

- How are my strengths and positionality related to the issue and/or potential social action?
- What strengths would I like to develop further?
- How does my positionality influence the way I use my strengths to support others or get out of the way?

Solidarity

I have a foundation for solidarity. Bringing together the relationships I have already built with the relationships I will soon build, I will be ready for stronger social action.

My Social Mosaic. Look back at Chapter 8, Activity 8.6, and feel free to add images or a web that depicts your social mosaic. Be sure to specify, in writing, how your social mosaic will come into play with respect to your social justice cause. It helps to write about every group you are a part of—even if you think they do not apply to your identified cause, include them! Be sure to reflect even on groups you are no longer technically a part of, but that you might be able to draw strength and connection from. For example, if you are no longer in K-12 school, were there folks you connected with that you might reach out to?

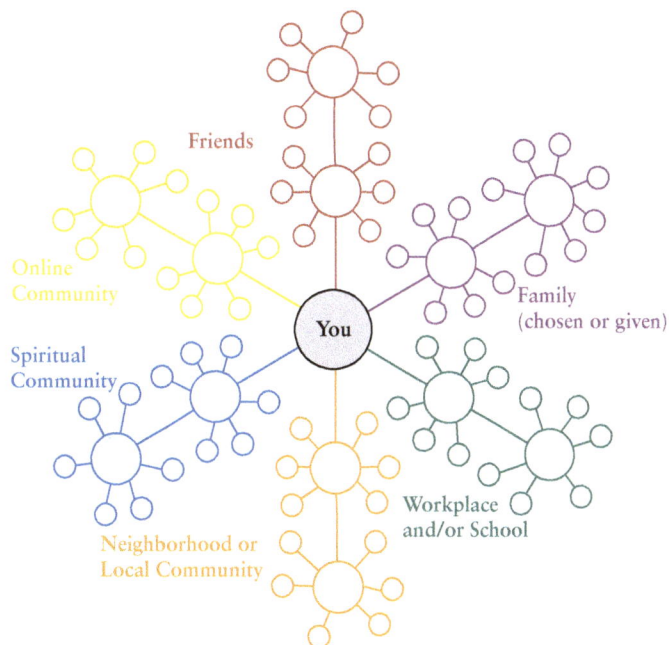

FIGURE 12.4 Social mosaic map

Allyship vs. Accompliceship. In developing solidarity, there is an important difference between becoming an accomplice and working together in accompaniment. Being an ally has an important role but sometimes does not include real partnership.

- How will I be an accomplice rather than an ally? An ally might support behind the scenes, but an accomplice is someone who will take the proverbial "bullet."
- How will I leverage my privilege to support the community without further marginalizing members? "Privilege can act as a buffer against negative repercussions that might arise," according to Toporek and Ahluwalia (2020, p. 18).
- What are some things I need to be mindful of as I reflect on my privilege and own social networks?

Microinterventions. Recognizing and intervening in microaggressions is one way to demonstrate solidarity.

- When I witness microaggressive behavior, these are some things I can say …
- If I notice someone who is engaging in inappropriate conduct against someone, I can intervene by naming the behavior …
- How can I use my helping skills to build culturally responsive relationships with the community I want to support?

Solidarity Within Mental Health Associations. As a mental health professional, these are professional organizations that I can be a part of (e.g., Counselors for Social Justice and other divisions of ACA such as SAIGE and AMCD, Divisions of APA, NASW, etc.).

- Which organization am I a member of (e.g., American Counseling Association [ACA], American Psychological Association [APA], National Association of Social Workers [NASW]?
- What are some committees within the professional association that work toward social justice? (If you can, identify committee leaders within these organizations to reach out to. You may want to look back at Chapter 10, Activity 10.2)
- What other organizations exist in my community (town, county, state, regional, national) that are doing the work. (If you are not drawn to your professional organizations, local organizations are a great way to go.)
  - o What is a brief history of this organization?
  - o What is their mission statement?
  - o Who can I reach out to? What is their contact information?

Coalitions. Refer back to Chapter 8, Activity 8.7: "Who's on the Team?" Is there anything else (or anyone else) that would be helpful to add?

"Point of Reflection: Solidarity

- What relationships do I have now related to my social action?
- Where can I expand my relationships to strengthen my connections with communities?
- How do my relationships with community reflect mutual care?

My Strategies

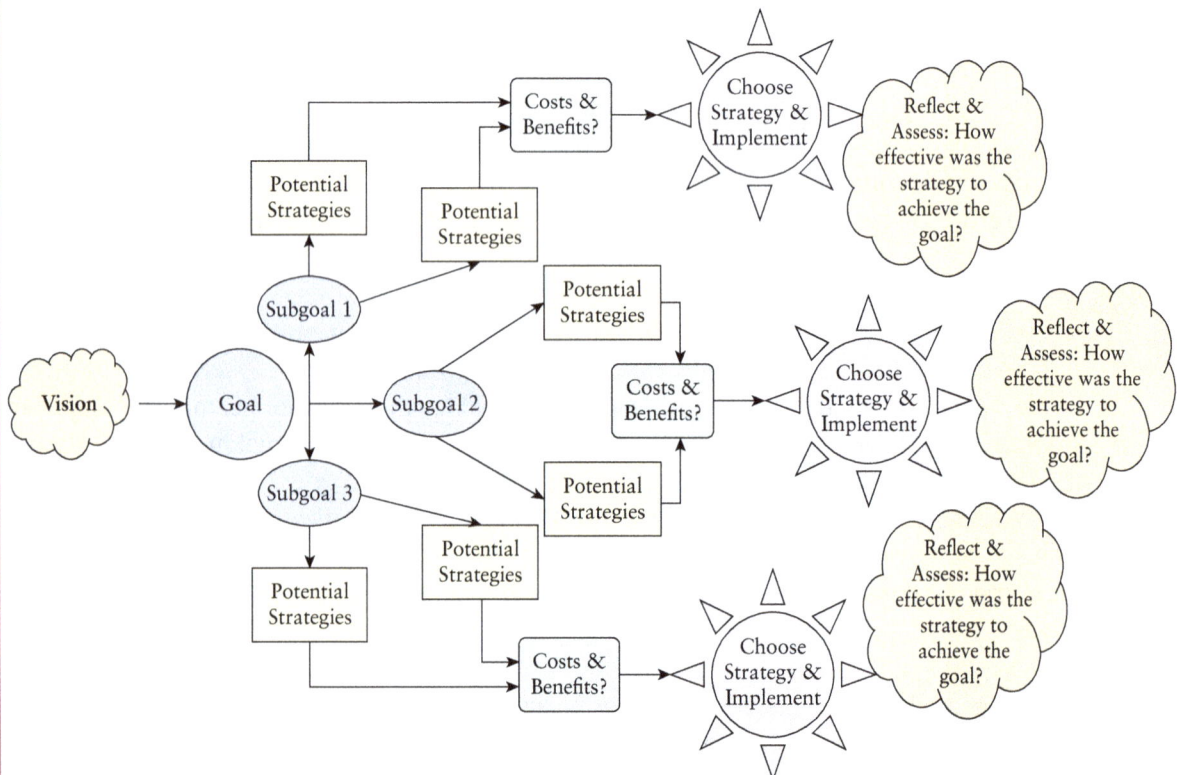

FIGURE 12.5 Strategy flowchart

Reflecting on the Issue. Narrowing down your issue to a concrete goal will help in identifying the strategies that will be most helpful. For example, if the broader issue is immigration rights, a more narrow focus might be to decrease the number of families who are separated when detained by Immigration and Customs Enforcement. Next, examining the issue will be helpful for developing a foundation for action.

- What is the issue or concern?
- Who is already working on the issue?
- Who has power in this issue?
- What advocacy organizations are related to this issue?

Analyzing One of My Causes. For the analysis process, reflect on the strengths, skills and knowledge you bring. Consider the relationships you already have with people most affected by the issue or problem. The wide range of action strategies discussed in Chapter 10 can be like a menu of action opportunities. Take a look and see where you might initiate action or contribute to existing actions.

- What do I want to see happen? What is my goal (or the goal of the community affected)?
- The skills and knowledge I have, as well as the solidarity and relationships I have relate to this issue in these ways …
- What levels are possible for action (e.g., individual, interpersonal, organizational, community, or state/national/global)?
- The strategies from Chapter 10 that might apply to my social justice issue are the following:
  - o Communicating and working with legislators/policymakers
  - o Professional writing
  - o Working with Groups
  - o Community Organizing
  - o Resisting publicly
  - o Creating art
  - o Creating blogs, podcasts, other media
  - o Changing your workplace
  - o Completing everyday actions
  - o Talking with people I don't agree with
  - o Boycotting
- I have chosen these five strategies that are the best fit for the issue, goal, my strengths, resources, and community. (List and include a brief description of how that strategy is relevant and/or how you might use it. While you do not have to speak to each strategy, you should select a minimum of five strategies.)
- Some of the benefits and costs of the strategies I have identified are … (describe for each strategy)
- I need to get more information to better understand how to implement the following strategies as well as possible benefits and costs about the following strategies …

Conceptualizing Action Through My Theoretical Orientation. One of our strengths is our training in human behavior, individually or in groups. Theoretical orientations can be helpful to explicitly describe our beliefs and the actions that align with those beliefs and the goals we have identified.

- My theoretical orientation is … (describe the lens, basic principles, types of interventions, etc.)
- These are the theories I use in my clinical or counseling work …

- These are ways my theoretical orientation describes justice work (or does not address it) …
- A social justice oriented theory (intersectionality, relational cultural, critical race theory, etc.) may help support my social action efforts in these ways …

Using the ACA Social Justice Advocacy Competencies to Guide My Justice Efforts. These competencies provide a structure for deciding what types of advocacy might be most appropriate and strategies for each type of advocacy.

Review the discussion of the Advocacy Competencies in Chapter 9 before considering the questions that follow:

- The specific domains of the competencies that are most relevant to my issue are …
- This is how and why these domains are relevant (describe specifically) …

Overcoming Barriers. Start by identifying the different types of barriers and negative consequences that might be related to the strategies you are considering.

- What barriers might be preventing me from taking action, and how can I challenge these barriers?
- Are they real and/or perceived?

  o If real, how can I process these to find a solution? Who can I reach out to for support? What resources (e.g. technology, processes, policies, laws) can help me reduce the potential negative consequences and isolation that sometimes comes with consequences

  o If perceived, what can I do to acknowledge and challenge this perceived barrier? What one, small, actionable step can I take today to challenge this and align my action and vision? (Consider SMART goals.)

Point of Reflection: Summary of Strategies and First Steps

- Based on the exploration of strategies above, the first strategy I will start with is …
- My first step is …
- Using the SMART goals (specific, measurable, attainable, realistic, and time-limited), this is my plan and timeline …

  o My goal …
  o Possible subgoals (steps, barriers to be changed to subgoals, skills and/or knowledge to build, relationships to develop, aspirational timeline)

Sustainability of My Project and My Personal Sustainability

Counseling and facilitating others' health and well-being requires a lot mentally, emotionally, and sometimes physically. Engaging in social action has its joys but also major obstacles, often making it difficult to stay healthy and even persist. This is especially true because we challenge large, entrenched oppressive systems that are slow to change and resist change. Active and intentional attention to sustaining my well-being is essential for my health and my ability to serve the populations I work with effectively.

For this section, it may be helpful to refer back to Chapter 11, Activity 11.1 "Prioritizing," Activity 11.4 "Where Do You Stand and Who Stands with You?" and Activity 11.5 "Good Times and Challenging Times." In addition to the sustainability we feel from engaging with loved ones, people in our lives can also help keep us accountable to our own wellness practices. They might even be a partner in our sustainability activities. We call them "sustainability buddies."

Point of Reflection: Sustainability. It's helpful to step back and get an overview of what sustainability might look like for you given the plan you create.

- For me, sustainability means …
- Currently, I have regular sustainability practices in place for …

  - mind and cognitive well-being
  - emotional well-being
  - relational well-being
  - physical well-being
  - spiritual well-being

- My "sustainability buddies" are …
- I believe it will be important for me to intentionally build in additional sustainability practices, and my menu to choose from is laid out in the following chart.

My Sustainability Menu (See Activity 11.7)

Activity	Mind	Heart: Emotions	Heart: Relational	Body	Spirit

Starting tomorrow, I will …
And the next day …

Chapter 13

Looking Ahead

Putting Your Plan into Action

"I think that is where I hope many of you will be—people that question why things are and why we have to do them the way we have always done them. I hope you will take some risks, exert some real leadership on issues, and if you will, dance along the edge of the roof as you continue your life from here."

—Wilma Mankiller, Commencement Address at Northern Arizona University, Dec. 18, 1992, https://awpc.cattcenter.iastate.edu/2017/03/21/commencement-address-at-northern-arizona-university-dec-18-1992/

In the previous chapter, you created your strategic professional and personal social action plan. This final chapter is an opening, not a closing. This is a call to action—to you—from you—for you. Are you ready? What do you need to be ready? You can revisit the activities you did throughout the book to help you move through the areas you are getting stuck in. You have an action plan (Chapter 12 and the culmination of the work you've done in this book). Your plan is not set in stone, and you will revise it as you learn the strengths, needs, and hurdles for yourself and for the communities you are partnering with.

Each of us has different things that *help us do* what is hard—and things that *keep us from doing* what is hard. As you reflect on the work you have done throughout this book, pay special attention to the personal reflections and awareness along the way. What did you notice about your emotional reactions; the thoughts or fears that might have come up; the excitement, hope and adrenaline that made your heart beat a little faster?

Our hope was to play some part in helping you to move a little further into social action, to make some noise, share some love, act for change, and to thrive—or at least survive—while doing it. So, before sending you off, we are going to ask you to do one more thing: Commit to acting on your plan starting today. Look at your timeline to see what is on the agenda and then consider and choose one of the following items:

- What are you doing tomorrow?
- What can you do right now that doesn't require extra training, skills, or resources?

- Who can help you do it? Or is there someone you can help who is already doing it?
- Are there barriers or obstacles that might keep you from moving forward? Are you missing something that you need in order to move in action? If so, is there an alternative strategy? If the barrier is "X," consider these questions as you transform these obstacles into subgoals:

    o How can I create or gain "X"?
    o How can I take action without "X"?
    o Where is this obstacle coming from and should I be challenging that?

As an example, we often hear (and sometimes feel like) there is not enough time, money, or resources to address a challenge. In that case, the questions can become the following:

- If time is critical to this strategy, are there alternative strategies to consider—or is this really the one that makes sense?
- How can I make more time (e.g., let go of other things)?
- How can I engage in this strategy without making more time (e.g., shifting the way I do things such as collaborating with others or finding better ways of doing things)?
- What is making me feel like I don't have enough time (e.g., a culture of busyness that serves the status quo)?

We want to end by saying that through it all, don't lose sight of what you are doing and why you are doing it. This does not mean you have to engage nonstop in social action. Not only is that impossible, it is also unhealthy for everyone involved. In your process of engaging in social action, be gentle with yourself and with humanity. And at the same time, be persistent and tenacious. Can you be both? We believe you can, but each moment will call for different kinds of engagement. You have to be intentional with what you do and keep your vision and the vision of the community as your guide.

Our Closing Letters to You

From Muninder

Each of us has had mentors who have given us invaluable advice. We didn't always listen in the moment, but we brought it with us. We bring these lessons or words of wisdom with us in our work. For me, Dr. Lisa Suzuki is one such mentor. She always has excellent advice, and I am sometimes not always ready or willing to hear it. Dr. Suzuki noticed that I had a tendency to get stuck in frustration and anger about large-scale issues I had little control over. She gave me one of her best pieces of advice: When pursuing a goal, "Focus on your hovel." She would hold up her arms to demonstrate the area that needed to be focused on. That reminder allows me to keep engaging in social justice action in ways that only I can.

Muninder

From Derrick

First, thank you for your engagement with this text. My hope is that your completion of this workbook serves as a launchpad for the work you're doing—or will do—in your communities for the causes you care about.

Since we began writing, many injustices have gained public awareness. Unfortunately, injustices occur often, even if they are not receiving significant public attention. Feel the feelings that arise within you as you witness and/or experience these injustices. You will likely find others feeling similarly. Those feelings can lead to forming a community with others and engaging in actions that can improve conditions and lead to liberation.

Remember that actions don't always have to be big, and that they don't always have to be your idea. As you engage with others, you'll learn what is needed. You don't have to be an expert to start taking action. However, it is important that you educate yourself on the causes that you are acting for.

Lastly, care for yourself and those around you. The work is rarely easy. But liberation and justice are worth the effort. I am sending you strength and the spirit of collaboration on your journey.

With deep gratitude and in solidarity,
Derrick

From Bryan

Dear Reader,

I hope this letter finds you well and filled with inspiration. I wanted to take a moment to express my deepest gratitude to each of you for being compañeros of our book on social action and for allowing us to come along with you for part of your journey. Your commitment, effort, and trust will be instrumental in making a positive impact in the world. Remember, you are not alone: Our ancestors, mentors, communities, and future descendants stand with each of us. I am humbled by the dedication, the commitment, and the love we know it takes to explore ideas and strategies for creating meaningful change. Your engagement and willingness to take action are the driving force behind the progress we see in society and the reason we wrote this book. Your passion for social justice and your desire to make a difference is a light of hope in a world that often feels overwhelmed by darkness.

Yet, we know that change does not come without resistance. Across the world, we witness efforts to silence marginalized voices, restrict bodily autonomy, colonize land, persecute the vulnerable, and dismantle hard-fought freedoms. In the face of this, our work is not just necessary—it is urgent. The very act of engaging with these ideas, of refusing to be silent, is resistance. The forces of oppression evolve, but so do we. Our movements are resilient, and our collective wisdom spans generations. When we stand together, we do more than resist; we reimagine and build anew.

Although this is the end of the book, it is not the end of our work for collective liberation. Creating lasting change can be a daunting task, but through determination and commitment, may we become an inspiration to others. In the same way a water drop will cut stone with time, we create change through consistent actions. Each step you take, no matter how small, contributes to the greater collective effort.

This book offered insights, tools, and strategies, but it is through your unique experiences and application of these principles that true transformation takes place. Knowledge and committed action lead to liberation. Embrace the lessons learned and adapt them to your communities and movement. Together, we can create a more inclusive, equitable, and compassionate world for all.

As you close this book, I invite you to choose one action—no matter how small—that aligns with your values. Perhaps it is mentoring a young leader, organizing in your community, or using your voice to challenge injustice. Let this be the beginning of your next chapter.

Wishing you continued strength, resilience, and unwavering determination on your path.

In Lak'ech,
Dr. Rojas-Araúz

From Rebecca

When I was in my doctoral program, I was meeting with Dr. Janet Helms, a beloved professor and mentor, and I expressed to her my frustration about a situation. In her style, she sat back and said, "The problem is that you still think that life should be fair, and you've always been allowed to believe that." (For context, she is a prolific scholar in Black and White racial identity. Prior to this meeting, I had shared the work I was doing to understand and undo my own White socialization.) To her comment I replied, "Yes, I know! But is it wrong to work toward fairness for everyone?" Her response was that it is not wrong and could be a good thing but allowing my frustration about the lack of fairness and equity and the presence of oppression to paralyze me interfered with taking action and became a problem. At least that was the message I took away. As more and more hatred, systemic violence and erasure erupts in this country, these words and the work of Dr. Helms and many others continue to bring me hope and inspiration.

Lessons come from so many different places and people. Some were hard lessons that came just at the right time while others were lessons I was not ready to integrate until later. At the very least, I have learned how important it is to acknowledge a sense of gratitude to the people who share their wisdom and heart, who have come before me, and those who have worked alongside me—sometimes invisibly—even when I felt alone. It fills my heart to honor mentors and elders who have laid the path that I am able to walk now. I am inspired by you and all the students and mentees that are carrying the world forward in a good way. Social action, addressing oppression and changing systems, is best done with others. We've emphasized that throughout the book, and it bears repeating. I have faith that with action, wisdom, solidarity and compassion, our community will grow, as we connect, do the work and find joy. Thank you for everything you are doing and will do.

With gratitude and in solidarity,
Rebecca

References

Adames, H. Y., & Chavez-Dueñas, N. Y. (2017). *Cultural foundations and interventions in Latino/a mental health: History, theory and within group differences.* Routledge/Taylor & Francis Group.

Ahluwalia, M. K., & Ali, S. R. (2016, April 29). *Islamophobia in the U.S.: A threat to justice everywhere* [Blog]. Psychology Benefits Society. https://psychologybenefits.org/2016/04/29/islamophobia-in-the-u-s-a-threat-to-justice-everywhere/

Ali, A., & Sichel, C. E. (2014). Structural competency as a framework for training in counseling psychology. *The Counseling Psychologist, 42*(7), 901–918. https://doi.org/10.1177/0011000014550320

American Arab, Middle Eastern and North African Psychological Association. (2022). *Our beginnings.* https://www.amenapsy.org/index.cfm?fuseaction=Page.ViewPage&pageId=472

American Association of University Professors. (n.d.). *Targeted harassment of faculty.* https://www.aaup.org/issues/fighting-targeted-harassment-faculty

American Civil Liberties Union. (n.d.). *Know your rights: Protesters' rights.* https://www.aclu.org/know-your-rights/protesters-rights

American Counseling Association. (n.d.). *What is counseling?* https://www.counseling.org/mental-health-counseling/what-is-counseling

American Counseling Association. (1995). *1995 ACA code of ethics & standards of practice.* https://www.counseling.org/docs/default-source/ethics/archived-code-of-ethics/code-of-ethics-1995.pdf?sfvrsn=a92f3a61_2

American Counseling Association. (2014). *2014 ACA code of ethics.* https://www.counseling.org/docs/default-source/default-document-library/2014-code-ofaP-ethics-finaladdress.pdf

American Counseling Association (2025, March 13). The U.S. Supreme Court to hear case on conversion therapy ban. https://www.counseling.org/publications/media-center/article/2025/03/13/us-supreme-court-to-hear-case-on-conversion-therapy-ban

American Psychological Association. (2011, June). *Revised competency benchmarks for professional psychology.* https://www.apa.org/ed/graduate/revised-competency-benchmarks.doc

American Psychological Association. (2014). *A career in counseling psychology.* https://www.apa.org/action/science/counseling

American Psychological Association. (2015). *Report of the independent reviewer and related materials.* https://www.apa.org/independent-review

American Psychological Association. (2017a). *Ethical principles of psychologists and code of conduct* (2002, amended effective June 1, 2010, and January 1, 2017). https://www.apa.org/ethics/code/

American Psychological Association. (2017b). *Multicultural guidelines: An ecological approach to context, identity, and intersectionality.* http://www.apa.org/about/policy/multicultural-guidelines.pdf

American Psychological Association. (2020a). *How to work with the media.* https://www.apa.org/pubs/authors/working-with-media

American Psychological Association. (2020b). *Building your resilience.* https://www.apa.org/topics/resilience/building-your-resilience

American Psychological Association. (2021). *Apology to people of color for APA's role in promoting, perpetuating, and failing to challenge racism, racial discrimination, and human hierarchy in U.S.* https://www.apa.org/about/policy/racism-apology

Amnesty International. (n.d.). *Protect the protest.* https://www.amnesty.org/en/what-we-do/freedom-of-expression/protest/#:~:text=Our%20goal%20is%20to%20enable,pushing%20for%20human%20rights%20change

Anderson, J., Hilert, A., Lara, M., Martinez, R., & Mavaneh, S. S. (2015). *The history of Counselors for Social Justice (CSJ).* https://www.counseling-csj.org/history.html

Annamma, S. A., Connor, D., & Ferri, B. (2013). Dis/ability critical race studies (DisCrit): Theorizing at the intersections of race and dis/ability. *Race, Ethnicity and Education, 16*(1), 1–31. https://doi-org.jpllnet.sfsu.edu/10.1080/13613324.2012.730511.

Anzaldúa, G. (1987). *Borderlands/La frontera: The new mestiza.* Aunt Lute Books.

APA Indigenous Apology Workgroup. (2023). *Report on an offer of apology, on behalf of the American Psychological Association, to First Peoples in the United States.* American Psychological Association. https://www.apa.org/pubs/reports/indigenous-apology.pdf

APA Office of General Counsel. (2023). *Chiles v. Salazar, et al.* https://www.apa.org/about/offices/ogc/amicus/chiles

Arredondo, P., Toporek, R., Brown, S. P., Jones, J., Locke, D. C., Sanchez, J., & Stadler, H. (1996). Operationalization of the multicultural counseling competencies. *Journal of Multicultural Counseling and Development, 24*(1), 42–78. https://doi.org/10.1002/j.2161-1912.1996.tb00288.x

Association of Black Psychology. (2021). *Official statement to the APA apology.* https://abpsi.org/abpsis-official-statement-to-the-apa-apology/

Association for Women in Psychology. (n.d.). *AWP herstory.* Retrieved December 4, 2021, from https://www.awpsych.org/awp_herstory.php

Banks, K., Beachy, S., Ferguson, A., Gobin, R., Ho, I., Liang, C., Maton, K., Miles-McLean, H.A., & Toporek, R. L. (2019). *Community advocacy: A psychologist's toolkit for state and local advocacy.* https://www.communitypsychology.com/wp-content/uploads/2019/06/2019_Community_Advocacy_A_Psychologist_Toolkit.pdf.

Barrett, (2021, October 22). Reflexive and reflective thinking practice: What's the difference? *Medium.* https://tombarrett.medium.com/reflexive-and-reflective-thinking-practices-whats-the-difference-4473c9f8142e

Bernal, D. D., & Villalpando, O. (2002). An apartheid of knowledge in academia: The struggle over the "legitimate" knowledge of faculty of color. *Equity and Excellence in Education, 35*(2), 169–180. https://doi.org/10.1080/713845282

Black Lives Matter. (n.d.). *Healing in action: A toolkit for Black Lives Matter healing justice and direct action.* https://blacklivesmatter.com/wp-content/uploads/2024/05/blm-healing-action-r1.pdf

Boggs, G. L. (2013). *American revolution: The evolution of Grace Lee Boggs* https://americanrevolutionaryfilm.com/

Briggs v. Elliott, 342 U.S. 350 (1952).

Brabeck, M., & Hunter, E. A. (2022). *Frequently asked questions regarding the ethical issues related to the recent Supreme Court decision overturning Roe v. Wade (1973).* https://www.apa.org/ethics/reproductive-rights.pdf

Bronfenbrenner, U. (1979). *The ecology of human development: Experiments by nature and design.* Harvard University Press.

brown, a. m. (2013, June 21). *Emergence* (speech from opening for allied media conference). https://adriennemareebrown.net/2013/06/21/emergence-speech-from-opening-for-allied-media-conference-2013/.

brown, a. m. (2017). *Emergent strategy: Shaping change, changing worlds.* A.K. Press.

Brown, M., Elizondo, S., & Ray, R. (2021, December 1). *Combating racism on social media: 5 key insights on bystander intervention.* Brookings Institution. media-5-key-insights-on-bystander-intervention/https://www.brookings.edu/blog/how-we-rise/2021/12/01/combating-racism-on-social-

Brown v. Board of Education, 347 U.S. 483 (1954). https://www.oyez.org/cases/1940-1955/347us483

Brownsmith, E. (2018, January 9). New to activism? Grow your practices of self-care. *Medium.* https://medium.com/@esther.brownsmith/new-to-activism-grow-your-practices-of-self-care-56c95cec1a32

Burton, M. (2012). *Liberation psychology: A constructive critical praxis.* https://libpsy.org/wp-content/uploads/2012/10/Liberation-Psychology_-a-constructive-critical-praxis.pdf

Cadenas, G. A., Campos, L., & Minero, L. (2022). The psychology of critical consciousness among immigrants: Reflection and activism responding to oppressive immigration policy. *Current Opinion in Psychology, 47.* https://doi.org/10.1016/j.copsyc.2022.101433

Campus Pride. (2012, September 27). *Ground rules.* https://www.campuspride.org/resources/ground-rules/

Carey, B. (2018, June 18). A troubling prognosis for migrant children in detention: 'The earlier they're out, the better.' *New York Times.* https://www.nytimes.com/2018/06/18/health/migrant-children-mental-health.html

Center for ArtEsteem. (n.d.). *Oakland super heroes mural project.* Attitudinal Healing Connection. https://www.ahc-oakland.org/oakland-mural-project

CEO Alliance for Mental Health (2025, March 18). Nations mental health leaders express concern about proposed cuts to SAMHSA. https://ceoallianceformentalhealth.org/nations-mental-health-leaders-express-concern-about-proposed-cuts-to-samhsa/

Chan, C. D., Cor, D. N., & Band, M. P. (2018). Privilege and oppression in counselor education: An intersectionality framework. *Journal of Multicultural Counseling and Development, 46*(1), 58–73. https://doi.org/10.1002/jmcd.12092

Chavez-Korell, S., Delgado-Romero, E. A., & Illes, R. (2012). The National Latina/o Psychological Association: Like a phoenix rising. *The Counseling Psychologist, 40*(5), 675–684. https://doi.org/10.1177/0011000012450421

Clay, R. (2017, January). Did you really just say that? *Monitor on Psychology, 48*(1), 46. https://www.apa.org/monitor/2017/01/microaggressions

Coates, T. (2015). *Between the world and me.* One World.

Cobb, J., Horwitz, S., Uppal, A., & Whitaker, A. (2023). *Decoding alternative education: Student demographics, coursework and budgeting in the five largest California County Offices of Education & tools for transparency.* ACLU of Southern California, National Center for Youth Law, and East Bay Community Law Center. https://youthlaw.org/sites/default/files/attachments/2023-03/2023%20Decoding%20Alternative%20Education%20FINAL.pdf

Comas-Díaz, L. (2009). Changing psychology: History and legacy of the Society for the Psychological Study of Ethnic Minority Issues. *Cultural Diversity and Ethnic Minority Psychology, 15*(4), 400–408. https://doi.org/10.1037/a0016592

Combs, D., & Rojas-Arauz, B. (2017). *DREAMless* [Documentary]. Vimeo. https://vimeo.com/221658847

Comstock, D. L., Hammer, T. R., Strentzsch, J., Cannon, K., Parsons, J., & Salazar II, G. (2008). Relational–Cultural Theory: A framework for bridging relational, multicultural, and social justice competencies. *Journal of Counseling & Development, 86*(3), 279–287. https://doi.org/10.1002/j.1556-6678.2008.tb00510.x

Cooper, S. (2023, June 26). ACA and SAIGE co-host webinar on LGBTQ+ advocacy and allyship. *Counseling Today.* https://ct.counseling.org/2023/06/aca-and-saige-co-host-webinar-on-lgbtq-advocacy-and-allyship/

Council for Accreditation of Counseling and Related Educational Programs. (2024). *2024 standards.* https://www.cacrep.org/for-programs/2024-cacrep-standards/

Council on Social Work Education. (2022). *Educational policy and accreditation standards for baccalaureate and master's social work programs.* https://www.cswe.org/getmedia/bb5d8afe-7680-42dc-a332-a6e6103f4998/2022-EPAS.pdf

Counselors for Social Justice. (2011). The Counselors for Social Justice (CSJ) Code of Ethics. *Journal for Social Action in Counseling & Psychology, 3*(2), 1–21. https://doi.org/10.33043/JSACP.3.2.1-21

Counselors for Social Justice. (2023). *We are advocates.* https://www.counseling-csj.org/

Crabtree, Mark (Ed.). (2003). *Ed Roberts: His words, his vision* [Video]. University of Kansas Research and Training Center on Independent Living. https://youtu.be/dLbrqMrVYL0?si=VG-CyPCDJ3IuUmdN

Crenshaw, K. (1989). *Demarginalizing the intersection of race and sex: A Black feminist critique of antidiscrimination doctrine, feminist theory and antiracist politics.* University of Chicago Legal Forum, *140,* 139–167. http://chicagounbound.uchicago.edu/uclf/vol1989/iss1/8

Crenshaw, K. (1991). Mapping the margins: Intersectionality, identity politics, and violence against women of color. *Stanford Law Review, 43*(6), 1241–1299. https://doi.org/10.2307/1229039

Crenshaw, K. W. (2011). Twenty years of critical race theory: Looking back to move forward. *Connecticut Law Review, 43*(5), 1253–1352.

Crenshaw, K. (2016, October). *The urgency of intersectionality* [Video]. TED Conferences. https://www.ted.com/talks/kimberle_crenshaw_the_urgency_of_intersectionality?utm_campaign=tedspread&utm_medium=referral&utm_source=tedcomshare

Crenshaw, K. (2017). *On intersectionality: Essential writings.* New Press.

Crowley, K., Garrison, J., & Snider, M. (2025, February 2025). Tracking federal layoffs 2025: Impacted agencies include IRS, FAA, TSA and more. *USA Today.* https://www.usatoday.com/story/news/politics/2025/02/21/federal-layoffs-2025-list/79415517007/

David, E. J. R., Nadal, K. L., & del Prado, A. (2022). SIGE!: Celebrating Filipina/x/o American psychology and some guiding principles as we "go ahead." *Asian American Journal of Psychology, 13*(1), 1–7. https://doi.org/10.1037/aap0000277

DeAngelis, T. (2003, March). When anger's a plus. *Monitor on Psychology, 34*(3), 44. https://www.apa.org/monitor/mar03/whenanger.aspx

DeBlaere, C., Brewster, M. E., Bertsch, K. N., DeCarlo, A. L., Kegel, K. A., & Presseau, C. D. (2014). The protective power of collective action for sexual minority women of color: An investigation of multiple discrimination experiences and psychological distress. *Psychology of Women Quarterly, 38*(1), 20–32. https://doi.org/10.1177/0361684313493252

DeGruy, J. (2013, May 14). *Cracking the codes: Joy DeGruy, a trip to the grocery store* [Video]. YouTube. https://www.youtube.com/watch?v=GTvU7uUgjUI

Delgado, R., & Stefancic, J. (2001). *Critical race theory: An introduction.* New York University Press.

Delgado, R., & Stefancic, J. (2017). *Critical race theory: An introduction* (3rd ed.). New York University Press.

Domonoske, C. (2018, April 2). Video reveals power of Sinclair, as local news anchors recite script in unison. *NPR.* https://www.npr.org/sections/thetwo-way/2018/04/02/598794433/video-reveals-power-of-sinclair-as-local-news-anchors-recite-script-in-unison

Downton Jr., J., & Wehr, P. (1998). Persistent pacifism: How activist commitment is developed and sustained. *Journal of Peace Research, 35*(5), 531–550.

Duggan, M. (2017, July 11). *Witnessing online harassment.* Pew Research Center. http://www.pewinternet.org/2017/07/11/witnessing-online-harassment/

Duran, A., & Jones, S. R. (2022). Intersectionality as a lens in qualitative research: Possibilities, problems, and practices. In P. A. Pasque & E. Alexander (Eds.), *Advancing culturally responsive research and researchers* (pp. 103–118). Routledge. https://doi.org/10.4324/9781003126621

Ellis, N., & Sitz, L. (2021, June 18). *What is White racial identity and why is it important? The Lily: The New Normal* [Video]. The Washington Post. https://www.washingtonpost.com/video/the-lily/what-is-white-racial-identity-and-why-is-it-important/2021/06/18/a7db496c-02a7-4128-9f4e-0f924df83976_video.html-2

Ellsworth, M. (2014, November 15). *Art as activism* [Video]. TED Conferences. https://www.youtube.com/watch?reload=9&v=KLg8LMK_Ct4

Elworthy, S. (2012). *Fighting with nonviolence* [Video]. TED Conferences. https://www.ted.com/talks/scilla_elworthy_fighting_with_nonviolence

The Ethics Centre. (2016, Sept. 27). *Ethics explainer: Ethics, morality and law.* https://ethics.org.au/ethics-morality-law-whats-the-difference/

Flaherty, J. (2016). *No more heroes: Grassroots challenges to the savior mentality.* AK Press. https://www.akpress.org/nomoreheroes.html

Flynn, A. W. P., Domínguez, S., Jr., Jordan, R. A. S., Dyer, R. L., & Young, E. I. (2021). When the political is professional: Civil disobedience in psychology. *American Psychologist, 76*(8), 1217–1231. https://doi.org/10.1037/amp0000867

Flores, L. A. (2017, March 6). Seeing through murals: The future of Latino San Francisco. *Boom, 6*(4), 16–27. . https://boomcalifornia.com/2017/03/06/seeing-through-murals-the-future-of-latino-san-francisco/

Freudenberger, H. J., & Richelson, G. (1980). *Burn out: The high cost of high achievement.* Anchor Press.

Friedman, V. (2023, January 15). The fashion sale of the century. *New York Times.* https://www.nytimes.com/2023/01/15/style/andre-leon-talley-auction.html

Freire, P. (1970). *Pedagogy of the oppressed.* New York: Seabury Press.

Funnell, A. (2017, October 24). From slacktivism to 'feel-good' protests, activism is broken: Here's how to fix it. *NBC News.* http://www.abc.net.au/news/2017-10-25/activism-is-broken-heres-how-we-fix-it/9077372

Gasch R., & Reticker-Flynn, J. (n.d.). *Youth activist toolkit.* Advocates for Youth. https://advocatesforyouth.org/wp-content/uploads/2019/04/Youth-Activist-Toolkit.pdf

Gilfoyle, N., & Dvoskin, J. A. (2017). APA's amicus curiae program: Bringing psychological research to judicial decisions. *American Psychologist, 72*(8), 753–763. doi: 10.1037/amp0000221.

Gómez, J. M., Smith, C. P., Gobin, R. L., Tang, S. S., & Freyd, J. J. (2016). Collusion, torture, and inequality: Understanding the actions of the American Psychological Association as institutional betrayal. *Journal of Trauma & Dissociation, 17*(5), 527–544. https://doi.org/10.1080/15299732.2016.1214436

Gorski, P. C., & Chen, C. (2015). "Frayed all over:" The causes and consequences of activist burnout among social justice education activists. *Educational Studies: Journal of the American Educational Studies Association, 51*(5), 385–405. https://doi.org/10.1080/00131946.2015.1075989

Goska, D. V. (2004). Political paralysis. In P. R. Loeb (Ed.), *The impossible will take a little while: A citizen's guide to hope in a time of fear* (pp. 47–57). Basic Books.

Gover, A. R., Harper, S. B., & Langton, L. (2020). Anti-Asian hate crime during the COVID-19 pandemic: Exploring the reproduction of inequality. *American Journal of Criminal Justice, 45*, 647–667.

Green, M. (2022, October 21). Kaiser mental health workers approve new contract, ending 10-week strike. *KQED.* https://www.kqed.org/news/11929713/kaiser-mental-health-workers-appove-new-contract-ending-10-week-strike

Harvard Kennedy School. (n.d.). *How to write an op-ed or column.* Communications Program. https://shorensteincenter.org/wp-content/uploads/2012/07/HO_NEW_HOW-TO-WRITE-AN-OPED-OR-COLUMN.pdf

Hays, P. A. (1996). Addressing the complexities of culture and gender in counseling. *Journal of Counseling & Development, 74*(4), 332–338. https://doi.org/10.1002/j.1556-6676.1996.tb01876.x

Hays, P. A. (2008). *Addressing cultural complexities in practice: Assessment, diagnosis, and therapy* (2nd ed.). American Psychological Association. https://doi.org/10.1037/11650-000

Hays, P. (2012). *Connecting across cultures: The helper's toolkit.* Sage Publications.

Hays, P. A. (2016). *Addressing cultural complexities in practice: Assessment, diagnosis, and therapy* (3rd ed.). American Psychological Association. https://doi.org/10.1037/14801-000

Heinze, J. L. (2022). *Online harassment resources.* National Sexual Violence Resource Center. https://www.nsvrc.org/blogs/online-harassment-resources

Herrnstein, R. J., & Murray, C. A. (1994). *The bell curve: Intelligence and class structure in American life.* Free Press.

Hickey, D., Fessler, D. M. T., Lerman, K., & Burghardt, K. (2025, February 12). X under Musk's leadership: Substantial hate and no reduction in inauthentic activity. *PLOS One.* https://journals.plos.org/plosone/article?id=10.1371/journal.pone.0313293#

Hoffman, D., Carter, D. J., Viglucci Lopez, C. R., Benzmiller, H. L., Guo, A. X., Latifi, S. Y., & Craig, D. C. (2015). *Independent review relating to APA Ethics Guidelines, national security interrogations, and torture.* Sidley Austin LLP. https://www.apa.org/independent-review/revised-report.pdf

Holliday, B. G. (2009). The history and visions of African American psychology: Multiple pathways to place, space, and authority. *Cultural Diversity and Ethnic Minority Psychology, 15*(4), 317–337. https://doi.org/10.1037/a0016971

Hook, J. N., Davis, D. E., Owen, J., Worthington, E. L. Jr., & Utsey, S. O. (2013). Cultural humility: Measuring openness to culturally diverse clients. *Journal of Counseling Psychology, 60*(3), 353–366.

Hudson, K. D., & Romanelli, M. (2020). "We are powerful people": Health-promoting strengths of LGBTQ communities of color. *Qualitative Health Research, 30*(8), 1156–70. doi:10.1177/1049732319837572.

Hunjan, R., & Pettit, J. (2011). *Power: A practical guide for facilitating social change.* Carnegie UK Trust and the Joseph Rowntree Foundation. https://d1ssu070pg2v9i.cloudfront.net/pex/pex_carnegie2021/2011/11/09211812/Power-A-Practical-Guide-for-Facilitating-Social-Change_0.pdf

Hunt, E. (2016). Alicia Garza on the beauty and the burden of Black Lives Matter. *The Guardian.* https://www.theguardian.com/us-news/2016/sep/02/alicia-garza-on-the-beauty-and-the-burden-of-black-lives-matter

Indivisible. (2016, December 11). Local advocacy tactics that work. In *Indivisible: A practical guide to resisting the Trump agenda.* https://www.indivisible.org/guide/advocacy-tactics/district-office-visits/

InterHelp. (2024). *Interhelp builds people's capacity to face the social–ecological demands of these complex times.* https://interhelpnetwork.org/

Internet Archive. (n.d.). *About the internet archive.* Accessed March 4, 2025, from https://archive.org/about/

Israel, T. (2020). *Beyond your bubble: How to connect across the political divide, skills and strategies for conversations that work*. APA Life Tools.

Jana, D. T. (2021, February 8). The differences between allies, accomplices & co-conspirators may surprise you. *Medium*. https://aninjusticemag.com/the-differences-between-allies-accomplices-co-conspirators-may-surprise-you-d3fc7fe29c

Katz, J. H. (1985, October). The sociopolitical nature of counseling. *The Counseling Psychologist, 13*(4), 615–624. https://journals.sagepub.com/doi/10.1177/0011000085134005

Kimmel, D. C., & Browning, C. (1999). A history of Division 44 (Society for the Psychological Study of Lesbian, Gay, and Bisexual Issues). In *Unification through division: Histories of the divisions of the American Psychological Association* (Vol. IV, pp. 129–150). American Psychological Association. https://doi.org/10.1037/10340-006

King Jr., M. L. (1967). *King's challenge to the nation's social scientists*. Retrieved March 12, 2021, https://www.apa.org/monitor/features/king-challenge

Kivel, P. (2012, winter). *A web of control*. https://paulkivel.com/resource/a-web-of-control

Kivel, P. (2017). Social service or social change. In INCITE! Women of Color Against Violence (Ed.), *The revolution will not be funded: Beyond the Non-Profit Industrial Complex* (pp. 129–150). Duke University Press, https://doi.org/10.1515/9780822373001-01

Klein, N. (2017, September). *How shocking events can spark positive change* [Video]. TED Conferences. https://www.ted.com/talks/naomi_klein_how_shocking_events_can_spark_positive_change

Kristofferson, K., White, K., & Peloza, J. (2014, April). The nature of slacktivism: How the social observability of an initial act of token support affects subsequent prosocial action. *Journal of Consumer Research, 40*(6), 1149–1166.

KU Center for Community Health and Development (n.d.-a). *Community tool box: Section 6. Coalition building II. Maintaining a coalition*. https://ctb.ku.edu/en/table-of-contents/assessment/promotion-strategies/maintain-a-coalition/main

KU Center for Community Health and Development (n.d.-b). Community toolbox: *Tools to change our world*. Center for Community Health and Development at the University of Kansas. https://ctb.ku.edu/en

Lee, K. (2018, February). How to write an op-ed. *Monitor on Psychology, 49*(2), 66. http://www.apa.org/monitor/2018/02/write-op-ed.aspx

Leong, F. T. L., & Okazaki, S. (2009). History of Asian American psychology. *Cultural Diversity & Ethnic Minority Psychology, 15*(4), 352–362. https://doi.org/10.1037/a0016443

Levine, B. (2015, September 29). *The 10 most egregious U.S. abuses of psychology and psychiatry*. Salon. https://www.salon.com/2015/09/29/10_worst_abuses_of_psychological_assns_partner

Lewis, J. A., Arnold, M. S., House, R., & Toporek, R. L. (2002). *ACA Advocacy Competencies*. Formerly available at http://www.counseling.org/Publications/, now available upon request.

Lewis-Giggetts, T. M. L. (2022, May 18). Black joy in pursuit of racial justice. *Yes! Magazine*. https://www.yesmagazine.org/issue/pleasure/2022/05/18/black-joy-racial-justice

Liu, R., & Shange, S. (2018). Toward thick solidarity: Theorizing empathy in social justice movements. *Radical History Review, 2018*(131), 189–198.

Lorde, A. (1984). *Sister outsider: Essays and speeches*. Crossing Press.

Lovell, J., & Scott-McLaughlin, R. (2023). Intersectional allyship & the importance of relationships. In B. Palmer II (Ed.) *Practical social justice: Diversity, equity, and inclusion strategies based on the legacy of Dr. Joseph L. White* (pp. 25–38). Routledge.

Malcolm X. (1964, June 28). *Malcolm X's speech at the OAAU founding rally (June 28, 1964)*, ICIT Digital Library. https://www.icit-digital.org/articles/malcolm-x-s-speech-at-the-oaau-founding-rally-june-28-1964

Malherbe, N., Ratele, K., Adams, G., Reddy, G., & Suffla, S. (2021). A decolonial Africa(n)-centered psychology of antiracism. *Review of General Psychology, 25*(4), 437–450. https://doi.org/10.1177/10892680211022992

Martín-Baró, I. (1996). *Writings for a liberation psychology*. (A. Aron & S. Corne, Eds.). Harvard University Press.

Maslach, C. (2003). Job burnout: New directions in research and intervention. *Current Directions in Psychological Science, 12*(5), 189–192. https://doi.org/10.1111/1467-8721.01258

Maslach, C., & Jackson, S. E. (1981). The measurement of experienced burnout. *Journal of Organizational Behavior, 2*(2), 99–113. https://doi.org/10.1002/job.4030020205

Maslach, C., & Leiter, M. (2005, Winter). Reversing burnout: How to rekindle your passion for your work. *Stanford Social Innovation Review*. https://ssir.org/images/articles/2005WI_Feature_Maslach_Leiter.pdf

McFerguson, M. (2016, March 16). *Art, social change, and uncomfortable conversations* [Video]. TED Conferences. https://www.youtube.com/watch?v=xjQRWWdocwg

Merriam-Webster. (n.d.-a). Power. *Merriam-Webster.com dictionary*. Accessed March 4, 2025, from https://www.merriam-webster.com/dictionary/power

Merriam-Webster. (n.d.-b). Sustainable. *Merriam-Webster.com dictionary*. Accessed March 4, 2025, from https://www.merriam-webster.com/dictionary/sustainable

Metzl, J. M., & Hansen, H. (2014). Structural competency: Theorizing a new medical engagement with stigma and inequality. *Social Science & Medicine, 103*, 126–133. https://doi.org/10.1016/j.socscimed.2013.06.032

Misawa, M. (2010). Racist and homophobic bullying in adulthood: Narratives from gay men of color in higher education. *New Horizons in Adult Education and Human Resource Development*, 24(1), 7–23. https://doi.org/10.1002/nha3.10370

Morse, G. S., & Blume, A. W. (2013). Does the American Psychological Association's Code of Ethics work for us? *Journal of Indigenous Research*, (3)1. https://digitalcommons.usu.edu/kicjir/vol3/iss1/2

Moyer, B. (2019, June 29). The four roles of social activism. *The Commons*. https://commonslibrary.org/the-four-roles-of-social-activism/

Mullin, B. (2025, February 26). Bezos orders Washington Post opinion section to embrace 'personal liberties and free markets'. *The New York Times*. https://www.nytimes.com/2025/02/26/business/media/washington-post-bezos-shipley.html

Myers & Briggs Foundation. (2025). *What is personality type and the MBTI assessment*. https://www.myersbriggs.org

Nam, E. (2023, May 19). How to have difficult conversations without burning bridges. *Harvard Business Review*. https://hbr.org/2023/05/how-to-have-difficult-conversations-without-burning-bridges

National Association of Social Workers. (n.d.). *Why choose the social work profession?* https://www.socialworkers.org/Careers/NASW-Career-Center/Explore-Social-Work/Why-Choose-the-Social-Work-Profession

National Association of Social Workers. (2015). *Standards and indicators for cultural competence in social work practice*. https://www.socialworkers.org/LinkClick.aspx?fileticket=PonPTDEBrn4%3D&portalid=0

National Association of Social Workers. (2021). *NASW apologizes for racist practices in American social work*. https://www.socialworkers.org/News/News-Releases/ID/2331/NASW-apologizes-for-racist-practices-in-American-social-work

National Center for Institutional Diversity. (2023, November 2). *Envisioning institutional responses to supporting scholar safety*. https://lsa.umich.edu/ncid/news-events/all-events/scholar-safety.html

National Sexual Violence Resource Center. (2014). *Healthy teens*. https://www.nsvrc.org/sites/default/files/saam_2014_becoming-an-agent-of-social-change_0.pdf

Neville, H. (2024). *Justice & joy: Transforming healing praxis in counseling psychology and beyond* [presidential initiative]. Society of Counseling Psychology. https://www.div17.org/presidential-initiatives

New Tactics in Human Rights. (2012, December 11). *Staying safe: Security resources for human rights defenders*. https://www.newtactics.org/conversations/staying-safe-security-resources-human-rights-defenders/

Nicole, C. (2017, May 3). *Black Lives Matter meditation for healing racial trauma* [Audio recording]. SoundCloud. https://soundcloud.com/drcandicenicole/black-lives-matter-meditation-for-healing-racial-trauma

Nobles, W. (1990). *The infusion of African and African-American content: A question of content and intent*. National Urban Alliance. http://www.nuatc.org/articles/pdf/Nobles_article.pdf

Norris, Z. (2020). *We keep us safe*. Beacon Press.

Novotny, A. (2023, June 29). *'The young people feel it': A look at the mental health impact of transgender legislation*. American Psychological Association. https://www.apa.org/topics/lgbtq/mental-health-anti-transgender-legislation

Nwangwu, N. C. (2023, April 24). Why we should stop saying "underrepresented." *Harvard Business Review*. https://hbr.org/2023/04/why-we-should-stop-saying-underrepresented

Ortutay, B. (2025, January 8). Meta rolls back hate speech rules as Zuckerberg cites 'recent elections' as a catalyst. *AP News*. https://apnews.com/article/meta-facebook-hate-speech-trump-immigrant-transgender-41191638cd7c720b950c-05f9395a2b49

Oxford English Dictionary. (n.d.). Privilege. *Oxford Old English Dictionary*. Accessed March 4, 2025, from https://www.oed.com/search/dictionary/?scope=Entries&q=privilege

P. v. Riles, 343 F. Supp. 1306 (N.D. Cal. 1972). https://law.justia.com/cases/federal/district-courts/FSupp/343/1306/1691183/

Padilla, A. M., & Olmedo, E. (2009). Synopsis of key persons, events, and associations in the history of Latino psychology. *Cultural Diversity and Ethnic Minority Psychology*, 15(4), 363–373. https://doi.org/10.1037/a0017557

Palmer II, B. (Ed.)(2023). *Practical social justice: Diversity, equity, and inclusion strategies based on the legacy of Dr. Joseph L. White*. Routledge.

Parham, T. A., & Parham, G. (2022). Healing in the broken places: Practical strategies for leaders and change makers. In B. Palmer II (Ed.), *Practical Social Justice* (pp. 83–109). Routledge.

Pérez Huber, L. (2009). Disrupting apartheid of knowledge: Testimonio as methodology in Latina/o critical race research in education. *International Journal of Qualitative Studies in Education*, 22(6), 639–654. https://doi.org/10.1080/09518390903333863

Pickren, W. E. (2009). Liberating history: The context of the challenge of psychologists of color to American psychology. *Cultural Diversity and Ethnic Minority Psychology*, 15(4), 425–433. https://doi.org/10.1037/a0017561

Plum Village. (n.d.). *The art of mindful living*. https://plumvillage.org/mindfulness-practice/

Pope, K. S. (2008). *Why I resigned from the American Psychological Association*. https://kspope.com/apa/

Pope, K. S. (2016). The Hoffman Report and the American Psychological Association: Meeting the challenge of change. In K. S. Pope & M. J. T. Vasquez, *Ethics in psychotherapy and counseling: A practical guide* (5th ed., pp. 361–369). John Wiley & Sons. https://kspope.com/kpope/Hoffman.php

Prilleltensky, I. (n.d.). *Fun for wellness*. https://www.professorisaac.com/diy-program

Prilleltensky, I. (1989). Psychology and the status quo. *American Psychologist, 44*(5), 795–802. https://doi.org/10.1037/0003-066X.44.5.795

Psychology Benefits Society. (n.d.). Blog series on race, racism, and law enforcement in communities of color. https://psychologybenefits.org/race-and-law-enforcement/

Rappaport, J. (1987). Terms of empowerment/exemplars of prevention: Toward a theory for community psychology. *American Journal of Community Psychology, 15*, 121–148.

Rath, T. (2007). *StrengthsFinder 2.0*. Gallup Press.

Ratts, V. J., Singh, A. A., Nassar-McMillan, S., Butler, S. K., McCullough, J. R. (2015). *Multicultural and social justice counseling competencies*. https://www.counseling.org/docs/default-source/competencies/multicultural-and-social-justice-counseling-competencies.pdf?sfvrsn=20

Ray, R., Brown, M., Summers, E., Elizondo, S., & Powelson, C. (2021, October 25). *Bystander intervention on social media: Examining cyberbullying and reactions to systematic racism*. Governance Studies at the Brookings Institution. https://www.brookings.edu/wp-content/uploads/2021/10/Bystander_Intervention_finalreport.pdf

Resolutions Northwest. (n.d.). *Resources*. Accessed March 4, 2025, from https://resolutionsnorthwest.org/resources/

Ricci v. DeStefano, 557 U.S. 557 (2009).

Right To Be. (n.d). *The 5Ds of bystander intervention*. https://righttobe.org/guides/bystander-intervention-training/

Roediger, D. R. (2018). *Working toward Whiteness: How America's immigrants became White: The strange journey from Ellis Island to the suburbs*. Basic Books.

Rojas-Araúz, B. O. (2021). *Undocumented healing: Strengths and resilience from the shadows* (Publication No. 28719603) [Doctoral Dissertation, University of Oregon]. ProQuest Dissertations & Theses Global.

Rosales, D., & Davis, K. (2023, May 15). The case for mental health in our social change worlds. *Stanford Social Innovation Review*. https://ssir.org/articles/entry/the_case_for_mental_health_in_our_social_change_worlds

SAIGE. (2020). *Our story*. https://saigecounseling.org/our-history/

Santoro, H. (2022, April 1). How to get comfortable talking with the media. *Monitor on Psychology, 53*(3), 72. https://www.apa.org/monitor/2022/04/career-talking-media

Sikh Coalition. (2021, November 22). *FlyRights tool updated*. https://www.sikhcoalition.org/blog/2021/flyrights-tool-updated/

Sayers-Roods, K. (n.d.). *Pocket guide to Ohlone solidarity for both native and non native allies and accomplices*. Mt. Diablo Peace and Justice Center. https://lapena.org/wp-content/uploads/2022/07/ohlone-solidarty-2018-3.pdf

Sloan, T. (2018). *Life choices: Understanding dilemmas and decisions*. Routledge.

Smith, D. (2003). The first code. *Monitor on Psychology, 34*(1), 65. https://www.apa.org/monitor/jan03/firstcode

Society for the Psychological Study of Culture, Ethnicity, and Race. (n.d.). *Brief history*. Retrieved December 2, 2021, from https://division45.org/about/history/

Solórzano, D., & Yosso, T. (2001). Maintaining social justice hopes within academic realities: A Freirean approach to Critical race/LatCrit pedagogy. *Denver Law Review, 78*(4), 595–621.

Southern Poverty Law Center. (2017a, August 14). *Ten ways to fight hate: A community response guide*. https://www.splcenter.org/20170814/ten-ways-fight-hate-community-response-guide

Southern Poverty Law Center. (2017b). *SPLC on campus: A guide to bystander intervention*. https://www.splcenter.org/resources/reports/splc-campus-guide-bystander-intervention/

Stern, J. A., Barbarin, O., & Cassidy, J. (2021). Working toward anti-racist perspectives in attachment theory, research, and practice. *Attachment & Human Development, 24*(3), 392–422. https://doi.org/10.1080/14616734.2021.1976933

Stephens, B. (2017, August 25). Tips for aspiring op-ed writers. *New York Times*. https://www.nytimes.com/2017/08/25/opinion/tips-for-aspiring-op-ed-writers.html

Stringer, H. (2018, September 1). Responding to a mental health crisis at the border. *Monitor on Psychology, 49*(8). https://www.apa.org/monitor/2018/09/crisis-border

Stuckey, J., & Lambert Snodgrass, L. (2021). Patchwork and paying it forward: Undocumented students' access to social capital. *Journal of Latinos & Education, 22*(4), 1341–1354.

Sue, D. W. (2010). *Microaggressions in everyday life: Race, gender and sexual orientation*. Wiley.

Sue, D. W., Alsaidi, S., Awad, M. N., Glaeser, E., Calle, C. Z., & Mendez, N. (2019). Disarming racial microaggressions: Microintervention strategies for targets, White allies, and bystanders. *American Psychologist, 74*(1), 128–142.

Sue, D. W., Capodilupo, C. M., Torino, G. C., Bucceri, J. M., Holder, A. M. B., Nadal, K. L., & Esquilin, M. (2007). Racial microaggressions in everyday life: Implications for clinical practice. *The American Psychologist, 62*(4), 271–286.

Tiefer, L. (1991). *A brief history of the Association for Women in Psychology (AWP) 1969–1991*. Montefiore Medical Center. https://www.awpsych.org/docs/AWP-Herstory-Part-1-1969-1991.pdf

Szymanski, D. M., & Owens, G. P. (2009). Group-level coping as a moderator between heterosexism and sexism and psychological distress in sexual minority women. *Psychology of Women Quarterly, 33*(2), 197–205. https://doi.org/10.1111/j.1471-6402.2009.01489.x

Toporek, R. L., & Ahluwalia, M. K. (2019). *Helping counselors and psychologists as advocates and activists: Strength, solidarity, strategy and sustainability* [Video]. Alexander Street Press.

Toporek, R. L., & Ahluwalia, M. K. (2020). *Taking action: Creating social change through strength, solidarity, strategy, and sustainability.* San Diego, CA: Cognella

Toporek, R. L., & Daniels, J. (2018). *American Counseling Association Advocacy Competencies. Endorsed by ACA 2003 and Updated in 2018.* https://www.counseling.org/docs/default-source/competencies/aca-advocacy-competencies-may-2020.pdf?sfvrsn=85b242c_8

Toporek, R. L., Lewis, J., & Crethar, H. C. (2009). Promoting systemic change through the advocacy competencies. Special Section on ACA Advocacy Competencies. *Journal of Counseling and Development, 87,* 260–268.

Trimble, J. E., & Clearing-Sky, M. (2009). An historical profile of American Indians and Alaska Natives in psychology. *Cultural Diversity and Ethnic Minority Psychology, 15*(4), 338–351. https://doi.org/10.1037/a0015112

Turshen, Julia. (2017). *Feed the resistance: Recipes + ideas for getting involved.* Chronicle Books.

Uniting Church in Australia. (n.d.). *Let us work together.* https://uniting.church/lilla-watson-let-us-work-together/

University of Kansas Research and Training Center on Independent Living. (2003). *Ed Roberts ILC Conference.* https://youtu.be/dLbrqMrVYL0

Viritual Knowledge Centre to End Violence against Women and Girls. (2012, January 3). *Demonstrations, marches and rallies.* UN Women. http://www.endvawnow.org/en/articles/1297-demonstrations-marches-and-rallies.html

Watson, L. B., Morgan, S. K., & Craney, R. (2018). Bisexual women's discrimination and mental health outcomes: The roles of resilience and collective action. *Psychology of Sexual Orientation and Gender Diversity, 5*(2), 182–193. https://doi-org.jpllnet.sfsu.edu/10.1037/sgd0000272

The WELLS Healing Center. (n.d.). *Welcome to WELLS.* https://www.wellshealing.org/

West, C. (2015). *Ware lecture by Cornel West, General Assembly* [Video]. Unitarian Universalist Association. https://www.uua.org/ga/past/2015/ware-west

White, J. L. (1969). *Hare & Hayakawa on-stage* [News Film]. 1968 San Francisco Student Strike. CBS5 KPIX-TV. Bay Area Television Archive. https://diva.sfsu.edu/collections/sfbatv/bundles/187275

White, J. L. (1984). *The psychology of Blacks: An Afro-American perspective.* Prentice-Hall.

Winerman, L. (2016). Students lead anti-racism efforts. *Monitor on Psychology, 47*(9), 16. https://www.apa.org/monitor/2016/10/anti-racism

Wright, K. C., Carr, K. A., & Akin, B. A. (2021). The whitewashing of social work history: How dismantling racism in social work education begins with an equitable history of the profession. *Advances in Social Work, 21*(2/3), Article 2/3. https://doi.org/10.18060/23946

Yosso, T. J. (2005). Whose culture has capital? A critical race theory discussion of community cultural wealth. *Race, Ethnicity and Education, 8*(1), 69–91.

Young, S. (2014, April). *I'm not your inspiration, thank you very much* [Video]. TED Conferences. https://www.ted.com/talks/stella_young_i_m_not_your_inspiration_thank_you_very_much

Zeitzoff, T. (2017). How social media is changing conflict. *Journal of Conflict Resolution, 61*(9), 1970–1991. https://doi.org/10.1177/0022002717721392

Zelizer, C. (2015, November 2). *A guide to blogging for peace and social change.* PCDN Social Change Careers. https://pcdn.global/guide-to-blogging-for-peace-and-social-change/

Index